Find It Quick

Handbook on Cults & New Religions

Ron Rhodes

HARVEST HOUSE PUBLISHERS

EUGENE, OREGON

Cover by Terry Dugan Design, Minneapolis, Minnesota

FIND IT QUICK HANDBOOK ON CULTS AND NEW RELIGIONS
Copyright © 2005 by Ron Rhodes
Published by Harvest House Publishers
Eugene, Oregon 97402
www.harvesthousepublishers.com

Rhodes, Ron.
    Find it quick handbook on cults and new religions / Ron Rhodes.
        p. cm.
    Includes bibliographical references.
    ISBN-13: 978-0-7369-1483-3
    ISBN-10: 0-7369-1483-8 (pbk.)
    Product # 6914838
    1. Cults—United States. 2. United States—Religion. I. Title.
    BL2525.R49 2005
    209—dc22   2005001910

To the survivors—
those who have come out of the kingdom of the cults
and found freedom and liberty in Jesus.

Acknowledgments

Kerri, David, and Kylie—
Thanks for your enduring love and support!

Contents

1
Defining Cults

SCRIPTURE OFTEN WARNS ABOUT spiritual deception (Matthew 7:15-23; 24:5; 2 Corinthians 11:4; Galatians 1:8; 1 John 4:1). God obviously does not want people to be deceived. This is one reason a study of the cults is important.

In this handbook, the term "cult" is not intended as a pejorative, inflammatory, or injurious word. The term is used simply as a means of categorizing certain religious or semireligious groups in modern Western culture.

The word "cult" comes from the Latin word *cultus*, which means "worship." In a sense, then, cults are groups that have distinguishable forms of worship. This definition, however, is far too broad to be of any real use. Modern usage is much more specific.

Today the word "cult" is often used in both a sociological and a theological sense. Sociologically, a cult is a religious or semireligious sect or group whose members are often controlled or dominated almost entirely by a single individual or organization. A sociological definition generally includes (but is not limited to) the authoritarian, manipulative, and sometimes communal features of cults. Some cults, such as the Children of God and the Moonies, manifest many of these sociological characteristics. Other cults—the Baha'i Faith and Unitarian Universalism, for example—manifest few if any of these characteristics. For this reason, a sociological definition of the cults is probably not precise enough.

Without meaning to discount insights we can gain from

sociology on the cults, I believe we are best served by defining cults theologically. Theologically, a cult is a religious group that derives from a parent religion (such as Christianity) but in fact departs from that parent religion by denying (explicitly or implicitly) one or more of the essential doctrines of that religion.[1] So, for example, the Jehovah's Witnesses and The Church of Jesus Christ of Latter-day Saints are cults in the sense that they both derive from the parent religion of Christianity but deny one or more of the essential doctrines of historic Christianity. For example, the Jehovah's Witnesses deny the doctrine of the Trinity and argue that Jesus is not eternal deity. The Mormons also deny the eternal deity of Jesus and argue that human beings can one day become gods. Obviously such beliefs separate them from mainstream historic Christianity.

Likewise, the Nation of Islam is a cult of Islam (the parent religion) because it denies one or more of the essential doctrines of Islam. The Hare Krishna sect is a cult of Hinduism (the parent religion) because it denies one or more of the essential doctrines of Hinduism. Such groups, then, are cults in this narrowly defined, non-pejorative sense.

If this definition is correct, then we must also clarify what the essential doctrines of Christianity are. Many churches and groups claiming to be Christian have differences of opinion over such issues as church government, the proper mode of baptism, and when the rapture of the church is going to happen. These issues do not define cults because these are considered peripheral doctrines (that is, they are minor doctrines over which people can freely disagree). Other doctrines of the Christian faith are so essential that if you deny one or more of them, you are no longer truly Christian. Five doctrines are especially important:

1. *Scripture.* The Bible is the inspired and authoritative Word of God.

2. *God.* The one true God is infinite and eternal, revealed in three persons: the Father, the Son, and the Holy Spirit.

3. *Jesus.* Jesus is eternal God as the second person of the Trinity. In the incarnation, He took on a human nature, being born of a virgin. He died for humankind's sins and three days later physically rose from the dead.

4. *Humanity.* God created human beings in His image, and they are morally accountable to him. They forever remain creatures who are morally accountable to the Creator.

5. *Sin and Salvation.* Every human being is born into the world in a state of dire sin and is estranged from God. People can do nothing to merit salvation before God. Salvation is by grace alone through faith alone, based solely on the atonement wrought by Christ.

When we talk about cults of Christianity, we are referring to groups that derive from the parent religion of Christianity but deny (explicitly or implicitly) one or more of the above essential doctrines of Christianity.

Doctrinal Characteristics of Cults

Among cults, one will frequently find one or more distinguishing characteristics, such as an emphasis on new revelation from God, a denial of the sole authority of the Bible, a distorted view of God and Jesus, and/or a denial of salvation by grace through faith. Not every cult manifests the characteristics below, but these characteristics are quite common. And those that do possess these characteristics don't do so to the same degree.

New Revelation. Many cult leaders claim to receive new revelations. Mormon presidents claim to receive revelations from God. New Agers claim to receive revelations from the Ascended Masters.

UFO cult leaders claim to receive revelations from space brothers. Spiritists claim to receive revelations from the great beyond. Typically in cults, in a conflict between the Bible (old revelation) and the new revelation, the new revelation supersedes the Bible.

Denial of the Sole Authority of the Bible. Many cults deny the sole authority of the Bible. Christian Scientists, for example, elevate Mary Baker Eddy's book, *Science and Health with Key to the Scriptures,* to supreme authority. Unification Church members elevate Reverend Moon's *Divine Principle* to supreme authority. New Agers often exalt *The Aquarian Gospel of Jesus the Christ.* Mormons place *The Book of Mormon* as the top authority.

A Distorted View of God. Many cults espouse a distorted view of God. The Jehovah's Witnesses deny the Trinity. New Agers believe that all in the universe is God (pantheism). Mormons believe human beings can become gods, and therefore many gods exist in the universe (polytheism). Witches and Wiccans believe in a Mother Goddess (paganism). Oneness Pentecostals believe Jesus is the one God and that he himself is the Father, the Son, and the Holy Spirit (modalism).

A Distorted View of Jesus Christ. Cults typically espouse a distorted view of Jesus Christ. Jehovah's Witnesses say Jesus was created as the archangel Michael and was a "lesser god" than God the Father. Mormons believe Jesus was the first spirit child of the heavenly Father and one of his unnamed wives. Spiritists say the human Jesus became the Christ through reincarnation. Hindu cults argue that Jesus was just an avatar or perhaps a guru. Some New Agers believe the human Jesus attained Christhood by learning from Indian gurus as a child in India. UFO cults suggest that Jesus was a hybrid being—half human and half alien (thus accounting for his miracles). Members of the Baha'i Faith argue that Jesus was just one of many manifestations of God.

Cults also have a distorted view of Jesus' work at the cross.

Jehovah's Witnesses say Jesus died on a stake as a mere man (not the God-man), and he died for the sins of Adam. Mormons say Jesus' death on the cross provided resurrection for all people but not full redemption. Some New Agers say Jesus died to balance world karma. Reverend Moon, of the Unification Church, believes Jesus did not complete the work of redemption, and therefore the Lord of the Second Advent (presumably Moon) must complete the job.

A Distorted View of the Holy Spirit. Cults typically espouse a distorted view of the Holy Spirit. The Jehovah's Witnesses believe the Holy Spirit is not a person but simply the force or power of God. The Way International also interprets the Holy Spirit as the force of God. The Children of God believe the Holy Spirit is the feminine aspect of God and is often depicted as a sensuous woman. Some New Agers equate the Holy Spirit with the Chi force. Oneness Pentecostals argue that the Holy Spirit is simply one of the modes of manifestation of Jesus.

A Distorted View of Humankind. Many cults espouse a distorted view of humankind. New Agers, for example, believe human beings are a part of God. Mind Science enthusiasts believe the same. Mormons believe that through a long process of eternal progression, human beings may become exalted to godhood.

Denial of Salvation by Grace. Cults typically deny salvation by grace, thus distorting the purity of the gospel. The Mormons, for example, emphasize the necessity of becoming increasingly perfect in this life. The Jehovah's Witnesses emphasize the importance of distributing Watchtower literature door-to-door as a part of "working out" their salvation. Oneness Pentecostals say that to be saved, one must have faith in Christ, repent of all sins, be baptized in water in the name of Jesus only, be baptized in the Holy Spirit as evidenced by speaking in tongues, and obey the holiness code throughout life. Hindu cults teach that one must become increasingly perfect in each successive lifetime through reincarnation.

Redefinitions of Biblical Terms. Cults often use words from the Bible—words like God, Jesus, sin, salvation, the cross, resurrection, and ascension—but redefine them to mean something entirely different from what historic Christianity teaches. This is known as the "terminology block." We must not forget that 2 Corinthians 11:4 warns of a different Jesus, a different spirit, and a different gospel (see also 2 Peter 2:1-3; Galatians 1:6-9; Acts 20:28-31; Matthew 24:24).

Sociological Characteristics of Cults

Cults are best defined theologically, but sociology helps us to understand the human dynamics of cultic groups. Sociological characteristics of cults can include such things as authoritarianism, exclusivism, isolationism, the fear of disfellowshipping, and threats of satanic attack. As with the doctrinal characteristics, not every cult manifests the following characteristics. And those that do possess them may do so to greater or lesser degrees.

Authoritarianism. Authoritarianism usually involves an authority figure—often an alleged prophet—whose word is considered ultimate and final. The late David Koresh of the Branch Davidians in Waco, Texas, is a tragic example. Members of this group followed Koresh to their death. Often such authoritarianism involves legalistic submission to the rules and regulations of the group that the leader established.

Exclusivism. Cults often believe that they alone possess the truth of God. The Mormons have a long history of teaching that they are the exclusive community of the saved on earth. The Jehovah's Witnesses believe they are the exclusive community of Jehovah on earth.

Isolationism. The more extreme cults sometimes create fortified boundaries. They sometimes require members to renounce and break off past associations with parents and siblings. The cult then functions as a surrogate family for those who have lost their biological families.

Fear of Disfellowshipping. Some cults disfellowship any member who questions or resists the teachings or instructions of the group. For example, if a Jehovah's Witness questions or resists the teachings of the Watchtower Society, he or she can be disfellowshipped and then shunned by family members and friends. The same is true in the Mormon church. Fear of disfellowshipping serves to keep cult members from causing any trouble in the cult.

Threats of Satanic Attack. Some cults warn new followers that friends and relatives may be used by Satan to try to dissuade them from remaining with the group. When a friend or relative actually does try to dissuade a new member in this way, the group appears to be in possession of God's truth. This, in turn, encourages the new convert to be even more loyal to the group.

How to Use This Book

I will briefly examine the history and teachings of 40 cults and cultic movements. You can read this book straight through or use it as a reference book.

A unique feature of this book is chapter 42: "Apologetic Power Points." The Apologetic Power Points represent concise biblical responses to cultic doctrinal errors. You will notice that the Power Points are numbered. At the end of each chapter in the book, I will provide the numbers of the Power Points that best answer the teachings of that particular cult. This information will equip you with a biblical response in the event that you encounter a member of this cult.

2
The Aetherius Society

THE AETHERIUS SOCIETY IS a popular UFO cult that claims to be a spiritual path to enlightenment.[1] It involves a group of dedicated people who cooperate with the Ascended Masters (also known as Cosmic Masters) to usher in a New Age of peace and enlightenment upon the world.[2] The Ascended Masters are allegedly historical persons who have finished their earthly evolutions and have moved on to higher planes of existence. They now voluntarily seek to help lesser-evolved human beings reach their exalted level.[3]

George King, a student of yoga, founded the Aetherius Society in 1954. While King was living in London, a spiritual "cosmic brotherhood" (made up of space brothers) informed him that he should prepare himself, for he was to become the voice of the "Interplanetary Parliament." He was to function as the "Primary Terrestrial Mental Channel." An Ascended Master had allegedly previously taught King how to obtain telepathic rapport with them.[4]

King claims that a little more than a week later, a Space Master entered his apartment when the door was locked. He gave King instructions in advanced yoga. From this initial meeting, King developed a rapport with the Ascended Master Aetherius, who resides on the planet Venus (an alleged spiritual planet).

King says that in 1958 he came into contact with the Ascended Master Jesus. Following his resurrection and ascension, Jesus reportedly went to live on Venus, where, in the company of other religious leaders such as Buddha and Ramakrishna, he continued his concern for the enlightenment of earthlings. Aetherians claim Jesus is one of the Great Masters and not the sole Son of God. This Master Jesus gave King the first chapter of his *Aquarian Age Bible*. King also continued to receive transmissions from Master Aetherius, which he published in a magazine entitled *Aetherius Speaks*.

The Cosmic Masters, King says, sincerely desire to help humanity. "The Cosmic Masters have been given permission to increase their help to mankind. To help mankind help himself and to guide us towards the New Age."[5] The Masters seek to give humans "cosmic knowledge" and increase their "spiritual energy."[6] This has become necessary because humanity is in danger of destroying itself.

> During World War II humanity once again found the power and means to cause global destruction through the use of atomic energy. We were in a position to allow our destructive tendencies to affect a system of life outside of our own world. If we destroyed this planet, it would affect the subtle balance of the Solar System itself.
>
> It became important for us to be watched to make sure this would not happen. It became important for us to be protected from the negative effects of our own actions and inactions. It became important to protect the life of the Mother Earth, herself, our great home.
>
> Since that time flying saucers, or UFOs, have been increasingly seen in our skies.[7]

The Aetherius Society teaches that physical flights between

distant planets are made possible by a special energy that facilitates flying at the speed of light. Aliens on highly developed planets are able to accomplish this by means of their advanced thought-power.

Presently the Aetherius Society rigorously studies UFO visitations to earth. Aetherius members say that UFO spacecrafts, normally functioning at a high vibratory rate, occasionally lower their vibratory rate so that humans on earth can see them. Like many others within the New Age UFO movement, Aetherians believe that the governments of the world have conspired to cover up reports of actual contacts with beings from outer space.

Beliefs

Ten pivotal doctrinal beliefs characterize the Aetherius Society:

1. Advanced, intelligent life exists on other planets.

2. UFOs are intelligently controlled extraterrestrial spacecrafts visiting earth to help humankind.

3. Jesus, Buddha, Krishna, and other religious leaders were of extraterrestrial origin and came to earth to help humanity.

4. Serving humankind is essential for spiritual progress to occur.

5. Human beings are a divine spark of God.

6. Religious people should cooperate with each other because all the world religions essentially teach the same thing.

7. Karma and reincarnation are laws of God. Karma refers to the debt a soul accumulates as a result of good or bad actions one commits during his or her life or past lives.

If one accumulates good karma, he or she will be reincarnated in a desirable state. If one accumulates bad karma,
he or she will be reincarnated in a less desirable state.

8. The earth is essentially a classroom on the evolutionary
   ladder of life back to the divine source from which we all
   came. Merging back with this divine source may take
   many lifetimes.

9. Mother Earth is a living, breathing entity, just as the Sun
   and galaxy are.[8]

10. The entire universe is a battleground between the
    opposing forces of good and evil. These forces battle on
    both the astral and physical planes. (The astral plane is
    allegedly an etheric spirit-plane of existence.) These forces
    advance from planet to planet by spaceships. "Because
    Terra [earth] is so underdeveloped spiritually, it could
    become easy prey and fall to an all-out assault by the
    forces of evil, led by a group with the ominous sounding
    name of the Black Magicians. What saves planet earth
    from destruction is the constant and repeated interven-
    tion on her behalf by the space masters."[9]

Aims

These are the primary aims of the Aetherius Society:

- To spread the teachings of the Cosmic (Ascended) Masters

- To create favorable conditions for contact with extraterrestrials

- To help New Age aspirants develop themselves spiritually
  through yoga and other spiritual disciplines

- To perform advanced metaphysical missions in cooperation with the Cosmic (Ascended) Masters to benefit both
  earth and humanity.[10]

The True Second Coming

The Aetherius Society espouses the idea that George King's
mother, Mary, met with Jesus aboard a spacecraft in 1959. Jesus
informed her that her son George had been chosen as a leader
among human beings in this New Age.

Some Aetherius members claim Mary King was the biblical
Mary in a previous life. In a way, then, this means that George
King is a form of Christ at his second coming.

King and the Aetherius Society are presently calling humanity
to open themselves to the new and imminent utopian age.

——— APOLOGETIC POWER POINTS ———

Other "Holy Books" Are Incompatible with the Bible. (11)

Jesus Is the Son of God. (33)

Jesus Is Unique. (37)

Humans Are Not Divine. (62)

Occultism Is Prohibited. (98)

Spiritism Is Prohibited. (99)

Reincarnation Is False. (103)

The World Religions Do Not Teach the Same
   Doctrines. (112)

The Space Brothers Are Demons in Disguise. (116)

The Ascended Masters Are Demons in Disguise. (117)

3

Anthroposophy

ANTHROPOSOPHY COMES FROM two Greek words: *anthropos*, meaning "man," and *sophia*, meaning "wisdom." Anthroposophy claims to be a spiritual science that embodies the wisdom of man. In reality, Anthroposophy is a blend of Christianity, Eastern religions, and various forms of occultism.

Rudolf Steiner (1861–1925) founded the Anthroposophical Society. He was a competent scholar with more than a hundred scientific, literary, and philosophical books published. He was particularly known for his work on Goethe's scientific writings.

Steiner had been an active member of the Theosophical Society and headed the German charter of the group (see chapter 33, "Theosophy"). However, when a Theosophical subgroup, the Order of the Star of the East, began promoting Eastern religious views and teachings that Krishnamurti was the new incarnation of the Christ, Steiner threatened to expel any member of the German charter who joined the Order. Annie Besant, who headed the Theosophical Society, retaliated by canceling Steiner's charter. Steiner promptly founded the Anthroposophical Society—also known as Anthroposophy—in 1912, and most of the German membership of Theosophy joined him.

Beliefs

Relationship with Theosophy. As an offshoot of Theosophy,

Anthroposophy has both similarities and differences with its parent cult. Researcher Timothy P. Weber makes this observation:

> Like Theosophy from which it came, Anthroposophy…affirms the existence of spiritual as well as material worlds and teaches that salvation consists of escaping the confines of the material world by obtaining esoteric spiritual knowledge about the true nature of things. Unlike Theosophy (wisdom of God), which holds that such knowledge comes from avatars (incarnations) and arhats (master teachers), Anthroposophy (wisdom of man) teaches that people possess the truth *within* themselves. By cultivating one's occult powers through certain mental, physical, and spiritual exercises, anyone can become a *Hellseher*, a master of clear vision, and thereby gain extraordinary spiritual insight.[1]

The most significant component of Steiner's theology is his Christology (doctrine of Christ), representing a significant departure from his Theosophical roots. Instead of arguing for a cosmic Christ who periodically incarnates into enlightened human beings throughout history, as Theosophy teaches, Steiner's emphasis was on what the Christ accomplished through his *decisive* incarnation in the human Jesus.

Revelations from the Akashic Records. Steiner's Christology is based on his investigation into the "Akashic Records." Occultists believe that the physical earth is surrounded by an immense spiritual field known as "Akasha" on which is impressed—like a celestial tape recording—every impulse of human thought, will, and emotion. It therefore constitutes a complete record of human history. Steiner, as a psychic, claimed to be able to read the Akashic

Records, thus enabling him to investigate human history without use of other written records. Based on this, he "discovered" that the descent of the Christ on the human Jesus was the absolutely central event of human evolution.

Humanity's Fall. Steiner believed the Christ's descent on the human Jesus became necessary because the consciousness of humankind had progressively become too focused on the material realm and had completely lost touch with the spiritual nature behind physical reality. This was humanity's fall. The danger was that this situation could become permanent.

The Christ's Solution. To prevent such a situation, the Christ's initial goal was to incarnate into a human being (Jesus) so he could accomplish his greater goal of incarnating from Jesus into the "etheric earth." Occultists believe an etheric earth exists behind the physical earth. The etheric earth is allegedly made up of a fine energy substance from which is created the mold for every form that is manifested in the physical plane. Every material object on the physical plane has an etheric counterpart. All material forms in the physical universe find their ultimate source in this energy substance of the etheric realm. The Christ desired to enter this etheric earth so he could bring about spiritual changes among people living on the physical earth. But in order to transfer from his spiritual realm to the etheric realm, he needed a human instrument through which to work. This instrument was Jesus.

The Centrality of the Crucifixion. The Christ incarnated into Jesus at his baptism. Three years later, at the crucifixion, the Christ left Jesus' body and incarnated into the etheric earth. Steiner explains this:

> The blood flowed from the wounds of Jesus Christ. This blood must not be regarded simply as chemical

substance, it must be recognized as something altogether unique. When it flowed from His wounds and into the earth, a substance was imparted to our earth which, in uniting with it, constituted an event of the greatest possible significance; this blood passed through a process of 'etherization'....Since the Mystery of Golgotha, the etherized blood of Christ Jesus has lived in the ether of the earth. The etheric body of the earth is permeated by what the blood that flowed on Golgotha became.[2]

Because of this, Steiner says, "ever since the Mystery of Golgotha man lives in a spiritual environment, an environment that has been Christianized because it has absorbed the Christ impulse."[3] Planet earth now mystically embodies the Christ.

The True Second Coming. Having mystically entered the etheric earth through his "etherized" blood, the Christ now seeks to "mass incarnate" into all humanity. This will lead to humankind's redemption. Steiner says that the "Christ impulse will penetrate humanity. He belongs to the whole earth and can enter all human souls, regardless of nation and religion."[4] This, says Steiner, is the true second coming.

Supersensible Perception of the Spiritual Worlds. Steiner argues that after Jesus' death on the cross, his spiritual, "phantom" (not bodily) resurrection was "clairvoyantly perceived" by the disciples. Steiner's techniques of meditation allegedly enable those who follow Anthroposophy to gain "supersensible perception of the spiritual worlds" and thereby recognize the Christ within them.[5] As Steiner explains it, "through such meditation a complete transformation takes place in the student. He begins to form quite new conceptions of reality."[6] This new conception of reality centers on the Christ within.

APOLOGETIC POWER POINTS

Jesus Is the Christ. (34)

Jesus Is Unique. (37)

Jesus Atoned for Sin. (40)

The Incarnate Jesus Had Two Natures. (47)

Jesus Will Return at the Second Coming. (51)

Humans Are Not Divine. (62)

Humans Are Fallen in Sin. (67)

Salvation Is by Grace Through Faith. (71)

Occultism Is Prohibited. (98)

Spiritism Is Prohibited. (99)

Mysticism Is Unreliable. (104)

Eastern Meditation Is Prohibited. (108)

The World Religions Do Not Teach the Same
Doctrines. (112)

4
The Arcane School

IN THE EARLY 1920S, ALICE AND FOSTER Bailey founded an occultic group called the Arcane School. Alice had been an active member of the Esoteric Section of the Theosophy—an inner group of trusted members who faithfully practiced Theosophy (see chapter 33, "Theosophy"). However, she eventually became critical of the organization's policy that one could not become a disciple or spokesperson of an Ascended Master (a highly evolved spiritual being who helps lesser evolved beings) unless one was notified by Annie Besant, president of the Theosophical Society.

This led to Alice Bailey's dismissal from the society. Shortly thereafter, in 1923, she and her husband, Foster, founded the Arcane School. Bailey describes this school as "non-sectarian, non-political, but deeply international in its thinking." She suggested that "service is its keynote. Its members can work in any sect and any political party provided that they remember that all paths lead to God and that the welfare of the one humanity governs all their thinking."[1]

Alice Bailey was convinced she was the "mouthpiece" of an Ascended Master known as the Tibetan. She reflects on her spiritistic encounters with this entity:

> I remain in full control of my senses of perception...I simply listen and take down the words that I hear and register the thoughts which are dropped one by one

into my brain....I have never changed anything that the Tibetan has ever given to me....I do not always understand what is given. I do not always agree. But I record it all honestly and then discover it does make sense and evokes intuitive response.[2]

Bailey produced 19 occultic books as the mouthpiece of the Tibetan. Two of the more significant of these, both very popular among today's New Agers, are *The Externalization of the Hierarchy* and *The Reappearance of the Christ*. Other well-known volumes include *A Treatise on Cosmic Fire* and *A Treatise on White Magic*.

Beliefs

Jesus: A Vehicle for the Christ. Bailey believed Jesus was a Master whose body served as a vehicle for a mighty cosmic being, "the Christ," some 2000 years ago. She writes about this in *The Externalization of the Hierarchy*:

Few mediums...know how to carry on this work in such a way that never for a moment are they unaware of what they themselves are doing and the purpose of their activity. Definitely and with purpose they lend their body temporarily to another soul for service, preserving their own integrity all the time. The highest expression of this type of activity was the giving of his body by the disciple Jesus for the use of the Christ.[3]

Buddha Prepared the Way. Bailey suggested that the Buddha prepared the way for the coming of the Christ in the human Jesus. "The Buddha came forth to...lay the foundation for a more enlightened approach to life, giving the teaching which would open the door to the work of the Christ who would, He knew, follow in His steps."[4] This is in keeping with Bailey's emphasis that all religions are paths to God.

The True Second Coming. According to Arcane thought, the Christ—along with his disciples, the Ascended Masters—will draw closer and closer to humanity and eventually appear on the physical plane. This is the true second coming. Bailey said this return necessitated three conditions that either have already come or are currently coming to pass: (1) catastrophic planetary conditions, (2) a spiritual awakening, and (3) a steadily mounting invocative prayer.

The Great Invocation. The last condition noted above refers to the use of the Great Invocation, a prayer intended to speed the reappearance of the Christ. This prayer expresses "truths common to all the major religions, and is now being used across the world by people of many differing faiths and creeds. It is a prayer which focuses the call for help from man to the Higher Worlds."[5] Here is the prayer:

> From the Point of Light within the Mind of God
> Let light stream forth into the minds of men.
> Let Light descend on Earth.

> From the point of Love within the Heart of God
> Let love stream forth into the hearts of men.
> May Christ return to the Earth.

> From the center where the Will of God is known
> Let purpose guide the little wills of men—
> The purpose which the Masters know and serve.

> From the center which we call the race of men
> Let the Plan of Love and Light work out
> And may it seal the door where evil dwells.[6]

Human Preparation. Preparation for the second coming is the responsibility of "attuned" human beings. Those who know about this coming are to help create conditions of "spiritual alignment" which will ultimately draw the Christ forth into our midst. Without this, the Christ is impotent to act. The more enlightened human beings—the more who pray the Great Invocation—the better.

Bailey believed the Christ will come again in a way that will create no divisions or separations between human beings, either religious, social, or ideological. When he comes, he will establish through precept and example the principles on which an interdependent world may create a new civilization.

Bailey taught that the second coming will be in a single Avatar, but she also affirmed that he will be mystically manifested in all humanity:

> Slowly, there is dawning upon the awakening consciousness of humanity, the great paralleling truth of God Immanent—divinely "pervading" all forms, conditioning from within all kingdoms in nature, expressing innate divinity through human beings and—two thousand years ago—portraying the nature of that divine Immanence in the Person of the Christ. Today, as an outcome of this unfolding divine Presence, there is entering into the minds of men everywhere a new concept: that of Christ in us, the hope of Glory. There is a growing and developing belief that Christ is in us, as He was in the Master Jesus, and this belief will alter world affairs and mankind's entire attitude to life.[7]

We can easily understand why the writings of Alice Bailey have remained popular among modern New Agers. Her influence has extended far beyond her lifetime.

—————— **APOLOGETIC POWER POINTS** ——————

Other "Holy Books" Are Incompatible with the Bible. (11)

God Is Transcendent and Immanent. (15)

Pantheism Is False. (26)

Jesus Is God. (30)

Jesus Is the Christ. (34)

Jesus Is the Only Way. (36)

Jesus Is Unique. (37)

Jesus Will Return at the Second Coming. (51)

Occultism Is Prohibited. (98)

Spiritism Is Prohibited. (99)

Mysticism Is Unreliable. (104)

The World Religions Do Not Teach the Same
  Doctrines. (112)

The Ascended Masters Are Demons in Disguise. (117)

5

The Association for Research and Enlightenment

EDGAR CAYCE IS PERHAPS HISTORY'S most thoroughly documented psychic. Born near Hopkinsville, Kentucky in 1877, Cayce was raised during a time of great religious revival, and this may account for his lifelong interest in the Bible.

Cayce's psychic abilities go back to his childhood. At just seven years of age, the youngster claimed he could see little invisible playmates who would disperse when real people entered the room. He also informed his parents he could see visions and could sometimes see relatives who had recently died. He claimed he could sleep with his head on his school textbooks and automatically learn their contents by means of his photographic memory without having to study.[1] He apparently derived his occultic interest from his grandfather, who was a water witch, and his father, a pied piper of snakes.

Cayce became well known for his psychic readings. Many of these readings related to health problems of people who came to see him. Typically, as his client was sitting in the room, Cayce would lie down, close his eyes, fold his hands, and drift into a self-induced sleep state—a deep altered state of consciousness. Because he uttered his psychic readings during a sleep state, he became widely known as the "sleeping prophet." During the sleep state, Cayce allegedly helped people with such health problems as cancer, diabetes, multiple sclerosis, gallstones, kidney stones, hay fever, digestive problems, epilepsy, hemorrhoids, ulcers, psoriasis, and even psychological problems. Many newspapers picked up on this, and Cayce enjoyed wide publicity.

Cayce used two primary sources for his readings: (1) the subconscious mind of his client, and (2) the Akashic Records. Occultists believe that the physical earth is surrounded by an immense spiritual field known as "Akasha" on which is impressed—like a celestial tape recording—every impulse of human thought, will, and emotion. It therefore allegedly constitutes a complete record of human history. Cayce claimed the ability to read the Akashic Records, thus enabling him to investigate human history without use of other written records.

Cayce gave more than 16,000 readings. Of these, 14,246 were stenographically recorded (on 49,000 pages) and are filed in indexed form—utilizing some 200,000 file cards—in the fireproof vaults at the Association for Research and Enlightenment headquarters building. Perhaps 5000 of these readings deal with religious matters, while the others deal with the health problems of his innumerable clients.

Cayce also spoke prophecies based on his psychic readings. These include the prediction that California would slide into the sea, that New York would sink beneath the waves, and that the lost continent of Atlantis would rise out of the ocean. Because no such events occurred, Cayce failed the test for a biblical prophet— 100 percent accuracy (Deuteronomy 18:22).

Beliefs

The theological doctrines Cayce derived from his psychic readings agree perfectly with current New Age ideas as well as the Mind Science cults:

- The Bible is one among many holy books, and we should interpret it symbolically or esoterically.

- God is a pantheistic, impersonal force.

- Because all is God, human beings are a part of God.

- Human beings are not morally fallen in sin but rather have fallen into a mental fixation on the world of matter, losing all awareness of their inner divinity.

- Salvation comes by recovering the awareness of one's divinity. Salvation is enlightenment.

- Death brings spiritual advancement through reincarnation. As people progressively overcome bad karma, they eventually attain eternal life with no further need to incarnate.

- Heaven and hell are just states of mind.

Cayce's Version of Jesus

Cayce's ideas about Jesus are worthy of more detailed attention. The person we know as Jesus, Cayce tells us, had 29 previous incarnations: "These included an early sun worshipper, the author of the Book of the Dead, and Hermes, who was supposedly the architect of the Great Pyramid. Jesus was also Zend (the father of Zoroaster), Amilius (an Atlantean), and other figures of ancient history."[2] Other incarnations include Adam, Joseph, Joshua, Enoch, and Melchizedek.

Since the soul who became Jesus of Nazareth had earlier incarnated as the biblical Adam, Jesus is the one, Cayce says, who sinned in the Garden of Eden. Cayce suggests that even when he fell in Eden, the soul who would become Jesus knew he would one day be the Savior of the world. In the soul who became Jesus, then, we have both the sinner and the Savior.

This particular soul did not become the Christ until his thirtieth incarnation—as Jesus of Nazareth. The reason Jesus had to go through so many incarnations is that he, like all other human beings, had karmic debt to work off. According to Eastern thought, karma refers to the debt a soul accumulates as a result of good or bad actions committed during one's life or past lives. People who accumulate good karma will allegedly be reincarnated in a desirable state. People who accumulate bad karma will be reincarnated in a less desirable state. In Cayce's thought, Jesus, in his earlier incarnation as Adam, accumulated karmic debt, and only in his thirtieth reincarnation, as Jesus of Nazareth, did he completely shed this karma.

Jesus thus saved himself by good works. Nonetheless, he did not atone for the sins of others. Jesus was merely a "way-shower." This is the only sense in which Jesus may be called a Savior. He modeled the way for human beings to find their way back to God. All of us will allegedly accomplish what Jesus accomplished, though this may require many lifetimes.

According to Cayce, Jesus received a comprehensive education. Prior to his twelfth year, he attained a thorough knowledge of the Jewish law:

> From his twelfth to his fifteenth or sixteenth year he was taught the prophecies by Judy [an Essene teacher] in her home at Carmel. Then began his education abroad. He was sent first again into Egypt for only a short period, then into India for three years, then into that later called Persia....From Persia he was called to Judea at the death of Joseph, then went into Egypt for the completion of his preparation as a teacher.[3]

During his alleged studies abroad, Jesus was tutored by such educators as Kahjian in India, Junner in Persia, and Zar in Egypt. He learned healing, weather control, telepathy, astrology, and other psychic arts.

When his education was complete, Jesus went back to his homeland, where he performed miracles and taught the multitudes for three years. The primary goal of his three-year ministry was not to provide salvation for humanity but to show others how they, like he, could save themselves. Following his short ministry, Jesus was put to death and then came to life in an esoteric manner—that is, "by forming from the ether waves."[4] But even this was nothing unique; what he accomplished, all human beings may accomplish.

The Association of Research and Enlightenment

Though Cayce died in 1945, the Association of Research and Enlightenment has continued to propagate his ideas and his primary psychic readings through the years. This association, founded in 1931, exists to "preserve, research and disseminate the psychic work of Edgar Cayce."[5] Toward this end, the worldwide association conducts workshops, conferences, and youth camps. People from all walks of life and various spiritual traditions have allegedly found life-transforming insights by studying materials from the association.

───────── **APOLOGETIC POWER POINTS** ─────────

Esotericism Is Illegitimate. (7)

Sound Hermeneutics Yields Proper Interpretation. (8)

Pantheism Is False. (26)

Jesus Is God. (30)

6

Astrology

ASTROLOGY IS THE SINGLE MOST predominant form of divination in the world. Some estimates place the number of people who believe in astrology at one fourth of earth's population, but at the very least some one billion people are advocates. More than 80 percent of the newspapers in the United States carry horoscope columns, and two-thirds of all Americans read them daily. Ten thousand professional astrologers live in this country and have at least 20 million clients. Of great concern is the fact that more than 10 percent of those claiming to be born-again Christians believe in astrology.[1]

What is the appeal? In short, astrology promises to bring answers to the questions people have about life (and the beyond). People think astrology can give them reliable information about how to be successful in life, how to remain healthy, how to understand one's emotions and personal characteristics, how to protect oneself from various dangers in the future, and much more. People latch on to astrology because of the perceived benefits it will bring them. What many do not realize is that in participating in astrology, they are also participating in occultism, which God clearly condemns (Deuteronomy 18:9-12).

Nancy Reagan, the wife of the late President Ronald Reagan, gave astrology a strong boost toward the mainstream in the late 1980s by consulting with an astrologer on a regular basis during the Reagan White House years. This gave an air of respectability to astrology on a worldwide level.

News of Nancy Reagan's involvement with astrology first surfaced in 1988 when Donald Regan, President Reagan's chief of staff for two years, disclosed in his book *For the Record* that astrology exercised an inordinately powerful influence in the Reagan White House. Some time later, Joan Quigley—Nancy Reagan's astrologer, who operated out of San Francisco—published a book entitled *What Does Joan Say? My Seven Years as White House Astrologer to Nancy and Ronald Reagan*, debuting with a first printing of 175,000 copies.[2] In this book Quigley documents her consultations with Nancy Reagan. Nancy Reagan also wrote a book entitled *My Turn*, which remained on the *New York Times* bestseller list for 14 weeks. In this book, Mrs. Reagan devotes ten pages to Joan Quigley. "I want to state one thing again and unequivocally," she writes. "Joan's recommendations had nothing to do with policy or politics—ever. Her advice was confined to timing—to Ronnie's schedule and to what days were good or bad, especially with regard to his out-of-town trips."[3]

Mrs. Reagan reportedly paid Quigley $3000 to $5000 per month for her services. "You learn something from living in the White House," Mrs. Reagan explains in her book, "and I didn't think an astrologer should be sent checks signed by the First Lady. And so I asked a friend back in California [Betsy Bloomingdale] to pay Joan, and I reimbursed her each month."[4]

Lloyd Shearer, who wrote a *Parade Magazine* article on Nancy Reagan's use of astrology, phoned Quigley to ask her how important a role she played as White House astrologer. Quigley claimed that "for seven years, she had selected the times for his press conferences, most of his important speeches, his State of the Union addresses, [and] many of the takeoffs and landings of Air Force One. 'I delayed President Reagan's first cancer operation from

July 10, 1985, to July 13,' she said, 'and I chose the time for Nancy's mastectomy.' "[5]

Astrology: A Form of Divination

Astrology is a form of divination that forecasts events on earth and among humans by observing and interpreting the planets, stars, sun, and moon. More specifically, astrology makes forecasts of a person's life by drawing up a horoscope chart that shows the positions of the planets and zodiacal signs at the moment of the person's birth, taking into account where the person was born. The positions of the planets at the moment of one's birth allegedly reflect one's character and destiny. The credo is "As above, so below." The planets and stars above are mystically connected to earth and human beings below.

Astrology's roots reach back to Babylon in 3000 BC.[6] The ancient Babylonians observed how orderly and rhythmically the planets moved across the sky and concluded that the planets were "gods of the night." They assigned godlike powers and character to the planets and worshipped them. These gods supposedly controlled the fate of human beings on earth in a broad sense—that is, they controlled the destiny *of nations*. The priests of Babylon sought to understand and predict the movements of these planets so that perhaps they could use this knowledge beneficially on their nation's behalf. To study and worship these deities, the Babylonians built towers called ziggurats. Apparently, the Tower of Babel was such a ziggurat.

Today astrology is a bit different. Instead of focusing broadly on nations, astrology promises information about individual people. Also, the old school of thought in astrology was fatalistic in the sense that it was considered deterministic (with little or no room for freewill decisions to change the course of one's destiny), but astrology today forecasts trends, likelihoods, and influences. Astrology today generally does not suggest an absolutely predetermined future. People use the trends and influences from horoscope charts to make wise decisions for the future.

The Horoscope Chart

The horoscope chart has three primary components: the planets, the signs of the zodiac, and the 12 houses. A person's horoscope chart constitutes a map of precisely where the planets and zodiacal constellations were at the moment of his or her birth, and this chart forecasts trends and influences for that person's life.

The Planets. The planets are placed on the chart according to mathematical formulas. These formulas consider two primary facts: one's time of birth and the latitude and longitude of one's birthplace. Each planet has its own personality or distinct character. For example, Venus is associated with love and beauty. Mars is associated with aggression and spontaneity. These characteristics can be modified by the "house" in which the planet is found (see below) as well as by the signs of the zodiac.

The Signs of the Zodiac. The zodiac is an imaginary belt in the heavens that comprises the 12 signs of the zodiac. The horoscope chart—a chart of the zodiac—is a circular diagram that contains 360 degrees. The 12 zodiac signs are equally divided among these 360 degrees, each containing 30 degrees. These zodiac signs are Aries the Ram, Taurus the Bull, Gemini the Twins, Cancer the Crab, Leo the Lion, Virgo the Virgin, Libra the Scales, Scorpio the Scorpion, Sagittarius the Archer, Capricorn the Goat, Aquarius the Water Bearer, and Pisces the Fish. These zodiac signs allegedly describe the ways that planets are limited or expanded.

The 12 Houses. The 12 houses on the horoscope chart represent various areas of one's life, including one's home, one's marriage, one's career, and so forth. As earth rotates, and the houses with it, the planets move into these various houses. The planets then influence that particular area of life with their distinct characteristics.

This may seem complicated to the uninitiated. The important point to remember is that the astrologer's goal is to interpret how the planets, houses, and signs of the zodiac relate to each other and influence each other. These relationships forecast trends, likelihoods, and influences for people. The astrologer's interpretation is based on personal knowledge of the meanings of the planets and their positions on the chart at the time of the client's birth.

Astrologers watch for "angular relationships." For example, a 90-degree aspect between two planets (called a "square aspect") reveals tension and disagreement. A 120-degree aspect between two planets (called a "trine aspect") reveals sympathy and cooperation. By analyzing such angular relationships, the astrologer draws conclusions regarding the client's future.

Is Astrology a Science?

Modern astrologers often deny any connection with occultism and argue that astrology is an objective science that uses scientific methodology. They claim to make mathematical calculations and then interpret the data.

Critics, however, maintain that the mere use of mathematical formulas to plot the position of planets at the time and place of one's birth does not remove astrology from the realm of occultism. Astrologers often delve into other forms of occultism, such as palmistry and numerology, and they often develop psychic powers.[7] Some astrologers admit that their practice is a form of occultism. Others admit that spirit guides help them properly interpret horoscope charts. Still others suggest that they have become adept at reading horoscope charts because they were astrologers in their past lives. All of this reeks with occultism.

Beliefs

God. Astrologers are generally pantheistic, holding that all things in the universe are divine. They are open to different ideas about God, but they are unanimous in rejecting a biblical God who sets forth moral requirements for human beings.

Jesus Christ. Jesus is not uniquely God in human flesh. He did not die for the sins of humankind and is not the Savior. Some astrologers suggest that Jesus died to pay off his own karmic debt.

Sin. Humankind is not fallen in sin and does not need a Savior. If human beings have any problem at all, they have simply become out of harmony with the divine forces of the universe.[8]

Salvation. To restore harmony with the divine forces of the universe, people must become aware of the effect of celestial patterns (by means of astrology).

——— APOLOGETIC POWER POINTS ———

Pantheism Is False. (26)

Jesus Is God. (30)

Jesus Is the Savior. (35)

Jesus Atoned for Sin. (40)

Humans Are Fallen in Sin. (67)

Salvation Is by Grace Through Faith. (71)

Occultism Is Prohibited. (98)

Spiritism Is Prohibited. (99)

Astrology Is Prohibited. (100)

Reincarnation Is False. (103)

7
The Baha'i Faith

SINCE ITS INCEPTION IN THE 1800s, the Baha'i Faith has established more than 17,000 Baha'i Local Spiritual Assemblies all over the world, with more than 4500 in the United States alone. Baha'is boast five million members in 235 countries. People can now read Baha'i literature in more than 700 languages.[1] Why has Baha'i touched a nerve with so many people? Baha'i's emphasis on the unity of world religions and their prophets is likely its most appealing teaching.

Unity is at the very heart of Baha'i. Every person in the world is considered a single drop in one ocean. Since we are all "one," we should work toward a universal brotherhood.[2] All of us have a single origin, so we have no reason for division. This principle applies to religion.

Baha'is believe the founders of the various world religions provided humankind with newly updated versions of the *same basic beliefs* from the *same God*.[3] The only differences between the religions are superficial and merely reflect the conditions of humankind that existed when the revelation was given.

Baha'is view religion as "a progressive, evolutionary process which needs to be updated as humanity evolves mentally, socially, and spiritually. Every so often a new prophet is sent to humanity to update religion to the current needs of mankind."[4] Each new manifestation of God—such as the Buddha or Jesus—brings progressively larger increments of truth.

The Baha'i Faith emerged out of Islam. This has caused no small suffering on the part of Baha'is worldwide. Islam teaches that Muhammad is the greatest of all prophets. Baha'i recognizes continual manifestations of God, the latest and greatest being Baha'u'llah. Muslims interpret this as a blasphemy against Muhammad and have persecuted—even executed—Baha'is through the years.

In 1844, Mirza Ali Muhammad—allegedly a direct descendent of Muhammad—proclaimed himself as the greatest manifestation of God to ever appear in human history.[5] Also known as "the Bab" (meaning "the Gate"), he claimed to be the fulfillment of prophecies from the various world religions. His revelations represent the actual beginnings of the Baha'i Faith.

The Bab prophesied that an even greater manifestation of God would follow him. The Bab considered himself to be a John the Baptist figure preparing the way for the coming of this greater manifestation.

No stranger to persecution, the Bab faced his own execution in 1850. Baha'i legend contends that hundreds of bullets were miraculously deflected. Some 750 Armenian soldiers opened fire on the Bab, and when the smoke cleared, he had disappeared, and the rope that had bound his hands was found in shreds. He was discovered back in his jail cell, giving final instructions to one of his followers. After this, the Bab instructed his captors that they could proceed with his execution. Following the execution, a fierce black whirlwind allegedly swept into the city.

The following decade, in 1863, one of the Bab's followers—Mirza Husayn Ali—proclaimed himself to be the fulfillment of the Bab's prophecy of a greater manifestation of God. He took the name "Baha'u'llah," meaning "The Glory of God." His followers became known as Baha'is, or "Followers of the Glory." According to legend, Baha'u'llah was an extraordinary person, even as child. He could supposedly answer any question posed to him.[6]

Not only was Baha'u'llah a new revelation from God, following in the footsteps of such spiritual luminaries as Moses, Buddha, Jesus, and Muhammad, but he was also the fulfillment of prophecies in the Christian Bible regarding the second coming, and he was the "other comforter" Jesus spoke of in the Upper Room Discourse (John 14:16). He is also Maitreya the Buddha (prophesied in Buddhist scripture), the new incarnation of Krishna for the Hindus, and a fulfillment of the "Day of God" spoken of in the Muslim Koran.[7]

Some 30 years after Baha'u'llah took over Baha'i leadership (1891), he proclaimed that his work was now finished, and the time had come for him to depart this world. He soon contracted a fever and died. Leadership of the group then passed to his son, Abbas Effendi (1844–1921). Effendi's primary goal was to rightly interpret his father's writings to followers of Baha'i, claiming infallibility in his interpretations. He did not claim to be a manifestation of God. Soon enough, Effendi took the name Abdul Baha (Servant of the Baha'i) and in 1912 brought the Baha'i Faith to the United States.

Upon his death, leadership passed to his Oxford-educated grandson Shoghi Effendi (the "Guardian of the Faith"). Effendi proved to be a prolific writer, and mainstream bookstores continue to distribute his books. Under his leadership, Baha'i became a global religion and spread to some 35 countries.

Effendi did not stipulate in his will who was to be his successor when he died. Subsequently, upon his death in 1957, Baha'i leadership passed to a Baha'i Universal House of Justice, composed of a nine-person board. This group has remained the supreme legislative and executive governing body of Baha'i. Members of this board come from three different religions—

Judaism, Christianity, and Islam—thereby symbolizing the unity of religions espoused by Baha'i.

Beliefs

God. Baha'is believe the various names for God in the different world religions—Yahweh, Allah, Brahma, and the like—all refer to the same God. However, God is so exalted, so ineffable, so beyond us that one cannot truly know him. It is impossible "for mortal men and women, with limited intellect and finite capacities, to directly comprehend or understand the Divine reality."[8] For this reason, Baha'is do not attempt to define God, except to say he certainly is not a Trinity. Rather, Baha'is simply refer to God with such terms as "the Most Exalted, the Inaccessible," "the Invisible and Unknowable Essence," and "the All-Pervading, the Incorruptible."[9]

Jesus Christ. Baha'is believe Jesus was one of many manifestations of God. Jesus was the way, the truth, and the life—but only for his time. He was certainly not God incarnate, he claimed no deity, he performed no miracles, and he never claimed to be the Son of God. As a manifestation of God, Jesus was inferior to Baha'u'llah. After all, Baha'u'llah is the fulfillment of biblical references to the second coming. As well, he is the fulfillment of messianic passages in the Old Testament, including Isaiah 9:2-7; 11:1-2; 40:1-5; and 53. Further, Baha'u'llah is the "other comforter" Jesus spoke of in the Upper Room Discourse (John 14:16).

Jesus' death on the cross did not attain human salvation. At most, his death was an example of self-sacrifice. Nor did Jesus rise from the dead. "Resurrection" is simply a metaphorical way of saying that Jesus' teachings and his cause found "new life" in the disciples' minds after three days of troublesome doubting.

Humanity. Human beings are not morally fallen in sin.

People err and make mistakes, but they are not intrinsically evil. No true messenger of God—including Jesus—ever taught the doctrine of original sin (a "false doctrine" that emerged in the sixteenth century).[10] People *learn* how to sin. The good news, Baha'is say, is that every person can live according to God's law, *un*learning sin and warranting salvation.

Salvation. Salvation comes as result of obeying God's law. The only salvation in any age is to "turn again towards God, to accept his Manifestation for that day, and to follow his teachings."[11] No Baha'i can know for sure that he or she is saved.

Heaven and Hell. Heaven and hell are not real places. They are mere states of being. People can experience heaven or hell on earth by obeying or disobeying God's laws. Those who obey experience "heaven" (existing in a happy state). Those who disobey experience "hell" (existing in an unhappy state).[12]

The afterlife is not clearly defined in the Baha'i Faith. It is a mystery. Baha'u'llah affirmed that "the nature of the soul after death can never be described."[13] Most Baha'is, however, expect to live with God in paradise.

APOLOGETIC POWER POINTS

Other "Holy Books" Are Incompatible with the Bible. (11)

God Is Personal. (12)

God's Attributes Reveal His Nature. (18)

God Is a Trinity. (22)

Jesus Is God. (30)

Jesus Is the Son of God. (33)

Jesus Is the Only Way. (36)

Jesus Is Unique. (37)

Jesus Performed Miracles. (39)

Jesus Atoned for Sin. (40)

Jesus Physically Rose from the Dead. (50)

Jesus Will Return at the Second Coming. (51)

The Spirit of Truth Is the Holy Spirit. (59)

Humans Are Fallen in Sin. (67)

All Humans Are Infected by Sin (Original Sin). (68)

The Law Cannot Save. (70)

Heaven Is Real. (77)

Hell Is Real. (78)

All Messianic Prophecies Point to Jesus. (95)

False Prophets Are Recognizable. (96)

The World Religions Do Not Teach the Same Doctrines. (112)

8
Christadelphians

THE WORD "CHRISTADELPHIANS" derives from two Greek words: *Christos* (meaning "Christ") and *adelphos* (meaning "brother"). The Christadelphians consider themselves the brothers of Christ.

Dr. John Thomas (1805–1871) founded the sect. Thomas, born in London, set out to immigrate to the United States in 1832, and while en route, the ship on which he was traveling encountered a severe storm. Fearing for his life, Thomas promised that if God saw him safely to the United States, he would devote his life to studying biblical truth.

Upon arriving in the United States, Thomas first joined up with the Campbellites, followers of Thomas and Alexander Campbell. In 1844, however, he left over differences he had with them, and some of the Campbellites accompanied him. For a time, his followers were casually known as "the Thomasites." Thomas eventually founded several magazines to spread his teachings.

When the Civil War broke out in 1861, Thomas and his followers took on the name "Christadelphians." They were pacifists, and they were taking a stand against fighting as a religious group, so they needed a formal name. "Christadelphians" seemed appropriate since they considered themselves to be "brothers of Christ."[1]

Today Christadelphian communities exist in America, Canada, Great Britain, and Australia. Smaller Christadelphian groups are in Central and South America, Africa, Eastern Europe, and the Pacific Rim.

Beliefs

Bible. The Bible is the only authoritative creed. It is the infallible and inerrant Word of God.

God. God is said to be "one" (Unitarian). There is no Trinity.[2] "We reject the doctrine that God is three persons."[3] Christadelphians believe the doctrine of the Trinity is a pagan teaching that infiltrated the apostate church. The Trinity is nowhere to be found in the Old Testament and is a doctrine that does not make sense.[4] "We reject the idea of a God with multiple independent personalities as not being in harmony with the teachings of Scripture."[5]

Jesus Christ. Jesus was not God in human flesh. He did not exist until he was born in Bethlehem. "We reject the doctrine that the Son of God was co-eternal with the Father."[6] "There is no hint in the Old Testament that the Son of God was already existent or in any way active at that time."[7] Jesus "did not actually come into being until He was begotten of the Holy Spirit and born in Bethlehem."[8] If Jesus were God, they argue, he could not have died on the cross, for God cannot die. If Jesus were God, he would be all-knowing, but he did not even know the day of his return (Mark 13:32). Further, if Jesus were God, he would be invisible, for God is invisible (1 Timothy 6:16).

Christadelphians also believe Jesus had a sin nature and was thus in need of redemption himself.[9] "It is not only that Jesus was called a sinner at his trial by his enemies or that he was 'numbered with the transgressors' when he was crucified between two thieves, but more particularly that he shared the very nature which had made a sinner out of every other man who had borne it."[10] Jesus inherited this sinful nature from Mary. "It was for that very reason—being a member of a sinful race—that the Lord Jesus himself needed salvation."[11]

Jesus did not finally and completely attain human salvation at the cross. "We reject as unbiblical the idea that Christ could die as a replacement for us, thus covering all our sins forever with that one act. Certainly it is through his sacrifice that we may be forgiven, but *only* if we walk the path of self-denial that he marked out for us."[12]

Holy Spirit. The Holy Spirit is not a person and is not God, but is simply the invisible impersonal power or energy of God. "The Spirit is not a 'separate' or 'other' person. It is God's own radiant power, ever out flowing from him, by which his 'everywhereness' is achieved." Further, the Spirit is personal only in the sense that "it is of God Himself: it is not personal in the sense of being some other person within the Godhead."[13] Through the Holy Spirit, the Father (God) is omnipresent. Through the Holy Spirit (as God's power), Jesus was able to perform miracles.

Humankind. God created human beings. They do not have an immortal soul that consciously survives death. "We reject the doctrine that man consciously exists in death."[14] "When we see someone die, no matter how nice it is to think that a part of them remains alive, the empirical evidence points to the fact that they are totally dead."[15] "Our only hope lies in the resurrection from the dead when Christ returns to this earth. In the meantime, the dead lie in the earth in the sleep of death, alive only in the memory of God, until Jesus comes."[16]

Church. The Christadelphians claim to have the only true church. All other churches are a part of apostate Christendom. One cannot be saved without being a Christadelphian. Christadelphians will not extend fellowship to those who hold to doctrines different from their own.

Salvation. Salvation is not by grace through faith. One must be perpetually obedient to God throughout life in order to be saved. "We reject the doctrine that the Gospel alone will save, without obedience to Christ's commandments."[17] Salvation is an extended process that includes a lifetime of obedience. Faith in Christ takes care of the sins of one's past, but obedience to God is necessary to retain God's favor and remain acceptable to Him. Baptism is necessary for salvation. Immortality is reserved for the future resurrection and is only for the truly righteous.[18] Once saved, believers can lose their salvation.

Satan. Satan is not a real supernatural angelic person. Rather, he represents the human tendency to engage in sin. "Satan" is an evil principle that is deep in human nature, inclining people to evil acts.

Hell. Hell is not an eternal place of punishment. "We reject the doctrine that the wicked will suffer eternal torture in hell."[19] The wicked experience no eternal conscious punishment, so such a hell is unneeded. The wicked will be annihilated.

——— APOLOGETIC POWER POINTS ———

God's Attributes Reveal His Nature. (18)

God Is a Trinity. (22)

The Trinity Is Not a Pagan Idea. (23)

Jesus Is God. (30)

Jesus Is Omniscient. (31)

Jesus Is the Son of God. (33)

Jesus Was Sinless. (38)

Jesus Atoned for Sin. (40)

The Incarnate Jesus Had Two Natures. (47)

Jesus Completed the Work of Salvation. (49)

Jesus' Death Does Not Detract from His Deity. (52)

The Holy Spirit Is a Person. (57)

The Holy Spirit Is God. (58)

The Law Cannot Save. (70)

Salvation Is by Grace Through Faith. (71)

Baptism Is Not Necessary for Salvation. (75)

Hell Is Real. (78)

There Is Conscious Existence After Death. (80)

Annihilationism Is False. (81)

Satan Is a Fallen Angel. (84)

9
Christian Identity

THE TERM "CHRISTIAN IDENTITY" refers to a social, political, and spiritual movement that emerged in the mid-1940s among religiously inclined racists.[1] It involves a loose-knit conglomeration of churches and individuals who are united in their view that the white Aryan race is God's chosen race and is the ten lost tribes of Israel. The Jews and other races are instruments of the devil. An influential preacher who gave momentum to the movement in the 1940s was Wesley Swift (more on him below). Among those who have been attracted to the movement are today's "skinheads."

Christian Identity is not categorized as a cult but rather as a cultic movement because adherents do not submit to one leader, and some doctrinal variation exists among member churches. Some in the movement have clear connections to occultism.

Beliefs

Some Orthodox Teachings. The strange thing about this group is that certain portions of an Identity doctrinal statement seem perfectly orthodox. YHVH (Yahweh) is the one true God. Jesus is the incarnate begotten Son of God, the Word made flesh, born of a virgin, who died on the cross to provide atonement. Salvation is by grace through faith. The Bible is inspired and inerrant. The red flag emerges, however, in the statement that the Bible was written about God's true children, who, as other portions of the doctrinal statement make clear, are white people.[2]

God's Chosen People. Christian Identity enthusiasts believe "identity" is an appropriate term for their title since they are convinced of their identity as God's chosen people. They believe they are the true inheritors of the promises made to Abraham and his descendants. Member churches may have unique distinctives, but they are united under the umbrella of Christian Identity in their hostility toward other races and their belief that the Bible, when properly understood, supports their viewpoint. The doctrinal statement of Kingdom Identity Ministries asserts this:

> WE BELIEVE the White, Anglo-Saxon, Germanic and kindred people to be God's true, literal Children of Israel. Only this race fulfills every detail of Biblical Prophecy and World History concerning Israel and continues in these latter days to be heirs and possessors of the Covenants, Prophecies, Promises and Blessings YHVH God made to Israel. This chosen seedline making up the "Christian Nations" (Gen. 35:11; Isa. 62:2; Acts 11:26) of the earth stands far superior to all other peoples in their call as God's servant race (Isa. 41:8, 44:21; Luke 1:54).[3]

The Jews: A Mongrel Race. Christian Identity proponents believe white people (good Aryan stock) are the only real descendants of Adam and Eve. Unfortunately, Eve was sexually seduced by the serpent (Satan) and gave birth to Cain (this copulation constituted "original sin"). Cain then mated with preexisting non-Adamic races—the "beasts of the field," also called mud people—that God created before Adam, and who had no souls (see Genesis 1:24-25). The result of this mating was a mongrel race called the Jews. This means that the true father of the Jews is Satan, and the Jews are enemies of white people (God's chosen people). The doctrinal statement of Kingdom Identity Ministries makes this position clear:

WE BELIEVE in an existing being known as the Devil
or Satan and called the Serpent (Gen. 3:1; Rev. 12:9),
who has a literal "seed" or posterity in the earth (Gen.
3:15) commonly called Jews today (Rev. 2:9; 3:9; Isa.
65:15). These children of Satan (John 8:44-47; Matt.
13:38; John 8:23) through Cain (I John 2:22, 4:3) who
have throughout history always been a curse to true
Israel, the Children of God...are contrary to all men
(I Thes. 2:14-15), though they often pose as ministers
of righteousness (II Cor. 11:13-15). The ultimate end
of this evil race whose hands bear the blood of our
Savior (Matt. 27:25) and all the righteous slain upon
the earth (Matt. 23:35), is Divine judgment (Matt.
13:38-42, 15:13; Zech. 14:21).[4]

A well-known proponent of this Identity viewpoint is Pastor
Arnold Murray, an Identity preacher in Gravette, Arkansas. He
claims that to call the Jews the chosen people of God is to commit
one of the gravest of sins against God: "Bless your heart if you
have ever been deceived by the Kenite [that is, the Jew], and I am
speaking now on the spiritual level, if you have ever really
believed that group was the chosen of God you were deceived by
Satan. Repent of that even more so than your personal sins in the
personal sense."[5]

Anglo-Israelism. An important component of Christian
Identity doctrine is Anglo-Israelism. Following the death of
Solomon, Israel split in two in 931 BC. The Northern Kingdom
was called Israel and consisted of ten tribes of Israel. The
Southern Kingdom contained the remaining tribes and was called
Judah because Judah was the most predominant tribe. Israel, the
Northern Kingdom, was taken into captivity by the Assyrians in

722 BC. Judah, the Southern Kingdom, was taken into captivity by the Babylonians in 605, 597, and 586 BC.

According to Anglo-Israelism, the ten tribes of Israel in the Northern Kingdom that were taken captive by the Assyrians in the eighth century BC were ultimately assimilated into Europe and Britain, thereby becoming the "ten *lost* tribes of Israel." Proponents of the theory thus reason that Anglo-Saxons are the lineal descendants and heirs of the promises made to Abraham and his descendants in the Old Testament.[6]

Anglo-Israelism was not originally an anti-Jewish doctrine. This theory first made its way to America in the late 1800s, started to become popular in the 1920s, and by the 1940s was being utilized by racists. A preacher named Wesley Swift first combined Anglo-Israelism, anti-Semitism, and political extremism. He taught this racist mix of ideas in a church he founded in California in the mid-1940s. He also founded a radio show where his views found a wider audience. A network of like-minded churches soon emerged. By the 1970s, the movement had reached theological maturity throughout the southern and western United States.

Interracial Marriages Prohibited. Christian Identity enthusiasts do all they can to prevent interracial marriage. They believe that one of the goals of the satanic Jews is to physically breed with white people and thereby contaminate the pure race of God. White supremacists therefore feel that the very preservation of the white race is at risk from the Jews and must be protected at all costs. This satanic plot must be stopped. One day, all of this *will* be stopped—after Armageddon is over.

Armageddon Approaching. Wesley Swift and others who hold to this viewpoint believe Armageddon is imminent. They believe it will be a violent and bloody race war in which millions of people will die. The powers of God (white people) will be in battle against the powers of the devil (people of other races). Even now, we are told, the Jews are engaged in a conspiracy to dominate the world and already control the United States government, the United Nations, and much of the media. The escalating resistance of white people will eventually result in Armageddon. America is a new kind of Promised Land where the whites will definitively stand against the Jews and other races in this diabolical scheme. After the final battle, God's kingdom will be established on earth, and at that time white people will finally be recognized as the one and true Israel.[7]

In preparation for Armageddon, Christian Identity enthusiasts are busy stockpiling food, weapons, and ammunition. They are also participating in survivalist training so they will prevail in the end.

Connections to Occultism. Critics have noted a connection of the Christian Identity movement to occultism. Some Christian Identity preachers, for example, incorporate occultic legends such as those about Atlantis and Lemuria in their sermons. Some hold to pyramidology—the idea that secret and esoteric knowledge may be discovered in the ancient pyramids. Many hold to astrology. Although many Identity proponents claim to derive all their teachings strictly from the Bible, their views are actually derived from a misinterpretation of the Bible and, in some cases, from occultic sources.

APOLOGETIC POWER POINTS

Sound Hermeneutics Yields Proper Interpretation. (8)

God Created All Races. (64)

Cain Was Not the Offspring of Satan and Eve. (65)

Anglo-Israelism Is Unbiblical. (66)

Occultism Is Prohibited. (98)

Astrology Is Prohibited. (100)

10

Christian Science

MARY BAKER EDDY (1821–1910), the founder of Christian Science, grew up in a Christian family (her parents were Congregationalists), though she had a strong dislike for certain Christian doctrines, such as predestination and hell.

Eddy was unhealthy as a child, something that would impact her developing theology as an adult. Because of her health problems, including spasmodic seizures, she developed a highly neurotic personality.[1]

As an adult, Eddy became involved in various forms of occultism, including spiritism. She sometimes fell into a deep trance, during which people asked her for advice on various matters. She claims she experienced mysterious encounters during the night, such as hearing strange rapping sounds and seeing dead people standing by her bedside. She sometimes received messages from the dead.

Eddy eventually came under the influence of Phineas Quimby (1802–1866), a famous metaphysical healer. Quimby held the unique viewpoint that sin, sickness, disease, and death exist only in the mind. He was convinced that wrong thinking or false beliefs caused physical diseases. Eliminate false beliefs, and the chief culprit for disease is thereby removed, yielding a healthy body. Quimby referred to his belief system by such names as "Science of Health" and even "Christian Science."[2] One cannot help but notice that Eddy was not an original thinker. A number of scholars have thoroughly documented that she plagiarized the great majority of her ideas directly from Quimby, even hijacking one of the names he used for his own system of thought.

Eddy initially contacted Quimby to seek treatment for a spinal ailment she suffered. She claims Quimby's treatment healed her, and she became a strong advocate of his methodology. Her spinal ailment soon returned, but she nevertheless remained convinced that Quimby's ideas must be true.

Following Quimby's death in 1875, Eddy published her book *Science and Health with Key to the Scriptures*, heavily plagiarizing Quimby's work. Even though she stole her ideas from Quimby, she claimed she had received new revelations of metaphysical truth. Because Quimby was so well known, people soon saw the connection between Quimby's teachings and Eddy's. A *New York Times* article presented irrefutable proof that Eddy plagiarized from Quimby.[3]

Regardless of such allegations, Eddy went on to found the Massachusetts Metaphysical College and taught the same plagiarized ideas contained in her book. Thousands of students graduated from this college, and Christian Science mushroomed and spread out all over the country. By 1896, proponents had established more than 400 Christian Science churches and societies. By the time of Eddy's death in 1910, more than a million people attended Christian Science services every week. Membership began to decline, however, in the 1960s. Today fewer than 250,000 people are affiliated with the cult.

Several factors account for the steady decline in membership. One is that in the 1990s, the church suffered a significant loss of income. More specifically, the Christian Science television network suffered a loss of $235 million, and the *Christian Science Monitor* newspaper lost $138 million. Church giving declined while church expenses escalated. The church thus had no choice but to sell off some of its media network.[4] This, in turn, caused many church members to question the competence of church leadership.

Worse came to worst in the 1990s when the church received a tidal wave of bad publicity due to a number of Christian Science children dying preventable deaths by parents who trusted Christian Science's healing techniques instead of taking their children to a doctor. Some Christian Science parents ended up going to jail for manslaughter.

At present, the Christian Science church operates 2300 branch churches in more than 60 countries (1600 are in the United States). The church headquarters is in Boston, Massachusetts.

Beliefs

The Bible. Christian Science proponents accept the Bible, but they interpret it esoterically, seeking hidden or secondary meanings in the biblical text.[5] The best way to ascertain such hidden meanings is to utilize Eddy's *Science and Health with Key to the Scriptures* as a guide. This guide provides the metaphysical meanings that lie behind the literal text of Scripture, enabling one to understand its mysteries.

Sin, Sickness, and Death. Sin, sickness, and death are allegedly illusions that people can conquer by correct thinking. The best way to obliterate these false beliefs is to follow Christian Science. The rationale behind the "illusion" explanation is that all things in the universe are ultimately God. If God is all that truly exists, then matter ultimately does not exist. If matter does not exist, then neither can sickness, pain, or death exist. Christian Science sets out to help one perceive the true nature of reality.

God. As noted above, Eddy believes that all things in the universe are God (pantheism). God is the only true reality; all else is an illusion of mortal mind. Eddy reinterprets the Trinity to refer to a triply Divine Principle: *Life, Truth,* and *Love.*

Jesus Christ. The human Jesus is not the divine Christ. Jesus, a mere human, embodied the Christ, which constituted the divinity of the man Jesus. Christ came not as a Savior but rather as a way-shower—to show humankind that sickness and death are illusions and should not be believed.

Humanity. A natural outgrowth of the idea that all is God is that humanity is also God. Human beings do not exist independent and separate from God. Christian Science proponents suggest that just as a drop of water is one with the ocean, so individual human beings are one with God. Just as God does not sin, neither do human beings sin because they are a part of God. Human beings are good and perfect, incapable of sin.

Salvation. Evil and sin are illusions of the mortal mind. Through the practice of Christian Science, human beings can deliver themselves from such mental errors. When people cease believing in sin, sickness, and death, they are "saved." All people will be saved in the end because nothing really exists except God.

The Crucifixion and Resurrection. Jesus did not shed his blood on Calvary. Because death is an illusion, Jesus could not truly die. Since there is no death, any discussion of a resurrection is a moot point. Eddy, utilizing esoteric methodology, suggests that the disciples "believed Jesus to be dead while he was hiding in the sepulcher, whereas he was alive, demonstrating within the narrow tomb the power of Spirit to overrule mortal, material sense."[6] Eddy explains, "In his final demonstration, called the ascension, which closed the earthly record of Jesus, he rose above the physical knowledge of his disciples, and the material sense saw him no more."[7]

——— APOLOGETIC POWER POINTS ———

Esotericism Is Illegitimate. (7)

Sound Hermeneutics Yields Proper Interpretation. (8)

God Is a Trinity. (22)

Pantheism Is False. (26)

Jesus Is the Christ. (34)

Jesus Is the Savior. (35)

Jesus Died on a Cross. (48)

Jesus Physically Rose from the Dead. (50)

Humans Are Not Divine. (62)

Humans Are Fallen in Sin. (67)

Death, Disease, and Sin Are Real. (79)

Occultism Is Prohibited. (98)

Spiritism Is Prohibited. (99)

Healing Is Subject to God's Will. (118)

11

The Church of Jesus Christ of Latter-day Saints

THE CHURCH OF JESUS CHRIST of Latter-day Saints, also known as the Mormon Church, was founded by Joseph Smith, Jr. He was born in Sharon, Vermont, on December 23, 1805, and lived with his large family in Palmyra, New York.

Beginning around 1819, Smith witnessed local revivals and "unusual excitement on the subject of religion." In 1820, at age 15, he was troubled by the conflict he witnessed among the people and clergy of the Methodist, Presbyterian, and Baptist churches. Because of such "great confusion and strife among the different denominations,"[1] he did not know what to do about joining a church. He was soon to receive divine direction on the issue.

One day in the spring of 1820, Smith was reading James 1:5 (KJV): "If any of you lack wisdom, let him ask of God, that giveth to all men liberally, and upbraideth not; and it shall be given him." The verse suddenly came alive to him. He determined he would ask God which church to join. He claims he was answered in a vision.

The two conflicting accounts of the vision suggest that the vision was not grounded in reliable history. In any event, the official version claims that the Father and Son appeared to Smith and told him not to join any church, for they were all corrupt.

Smith accordingly did not join any of the denominations. But neither did he attempt to live a virtuous life. Instead, Smith later confessed, during the next three years he frequently "fell into many foolish errors, and displayed the weakness of youth, and the foibles of human nature."[2]

On September 21, 1823, after Smith had gone to bed, he prayed for forgiveness of his sins and requested a manifestation. This time, a "messenger sent from the presence of God" named Moroni appeared to Smith and said "there was a book deposited, written on gold plates, giving an account of the former inhabitants of this continent, and the source from whence they sprang. He also said that the fullness of the everlasting Gospel was contained in it, as delivered by the Savior to the ancient inhabitants."[3] Moroni further informed Smith that the "Urim and Thummin"— seer stones that served as a translation device—were buried with the plates.

Moroni eventually allowed Smith to retrieve the plates with the charge to keep them safe until the angel "should call for them." Smith translated the sacred records from "Reformed Egyptian" into English. He accomplished this with the "seer stones," which allegedly enabled Smith to precisely render one character at a time by the "power of God."[4] After the translation of the Book of Mormon was complete, the golden plates were removed by Moroni and are therefore unavailable for inspection.

In May 1829, Smith and Oliver Cowdery, an associate, went into the woods to pray about baptism for the remission of sins. While there, John the Baptist allegedly appeared, conferred the Aaronic priesthood upon them, and gave them instructions regarding how to baptize each other. Later, Peter, James, and John conferred the Melchizedek priesthood upon them.

Because Jesus had told Smith that all other churches were false, the "one true church" was organized on April 6, 1830, by Smith and five others in Fayette, New York. At the founding meeting, God gave Smith a revelation that he was to be "a seer, a translator, a prophet, and an apostle."[5]

As the church grew, so did public opposition—due not only to their doctrines but also to the polygamy Joseph Smith espoused. This opposition forced the Mormons to move on to other areas. They settled for a while in Kirtland, Ohio; then in Independence, Missouri; then in various other counties in Missouri; then in Nauvoo, Illinois, where Smith became the mayor of the city. During this time, Smith's continued revelations yielded other Mormon Scriptures: *Doctrine and Covenants* and *The Pearl of Great Price.*

Trouble continued to escalate for the Mormons. On June 7, 1844, a group of dissident Mormons published a newspaper detailing grievances they had against Smith. It was the first and last issue of the *Nauvoo Expositor.* Smith knew the charges of polygamy and of his mishandling of church funds would cause trouble for him. Days later, his city council decided to destroy the printing office and the presses. This act resulted in Smith's arrest for treason, and he, his brother Hyrum, and two other Mormon leaders were jailed in Carthage, Illinois.

On June 27, a mob formed and stormed the jail, killing Joseph and Hyrum Smith and wounding the other men. Before Smith died, however, he used a six-shooter to wound a few of the men in the mob during the blazing gun battle. Smith's role as God's "Prophet, Seer, and Revelator" came to an abrupt end in bloody violence.

Brigham Young, the senior Mormon apostle at the time of Smith's death, immediately assumed leadership. He led a company of the Latter-day Saints across the treacherous Great Plains, reaching the valley of the Great Salt Lake in Utah in July of 1847, where they built their new Zion, Salt Lake City. He ruled Mormons with an iron hand and both practiced and encouraged polygamy throughout the remainder of his life.

The practice of polygamy ended on September 24, 1890, when

a "manifesto" was issued by Wilford Woodruff, fourth president of the Mormon Church, declaring that all Mormons must give up the practice. Failure to do so would result in the jailing of Mormon leaders, the confiscation of Mormon temples and other property, and the United States' refusal to admit Utah to statehood.

Beliefs

The Restored Church. Mormons teach that total apostasy engulfed the church soon after the death of the last apostle, and so the "one true church" needed to be restored. Among that which was lost was the true gospel, proper church organization with its respective offices, and the Aaronic and Melchizedek priesthoods. Joseph Smith allegedly restored all this in the Mormon church, and so the Mormons alone constitute the one true church.

The Book of Mormon. Joseph Smith said the Book of Mormon is "the most correct of any book on earth, and the keystone of our religion, and a man would get nearer to God by abiding by its precepts, than any other book."[6] This book is an abridged account of God's dealings with the original inhabitants of the American continent from about 2247 BC to AD 421. It is allegedly God's uncorrupted revelation to humankind, the "fullness of the everlasting gospel," and "another Testament of Jesus Christ." Smith said he infallibly translated the Book of Mormon from gold plates—a single character at a time—using "seer stones." Following the translation, Smith claimed he heard a divine voice from out of a bright light above him that affirmed the translation was correct.

The Bible. The Mormons' eighth "Article of Faith" makes this affirmation: "We believe the Bible to be the Word of God, as far as it is translated correctly."[7] Mormons believe that large portions of the Bible have been lost through the centuries. The portions that have survived have become corrupted because of faulty transmission. Mormon apostle Orson Pratt asked, "Who, in his right mind, could, for one moment, suppose the Bible in its present form to be a perfect guide? Who knows that even one verse of the Bible has escaped pollution?"[8]

Joseph Smith is credited with the "translation" of the Inspired Version of the Bible. Smith did not come up with a new translation but rather took the King James Version (KJV) and added to and subtracted from it—not by examining Bible manuscripts but allegedly by "divine inspiration." Smith "corrected, revised, altered, added to, and deleted from" the KJV.[9] Thousands of changes were introduced. Smith even added a verse in Genesis 50 that predicted his own coming: "That seer will I bless...and his name shall be called Joseph."[10]

God. Mormon prophets and apostles teach that God the Father was once a mortal man who continually progressed to become a God—an exalted man. Mormon general authority Milton R. Hunter said that "God the Eternal Father was once a mortal man who passed through a school of earth life similar to that through which we are now passing. He became God—an exalted being—through obedience to the same eternal Gospel truths that we are given opportunity today to obey."[11] Today, then, "God the Eternal Father, our Father in Heaven, is an exalted, perfected, and glorified Personage having a tangible body of flesh and bones."[12]

Mormons often cite verses from the Bible to prove God is a physical being. They suggest that since Adam was a physical being and was created in the "image of God" (Genesis 1:26-27), God too must have a physical body. This physicality is also evident in the fact that Moses spoke to God "face to face" (Exodus 33:11). Further, since Jesus (a physical being) said that "anyone who has seen me has seen the Father" (John 14:9), the Father too must have a physical body.

The Trinity. Mormonism teaches that the Father, Son, and Holy Spirit are not three persons in one God, as historic Christianity has always taught; rather, they are three separate Gods. They are said to be "one" only in their common purpose and in their attributes of perfection. Many other gods also exist.

In Mormon theology, just as Jesus has a Father, so the Father allegedly has a Father, and the Father of Jesus' Father has a Father, and so on. This endless succession of Fathers goes on and on through the endless hierarchy of exalted beings (gods) in the universe.

Each of the numerous Father-gods has a heavenly wife (or wives). Mormon apostle Orson Pratt explained, "Each God, through his wife or wives, raises up a numerous family of sons and daughters....As soon as each God has begotten many millions of male and female spirits...he, in connection with his sons, organizes a new world, after a similar order to the one which we now inhabit, where he sends both the male and female spirits to inhabit tabernacles of flesh and bones."[13] The inhabitants of each world then render worship to the particular heavenly Father of their world. All of this is part and parcel of the polytheistic world of Mormonism.

Humanity. The ultimate goal for human beings in Mormonism is godhood. Brigham Young said that "the Lord created you and me for the purpose of becoming Gods like himself." We were created "to become Gods like unto our Father in heaven."[14]

This exaltation to godhood is known among Mormons as attaining "eternal life." The official *Gospel Principles* manual tells us that "exaltation is eternal life, the kind of life that God lives....We can become Gods like our heavenly Father. This is exaltation."[15] Joseph Fielding Smith said that "eternal life is the name of the kind of life possessed by the Father and the Son; it is exaltation in the eternal realm."[16]

Fundamental to understanding the Mormon concept of exaltation is the doctrine of eternal progression. Mormons say we do not just seek perfection in this life. It begins before birth and continues beyond the grave. Exaltation to godhood ultimately involves not just what one does in this earthly life *(mortality)* but what one has already done in *premortality* (one's "preexistence" as a spirit child) and in *postmortality* (one's return to the spirit world following physical death).

Mormons believe the Bible supports their belief that they can become gods. Jesus in John 10:34 told some Jews, "You are gods." The apostle Paul in 1 Corinthians 8:5 made reference to gods in heaven and on earth. Romans 8:16-17 makes reference to believers as "heirs of God and coheirs with Christ," and says believers will "share in his glory."

Jesus Christ. Jesus was allegedly "begotten" as the first spirit-child of the Father (Elohim) and one of his unnamed wives ("Heavenly Mother") (see Psalm 2:7). Jesus is the first and highest of all the spirit children. After all, Jesus is called the "firstborn" (Colossians 1:15). Because the Heavenly Father and Mother had many other spirit children who have now been born as humans, Jesus is often referred to by Mormons as "our elder brother." (Lucifer is also the spirit-brother of Jesus.)

Jesus progressed by obedience and devotion to the truth in the spirit world until he became a God. This allegedly took aeons of time. Prior to his incarnation, Jesus was the Jehovah of the Old Testament. (The Father, a separate God, was Elohim.)

When the time for his birth on earth had come, Jesus in his mortal state was "begotten" through sexual relations between a flesh-and-bone Heavenly Father and his daughter Mary. There is nothing figurative in the word "begotten."[17]

In terms of Christ's work, Mormons speak of Christ accomplishing atonement—but they do not mean by these words what Christians mean. Jesus "atoned for Adam's sin, leaving us responsible only for our own sins."[18] The Mormon second Article of Faith affirms: "We believe that men will be punished for their own sins, and not for Adam's transgression."[19] Salvation therefore begins with Jesus' atonement, but each person must complete the process by doing good works. The official *Gospel Principles* manual tells us that Jesus "became our savior and he did his part to help us return to our heavenly home. It is now up to each of us to do our part and to become worthy of exaltation."[20]

The result of Jesus' atonement is that all humankind will be resurrected. Jesus was able to overcome physical death for us. He "opened the door of immortality for all to walk through. He paid the price for us to rise from the grave. Through His own willful sacrifice—the infinite and eternal atonement—we all shall live again."[21]

Sin. Mormons define "sin" as a wrong judgment, a mistake, an imperfection, or an inadequacy. The moral sting is thereby taken out of sin. Moreover, instead of holding to original sin—which says that all people are born into the world in a state of sin—Mormons say children are "innocent" until they reach the age of accountability, which is the age of eight. Children are said to be born innately good.

Salvation. Though Jesus provided "general salvation" (resurrection) for all people, "individual salvation" refers to that which a person merits through his own acts throughout life by obedience to the laws of the gospel. Mormons teach that people must become increasingly perfect as they work toward salvation. They often cite Matthew 5:48 in support of the goal of perfection: "Be perfect, therefore, as your heavenly Father is perfect." Baptism is necessary for salvation. Mormons reject the doctrine of justification by faith.

The Afterlife. At the end of the world, Mormons believe people will end up in one of three kingdoms of glory: the celestial kingdom, the terrestrial kingdom, or the telestial kingdom. Mormons believe 1 Corinthians 15:40-42 offers biblical support for these three kingdoms. Our level of worthiness will determine which of these three realms we end up in.

The celestial kingdom is the highest degree of glory and is inhabited by faithful Mormons—the "righteous, those who have been faithful in keeping the commandments of the Lord, and have been cleansed of all their sins."[22] The second of the three degrees of glory is the terrestrial kingdom, and is reserved for non-Mormons who live moral lives as well as for "less than valiant" Mormons (those who did not live up to their church's expectations or requirements). The lowest of the three degrees of glory is the telestial kingdom, which is reserved for those who have been carnal and sinful throughout life.

——— APOLOGETIC POWER POINTS ———

The Bible Should Not Be Added To. (2)

The Bible Is Reliable. (3)

The Bible Is Authoritative. (6)

Joseph Smith's "Inspired Version" Is Untrustworthy. (9)

The Book of Mormon Is Unreliable. (10)

God Is a Spirit. (13)

God Is Not an Exalted Man. (14)

God Is Immutable. (17)

God's Attributes Reveal His Nature. (18)

God Is a Trinity. (22)

Polytheism Is False. (27)

Jesus Is God. (30)

Jesus Atoned for Sin. (40)

Jesus Was Not the Spirit-Brother of Lucifer. (43)

Jesus Completed the Work of Salvation. (49)

Humans Are Not Divine. (62)

All Humans Are Infected by Sin (Original Sin). (68)

The Law Cannot Save. (70)

Salvation Is by Grace Through Faith. (71)

Salvation Involves Justification. (72)

Heaven Is Real. (77)

Hell Is Real. (78)

The Mormon Church Is Not the Restored Church. (90)

The Mormon Priesthoods Are Unbiblical. (94)

Polygamy Is Prohibited. (114)

12

The Church Universal and Triumphant

OCCULTIST MARK PROPHET (1918–1973), who claimed to be in contact with the Ascended Master El Morya, founded the Church Universal and Triumphant in 1958. (Ascended Masters are allegedly historical persons who have evolved spiritually and have ascended to a more exalted plane of existence, now seeking to help lesser-evolved humans reach their same level.) The church is now headed by Mark's widow, Elizabeth Clare Prophet, also an occultist in contact with the spirit world. Upon Mark's death, Elizabeth claimed Mark himself had now become an Ascended Master named Lanello. Elizabeth is affectionately known among followers as "Guru Ma." The Prophets borrowed much of their theology from the I AM movement, which Guy and Edna Ballard began in the 1930s (see chapter 16).[1]

Beliefs

Revelation. The revelations Elizabeth Clare Prophet receives from Ascended Masters are considered authoritative for the group. The Bible is also used, but it is interpreted esoterically (seeking hidden or secondary meanings in the text). An example of this esotericism is Prophet's interpretation of Jesus' words in Matthew 11:29: "Take my yoke upon you and learn from me." When Jesus said this, the Prophets argue that he was teaching his disciples to "take my yoke, *yoga*, upon you and learn of me [take my consciousness of my sacred labor, my Christhood bearing the burden of world karma…and learn of my Guru, the Ancient of Days]; for I am meek and lowly in heart, and ye shall find rest unto your souls. For my yoke, *yoga*, is easy and my burden in heaven and on earth is truly Light."[2]

God. The church holds to a pantheistic concept of God—that is, God and the universe are essentially one and the same. God possesses both male and female characteristics, and members sometime refer to God as "Father-Mother." The Holy Spirit is a depersonalized energy or power in nature whose function is to charge all life with the knowledge of God.

Humanity, Sin, and Salvation. The Prophets believe that an "I AM Presence" resides in each person and represents a point of contact with divine reality. This "I AM Presence" is equated with "the Christ," who is distinct from the human Jesus. The "Christ" of "I AM" theology represents the divinity within all men: "God dwells in every man and not alone in His son, Jesus the Christ. The only begotten Son of the Father, full of grace and truth, is the Christ whose Image the Lord has reproduced over and over again as the Christ-identity of every son and daughter who has come forth from the infinite Spirit of the Father-Mother God."[3] The Prophets conclude that "to become the Christ, then, is the goal of every child of God."[4]

Jesus allegedly taught that all human beings have the I AM Presence in John 8:58: "I tell you the truth…before Abraham was born, I am!" When Jesus said this, the Prophets are sure he did so "in the full awareness that the 'I AM' of him had always been the Christ. And he also knew that the permanent part of each one of you was and is that same Christ."[5] They tell us that "Jesus' I AM Presence looks just like yours. This is the common denominator. This is the coequality of the sons and daughters of God. He created you equal in the sense that he gave you an I AM Presence—he gave you a Divine Self."[6] One can allegedly attune to the I AM Presence by chanting I AM decrees.

The Atonement. If all human beings have an I AM Presence, then Jesus' work on the cross is unnecessary. Mark and Elizabeth Clare Prophet completely dismiss the idea of Jesus' atonement on the cross:

> The erroneous doctrine concerning the blood sacrifice of Jesus—which he himself never taught—has been perpetuated to the present hour. God the Father did not require the sacrifice of His son Christ Jesus… as an atonement for the sins of the world; nor is it possible according to cosmic law for any man's sacrifice to balance either the original sin or the subsequent sins of the one or the many.[7]

The Prophets reinterpret the crucifixion of Jesus in terms of reincarnation and karma. They argue that a lot of bad karma existed on the earth at the time Jesus lived, and the planet was in danger of self-destruction. Jesus' crucifixion helped balance the planetary karma: "Avatars—souls of great Light and spiritual attainment, such as Jesus the Christ and Gautama Buddha—were sent to take upon themselves a certain portion of mankind's planetary karma. This they were able to do because they themselves were 'without blemish and without spot,' having expiated what karma they had, if any, in previous lives."[8]

The Christhood of Jesus. Elizabeth Clare Prophet argues that Jesus traveled to India as a child and underwent a learning process under Hindu gurus that led to his eventual Christhood.[9] In her book *The Lost Years of Jesus*, Prophet champions the Nicolas Notovitch theory.

As the story goes, in 1887 Nicolas Notovitch—a Russian war correspondent—went on a journey through India. While en route to Leh, the capital of Ladakh (in Northern India along the Tibetan border), he heard a Tibetan lama (that is, a monk) in a monastery refer to a grand lama named *Issa* (the Tibetan form of "Jesus"). Notovitch inquired further and discovered that a chronicle of the life of Issa existed with other sacred scrolls at the Convent of Himis, about 25 miles from Leh.

Notovitch visited this convent and learned from the chief lama that a scroll did in fact exist that provided details about the prophet Issa. This holy man allegedly preached the same doctrines in Israel as he earlier did in India. The original scroll, the lama said, was written in the Pali language and later translated into Tibetan. The Convent of Himis possessed the Tibetan translation, and the original was kept in the library of Lhassa, the capital of Tibet.

Notovitch persuaded the lama to read the scroll to him and had it translated from Tibetan by an interpreter. According to Notovitch, the literal translation of the scroll was "disconnected and mingled with accounts of other contemporaneous events to which they bear no relation," and so he took the liberty to arrange "all the fragments concerning the life of Issa in chronological order and [took] pains to impress upon them the character of unity, in which they were absolutely lacking."[10] He went without sleep for many nights so he could order and remodel what he had heard.

From the scroll, Notovitch learned that "Jesus had wandered to India and to Tibet as a young man before he began his work in Palestine."[11] According to Notovitch, the scroll explains that after briefly visiting with the Jains, young Issa studied for six years among the Brahmins at Juggernaut, Rajagriha, Benares, and other Indian holy cities. The priests of Brahma "taught him to read and understand the Vedas, to cure by aid of prayer, to teach, to explain the holy scriptures to the people, and to drive out evil spirits from the bodies of men, restoring unto them their sanity."[12]

While there, the story continues, Issa sought to teach the scriptures to all the people of India—including the lower castes. The Brahmins and Kshatriyas (higher castes) opposed him in this and told him that the Sudras (a lower caste) were forbidden to read or even contemplate the Vedas. Issa denounced them severely for this.

Because of Issa's controversial teachings, members of the higher castes devised a death plot against him. But the Sudras warned him, and he left Juggernaut, establishing himself in Gautamides (the birthplace of the Buddha Sakyamuni), where he studied the sacred writings of the Sutras. "Six years after, Issa, whom the Buddha had elected to spread his holy word, had become a perfect expositor of the sacred writings. Then he left Nepal and the Himalayan Mountains, descended into the valley of Rajputana, and went towards the west, preaching to diverse peoples the supreme perfection of man."[13] Following this, we are told, Issa briefly visited Persia, where he preached to the Zoroastrians. Then, at 29, he returned to Israel and began to preach all that he had learned.

According to Notovitch's "scroll," by the end of Issa's three-year ministry, Pilate had become so alarmed at his mushrooming popularity that he ordered one of his spies to accuse him falsely. Issa was then imprisoned and tortured by soldiers to force a confession that would permit his being executed. The Jewish priests tried to act in Issa's behalf but to no avail. Issa was falsely accused, and Pilate ordered the death sentence. Yet even in death, Elizabeth Clare Prophet argues, Issa (Jesus) accomplished the wonderful work of balancing world karma.

APOLOGETIC POWER POINTS

Esotericism Is Illegitimate. (7)

Sound Hermeneutics Yields Proper Interpretation. (8)

God Is Personal. (12)

Pantheism Is False. (26)

Jesus Is God. (30)

Jesus Is Unique. (37)

Jesus Atoned for Sin. (40)

Jesus Did Not Go East. (46)

The Holy Spirit Is a Person. (57)

The Holy Spirit Is God. (58)

Humans Are Not Divine. (62)

Humans Are Fallen in Sin. (67)

Occultism Is Prohibited. (98)

Spiritism Is Prohibited. (99)

Chanting Is Prohibited. (102)

Reincarnation Is False. (103)

The Ascended Masters Are Demons in Disguise. (117)

13
Eckankar

In 1965, Paul Twitchell FOUNDED Eckankar, a New Age Hinduistic style of cult. He claimed to be the nine hundred, seventy-first "Living ECK Master," a *Sugmad* (a living oracle of God), and the *Mahanta* (a title indicating the highest state of God consciousness on earth) for the current age. Prior to his role as Living ECK Master, Twitchell had long been involved in mysticism, cultism, and occultism. He says he experienced "God realization" (a state of complete and conscious awareness of God) in 1956. He claims to have been initiated by spiritual masters known as the "Order of Vairagi Masters," who trained him to become a Living ECK Master. After founding Eckankar, he asserted that Eckankar was the oldest true religion in the world, embodying ancient wisdom, and that any truth found in other religions ultimately derived such truth from Eckankar.

When Twitchell died in 1971, Darwin Gross took over as the next Living ECK Master from 1971 to 1981. Harold Klemp then took over the leadership in 1981 and continues leading the group to the present day.

Present membership is approximately 50,000 in more than 100 countries. The organization has facilities in North and South America, Europe, Africa, Asia, and Australia. Members give dues to support the organization. Individual churches are subordinate to the parent church in Minneapolis, Minnesota. Clergy are ordained after training and operate on a volunteer (nonpaid) basis. ECK worship services last one hour and include a reading from an ECK book, singing, silent contemplation, and discussion. Various kinds of services are available for infant consecration, rites of passage for the youth, weddings, and funerals.[1]

Beliefs

Centrality of the ECK Master. Eckankar teaches that one can obtain enlightenment over the course of many lifetimes (reincarnation) by practicing the spiritual exercises set forth by the ECK Master. "ECK" refers to the "Life Force" or "Divine Spirit" or "the Holy Spirit" which sustains all life.[2] ECK Masters are viewed as Spiritual Masters or agents of God, vehicles of the Divine Spirit who provide spiritual guidance. ECK Masters of the past allegedly include such "God-realized" luminaries as Socrates, Plato, Moses, Jesus, Mozart, Martin Luther, and Albert Einstein. Eckankar is exclusivistic in the sense that it claims to be the only true means of enlightenment because it alone has ECK Masters.

Humanity. Eckankar teaches that every person is Soul, a particle of God, a spark of God sent into the world to gain spiritual experience. Soul is eternal and is a person's true identity, the permanent center of his or her being. Each Soul is on a journey seeking God-realization.

Spiritual Exercises. Eckankar claims to provide spiritual exercises that open one's heart to Divine Spirit, bring purification, and enable one to experience the Light and Sound of God (also known as the Holy Spirit). "The inner Sound is the Voice of God calling us home. The inner Light is a beacon to light our way. All the Spiritual Exercises of ECK are built on these two divine aspects of the Holy Spirit."[3]

These exercises also facilitate soul travel, enabling one to recover a fully spiritual viewpoint and move into greater states of consciousness.[4] Such soul travel involves "the ability of Soul to transcend the physical body and travel into the spiritual worlds of God."[5]

Though practitioners can choose from more than 100 exercises, one of the more common is to simply relax by sitting down or laying down, closing the eyes, and singing the word "HU," which is supposedly an ancient name of God. People who engage in such spiritual exercises (ideally, at least 20 minutes each day) become spiritually revitalized and recognize the presence of the Holy Spirit—which then provides further guidance. People who mature spiritually learn to express God's love through serving others.[6]

Reincarnation. Because Soul is eternal, we will all live forever, and death cannot destroy us. Through reincarnation, we have many lifetimes available in which to attain enlightenment. As we spiritually mature through many lives of existence, we can progress upward through various planes of existence, including the Astral, the Causal, the Mental, the Etheric, and the Soul Planes.[7] As we obey the teachings of the ECK Masters, the ECK (the Holy Spirit or "Life Force") can purify us of bad karma and speed our spiritual progression.[8] Such purification also enables us to accept the full love of God in the present lifetime.[9]

─────────── **APOLOGETIC POWER POINTS** ───────────

Jesus Is the Only Way. (36)

The Holy Spirit Is a Person. (57)

The Holy Spirit Is God. (58)

Man Is a Creature. (60)

Man Is Both Material and Immaterial. (61)

Humans Are Not Divine. (62)

Salvation Is by Grace Through Faith. (71)

Occultism Is Prohibited. (98)

Spiritism Is Prohibited. (99)

Reincarnation Is False. (103)

Mysticism Is Unreliable. (104)

Eastern Meditation Is Prohibited. (108)

14

The Family
(The Children of God)

ONE HALLMARK SOMETIMES FOUND among false religions is the corruption and distortion of human sexuality.[1] Perhaps this is nowhere better illustrated than with a cult known as the Family or as the Children of God.

The Children of God emerged out of the teachings of David Berg and experienced fast growth during the 1970s in the hippie movement. During these years, many people joined Berg, not knowing what they were getting into. The movement suffered some decline in the 1980s and is today a rather insignificant group—but it is still alive and well, as their website attests. The purpose of the group is to continue spreading the teachings of the late David Berg and warn people that the end of the world is near.

Berg was born in California in 1919. As a boy, he apparently suffered loneliness and had very few friends. Some sources indicate he suffered a sense of shame and insignificance as a youngster.

Berg's father, Hjalmer Emmanuel Berg, was a pastor and administrator of a Christian college in Santa Barbara, California. His mother, Virginia Lee Brandt-Berg, was a radio evangelist affiliated with the Christian and Missionary Alliance. As young David grew up, he experienced constant conflict with his father.

After joining the Christian and Missionary Alliance, Berg met his wife, Jane Miller, whom he married in 1944. Throughout the 1950s, Berg and his wife wandered about the country, trying to find a place where he could belong. During these years, Berg fell into secret immorality, committing adultery by visiting prostitutes.[2]

In 1968 Berg became involved with a ministry in Huntington Beach, California. He worked with his evangelist-mother at a Teen Challenge coffee house. While there, he ministered among hippie audiences and started to gain a following among the "Jesus people." His work at the coffee house was short-lived, however, as he became increasingly dissatisfied with organized religion. He left and began preaching rather harsh sermons, condemning mainstream churches and ministries and becoming increasingly exclusivistic.

Berg left California in 1969. He and his followers—now called "Revolutionaries for Jesus"—resettled in the wilderness near Tucson, Arizona. After leaving California, he prophesied that a huge earthquake would destroy the state, sweeping it into the Pacific Ocean.

In 1970 Berg met a woman named Maria in Tucson and began living with her. He did not divorce his wife or send her away; he slept with her every other night. Berg claimed he received revelation from God that justified this scenario. He claimed his wife represented the old religion while Maria represented a new religion.

Berg's authority continued to increase among his followers, and he often referred to himself in exalted terms. He claimed to speak for God as "Moses" and claimed to rule God's theocracy as "King David." He positioned himself as God's prophet for this age.

As God's prophet, he communicated to his many followers through the *Mo Letters*. He penned them himself, but he claims

God was actually the author. The Children of God consider these letters, which addressed a wide variety of issues, to be God's revelation for today, replacing the old revelation found in the Bible.

Beliefs

Occultic Revelations. Berg was involved in various forms of occultism. He claimed to be a follower of astrologer Jeanne Dixon. He was also involved in spiritistic contact with the dead, including the likes of Martin Luther, the Pied Piper, Peter the Hermit, Anne Boleyn, Ivan the Terrible, and other historical figures. He claimed he had a personal spirit guide named Abrahim.

God. Berg flatly denied the doctrine of the Trinity, noting that the word is not even in the Bible. He viewed Jesus as "partly God," having been created as the Son of God. He viewed the Holy Spirit as the feminine aspect of God, referring to "her" as the "Holy Queen of Love" and God's "Elixir of Love." The Holy Spirit is often portrayed in the *Mo Letters* as an enticing and sensual young woman.

Salvation. Berg advocated the necessity of works, but the only law one was required to obey was Christ's "law of love." Christians can do just about anything they want, including open sex, so long as it is done in love. Berg believed that in the end, even among those who failed to obey Christ's law of love, all people would be saved (universalism). Some will have to spend time in the lake of fire to be purged of sin, but following that they will be saved.

Evangelism through "Flirty Fishing." "Flirty fishing" involves bringing people into the cult via sex. One Children of God document shockingly states: "May God help us all to be flirty little fishies for Jesus to save lost souls....God bless and make you a flirty little fishy for Jesus!"[3]

Berg prayed for the typical Children of God witness this way: "Help her, O God, to catch men! Help her to catch men, be bold, unashamed and brazen, to use anything she has, O God, to catch men for Thee!—Even if it be through the flesh, the attractive lure, delicious flesh on a steel hook of Thy reality, the steel of Thy Spirit!"[4]

In the late 1970s, a Children of God annual report boasted that "our dear Flirty Fishers are still going strong, God bless'm, having now witnessed to over a quarter-of-a million souls, loved over 25,000 of them, and won nearly 19,000 to the Lord, along with about 35,000 new friends."[5] Berg boasted that "there is nothing wrong with a sexy conversion. We believe sex is a human necessity, and in certain cases we may go to bed with someone to show people God's love."[6]

Even Children Involved. Children were not exempt from Berg's sexual perversions. He suggested that parents masturbate their young boys at bedtime. He encouraged adults to "play" and sleep together nude among their children, allowing full sexual exploration and activity:

> They should be encouraged in nude mixed bathing and nude mixed play where socially, legally, and climatically permissible, acceptable, and advisable. They should also not be inhibited from mutual and self-sexual examination, experimentation, or interplay when playing or sleeping together where legally possible and social and housing conditions permit.[7]

Berg tried to garner support for his view from a perverted interpretation of the life of Jesus. He argued from John 11:1-44 that Jesus had sexual relations with Mary and Martha: "I even believe that he [Jesus] lived with…Mary and Martha later, which was no sin for Him, because He couldn't commit sin. Everything that He did He did in love, He probably did it for their sakes as much as His own—He had physical needs just like they did."[8]

A Cult on the Run

Not surprisingly, Berg eventually found himself in trouble on many fronts. Virtually hundreds of complaints and charges emerged from former followers, parents of children in the cult, and law officials. They accused Berg's group of kidnapping, holding members against their wills, brainwashing them, and committing fraud in fund raising (claiming money was being raised to help get kids off of drugs or to support students going to Bible college). Even Berg's disenfranchised daughter, Deborah Davis, accused him of incest.[9] As well, the group suffered significant bad publicity when disease broke out among cult members as a result of widespread open sex, which caused the government to begin investigating the group. Berg and his followers retorted that they were just being persecuted as the true people of God.

Berg and his followers left the United States in 1972, settling in England and renaming themselves the Family of Love. By the mid-1970s, Children of God colonies surfaced in most of the countries of Western Europe. By the late 1970s, more than 70 countries had colonies—probably totaling about 400.

By 1980, Berg had dropped out of sight, though he continued to exercise control over the Children of God through *Mo Letters*. In the early 1990s, the group resurfaced in the United States, now calling itself the Family, with a newly sanitized image. A singing troupe affiliated with the Family sang during the Christmas season at the White House during the presidency of George Bush Sr., who was unaware of the sect's perverted past.

The Children of God claimed to have changed their ways in

the 1990s, but cult watchers and former cult members remained skeptical—and for good reason. A former Children of God member, Ruth Gordon, suggested that "part of their plan is to lay a fresh groundwork as if alleged past practices of child sexual abuse and sexual deviancy never occurred. It is no different from a brand-name company changing their label but not their content."[10]

Police raids conducted in 1993 against the Family (Children of God) would seem to confirm that the cult had continued its emphasis on perverted sex. In September of 1993, 180 police officials raided a complex of seven residences in an upscale Buenos Aires neighborhood that housed the Argentine headquarters of the Family. According to news reports, "authorities detained 30 adults, took 268 children into protective custody, and seized an undisclosed number of allegedly pornographic videos and other materials."[11]

The *Christian Research Newsletter* makes this report:

> A Reuters news dispatch told of "grisly details" emerging "about hard-core videos of sex between adults and children" and Argentine officials' claims that "at least some of the children…appear to be mentally impaired." The Brazilian newsweekly *Veja* reported that authorities apprehended at least one video showing scenes of boys masturbating before adults, and another depicting sexual acts between a father and his daughter.[12]

More than a decade later, the Family remains alive and well. Their website provides a revisionist account of David Berg, making no mention of his sexual deviations but nevertheless affirming he used an "unconventional approach." Amazingly, we are told that Berg decried the "decay in moral values of Western society."[13] Whether any true reformation in the group has taken place is not known.

——— APOLOGETIC POWER POINTS ———

The Bible Is Authoritative. (6)

Sound Hermeneutics Yields Proper Interpretation. (8)

God Is a Trinity. (22)

Jesus Is God. (30)

Jesus Is the Son of God. (33)

The Holy Spirit Is a Person. (57)

The Holy Spirit Is God. (58)

Humans Are Fallen in Sin. (67)

Universalism Is False. (73)

False Prophets Are Recognizable. (96)

Occultism Is Prohibited. (98)

Spiritism Is Prohibited. (99)

Astrology Is Prohibited. (100)

Sexual Immorality Is Prohibited. (113)

15
Hare Krishna (ISKCON)

THE HARE KRISHNA SECT IS AN offshoot of Hinduism that became popular in the 1960s. Known for their orange robes, shaved heads (except for a ponytail), and two marks on their foreheads, Krishna devotees were often seen pounding drums, clanging little cymbals, and chanting on street corners. Their goal was to collect donations for their full-color magazine, *Back to Godhead,* as a means of raising funds for the group. Today Hare Krishna devotees no longer dress in orange robes and have essentially merged with the popular culture.

The Hare Krishna sect first emerged under the teachings of the guru Chaitanya, born in 1486. His primary teaching was that the Lord Krishna was supreme over all Hindu deities. Chaitanya chanted and danced through the streets in Krishna's name and quickly gained a substantive following in Bengal, India. Others began to do as he did, mimicking his strange actions.[1] Many came to believe that Chaitanya was an incarnation of Krishna.

Four hundred years later, a guru who was a descendant of Chaitanya initiated and commissioned Abhay Charan De Bhaktivedanta Swami Prabhupada (1896–1977) to spread Chaitanya's teaching. Prabhupada founded the International Society for Krishna Consciousness (ISKCON) in the United States and established *Back to Godhead* magazine, which is the major voice in the United States for the promotion of Hare Krishna beliefs.

Prabhupada's work began humbly in Greenwich Village in

New York City, where many in the hippie subculture were open to new and different ideas. Disciples joined the movement, and it grew quickly as a result of heavy media attention (the colorful robes, chanting, and dancing through the streets could hardly fail to attract attention). In just a matter of years, 70 ISKCON centers emerged across the United States and Canada, and others spread into Mexico, the West Indies, Japan, Hong Kong, India, Sweden, France, Germany, Holland, Switzerland, England, Scotland, New Zealand, and Australia.

Prabhupada died in 1977. Senior Hare Krishna devotees have continued to direct the sect, disseminating the teachings of Prabhupada throughout the world.

Beliefs

The Supremacy of Krishna. Hare Krishna theology views Krishna as the eighth avatar of Vishnu (that is, he is the eighth person in whom Vishnu has incarnated). Vishnu is one of the preeminent gods of Hinduism[2] and is considered to be the preserver and protector of the universe.[3] Understandably, he has high standing among Hindus. Interestingly, however, Hare Krishna devotees worship Krishna *above* Vishnu. They consider Vishnu to be a "plenary expansion" of Krishna.

Krishna devotees often refer to Krishna as the "Supreme Personality of the Godhead." He is the ground of all existence in the universe and is everywhere-present.[4] Devotees respect Jesus but say he is lesser to and subordinate to Krishna. He is a son of Krishna.

Humanity's Problem. Like traditional Hinduism, Hare Krishna devotees believe that the main problem human beings have is that they are ignorant of their true divine nature. Instead of recognizing their true nature, people have tended to identify themselves with their material bodies and have thus become entangled in illusion, which Hindus call *maya*. This ignorance will continue until it is somehow dispelled. Until that time, human beings are reincarnated in one life after another, making steady progress toward enlightenment.

Humanity's Solution. Hare Krishnas teach that the single best way to dispel ignorance and to burn off bad karma is to express loving devotion to Krishna through dancing and chanting, accompanied by the use of brass finger cymbals.[5] This ritual is known as *sankirtana*. The dance-chant-cymbal combination allegedly burns out all the "garbage" in one's life and produces a divine influence. People who continue to practice *sankirtana* come to experience ecstasy (Krishna himself is viewed as an ocean of bliss). This is called "Krishna consciousness." In engaging in this ritual, one's goal is to terminate the cycle of continual rebirths caused by karma. The ritual can enable one to be liberated from the slow cycle of reincarnation and go "back to Godhead" (with Krishna).

This is the Hare Krishna chant:

Hare Krishna, Hare Krishna
Krishna, Krishna, Hare, Hare
Hare Rama, Hare Rama
Rama, Rama, Hare, Hare.

In this phrase, the word *Rama* is another name for Krishna, while *Hare* refers to the "pleasure potency of Krishna." These words are chanted 1728 times a day (16 rounds per day, each round consisting of chanting the phrase 108 times. Devotees use 108 prayer beads to keep track of their chants).

The Afterlife. Hare Krishnas depart from their Hindu roots in their teaching on the afterlife. Hindus believe that after many lifetimes of reincarnation, one finally comes to the realization that there is no separation between himself and Brahman (the impersonal deity that underlies all existence). This realization breaks the wheel of karma (reincarnation), and the devotee merges with the Absolute (Brahman). Hare Krishna devotees, by contrast, look forward to fellowship and transcendental love in the presence of Lord Krishna. "This is salvation—to live forever in the joy of Krishna's service."[6]

Submission to a Master. In order to become a Hare Krishna devotee and serve Lord Krishna, worshippers must be in submission to a Hare Krishna spiritual master who is directly connected to Krishna via "disciplic succession." One becomes connected to the spiritual master, or guru, through an initiation ceremony. Without this connection, Krishna consciousness is impossible to attain. With the connection, a relationship with Krishna becomes a reality, with the devotee worshipping the guru himself as God. The devotee's relationship with Krishna is through the *mediacy* of the guru. Once this relationship is made, the devotee is free to go about his day chanting in order to gain Krishna consciousness. After worshippers realize their true identity, they are delivered from the cycle of rebirths and deaths and are transported to a spiritual world known as *Goloka-Vrindavan,* where Krishna lives eternally.

Living Arrangements. Hare Krishna devotees have different views regarding whether they should live in the broader culture or more exclusively within a Krishna communal setting. Some choose to withdraw from life in the broader culture in order to devote sole attention to Krishna. Communal living for such devotees involves obedience to a variety of rules that prohibit sports, drugs, alcohol, tobacco, coffee, tea, and illicit sex. The diet contains no meat, fish, or eggs, and most end up sleeping on the floor in sleeping bags. No discussions unconnected with Krishna consciousness are permitted.

Married couples in the sect generally practice sexual abstinence except when seeking to have children. Sexual relations are limited to once per month (on the most likely day for conception). The sexual act must be preceded by 50 rounds of chanting (each round consisting of 108 chants)—taking perhaps four or five hours—for purification purposes.[7] Once children reach the age of five, they are raised apart from the parents in a Hare Krishna boarding school.

Today the number of ISKCON devotees in the United States is probably around 10,000.[8]

APOLOGETIC POWER POINTS

Pantheism Is False. (26)

Polytheism Is False. (27)

Jesus Is God. (30)

Jesus Is the Son of God. (33)

Jesus Is the Only Way. (36)

Jesus Atoned for Sin. (40)

Humans Are Fallen in Sin. (67)

Heaven Is Real. (77)

Hell Is Real. (78)

False Prophets Are Recognizable. (96)

Chanting Is Prohibited. (102)

Reincarnation Is False. (103)

Mysticism Is Unreliable. (104)

Eastern Meditation Is Prohibited. (108)

16
The I AM Movement

MINING ENGINEER GUY BALLARD (1878–1939) and his wife Edna (1886–1971) were Theosophists until Guy claimed he was contacted by Saint Germain, an Ascended Master who appeared to him in a physical body. (The Ascended Masters are alleged historical persons who have finished their earthly evolutions and have moved on to higher planes of existence, now seeking to help lesser-evolved humans reach their exalted level.) Saint Germain informed Guy that he lived on Mount Teton with 98 other Ascended Masters. I AM followers revere revelations from these Ascended Masters more than the Bible.

In the early 1930s Saint Germain appointed Guy, Edna, and their son Donald as the only "accredited" spokespeople for the Ascended Masters. Many of the revelations received from the Masters are contained in Guy's book, *Unveiled Mysteries*. One purpose of these revelations was to prepare humanity for the emergence of the Aquarian Age and a planetary rise in "Christ-consciousness."[1]

Saint Germain informed Guy that he had attained his exalted status as an Ascended Master by means of continual reincarnations throughout human history. Guy also learned that he himself had been reincarnated many times, and that he had been George Washington in a former life.

At the height of its popularity in the late 1930s, the I AM movement claimed to embrace more than three million adherents, though this figure is hard to verify. The Ballards did in fact speak to capacity crowds in large convention centers all across America.

The Gnostic backdrop to the idea of Ascended Masters is obvious. Gnostic speculation begins with a single eternal principle (God) from which multiple aeons (intermediate beings or manifestations) spring in a declining hierarchy. Christian theologian Louis Berkhof, in *The History of Christian Doctrines*, tells us that in the Gnostic view, the Supreme or High God "interposes between Himself and finite creatures a long chain of aeons or middle beings, emanations from the divine, which together constitute the Pleroma or fullness of the divine essence. It is only through these intermediate beings that the highest God can enter into various relations with created beings."[2] In the case of I AM theology, these intermediate beings are the so-called Ascended Masters, each of whom is at a different level of spiritual evolution.

Beliefs

Chanting I AM Decrees. Saint Germain taught Guy about the "Great Creative Word" (I AM). The "I AM Presence" is in each person and represents a point of contact with divine reality. The I AM Presence is "the Christ." One can attune to this I AM Presence (or "the Christ") by chanting I AM decrees. Such chanting reportedly brings about dramatic results in the life of the one chanting.

The Supremacy of Saint Germain. The Ballards' Christology is distinct in that Saint Germain is more important in the dawning Aquarian Age than Jesus and is the primary object of worship among I AM devotees. Jesus—himself an Ascended Master—said that Saint Germain is "the Greatest Blessing that has ever come to mankind."[3] The reason for this devotion to Saint Germain is that he has brought the Violet Consuming Flame:

"The conscious use of the Violet Consuming Flame is the only means by which any human being can free himself or herself from his or her own human discord and imperfection."[4] The I AM Presence is invoked by chanting decrees, and this in turn activates the Violet Consuming Flame. This Flame then burns away undesirable conditions in one's life (such as bad karma). Of course, this nullifies any need for Jesus' work of atonement on the cross.

God. The I AM movement espouses a pantheistic concept of God—that is, the impersonal God and the universe are essentially one and the same. God possesses both male and female characteristics and is thus sometimes referred to as "Father-Mother." The Holy Spirit is a depersonalized energy or power in nature (essentially the I AM Presence) whose function is to charge all life with the knowledge of God.

Humanity. Humanity is greatly elevated in I AM theology. Salvation consists of becoming free of all physical limitations, coming to the realization that one is divine, and ultimately attaining "ascension" (like the Ascended Masters). Jesus allegedly claimed that human beings are "Gods and Goddesses in embryo."[5]

Afterlife. Because of their belief in reincarnation, I AM enthusiasts do not fear death. Hell is simply a state of consciousness.

Guy's Ascension. The I AM movement was dealt a hard blow when Guy Ballard suddenly died in 1939. The Ballards had taught that people could bypass physical death in the process of attaining spiritual enlightenment. Many followers left the movement upon hearing of Guy's death.[6] Edna Ballard, however, claimed her husband had now become an Ascended Master, and she began communicating revelations from him to I AM devotees who remained with the movement. Others eventually left the Ballards' group to join the Church Universal and Triumphant, a modernized and popularized offshoot of the I AM movement.

─────── **APOLOGETIC POWER POINTS** ───────

The Bible Is Authoritative. (6)

Pantheism Is False. (26)

Jesus Is God. (30)

Jesus Is Unique. (37)

Jesus Atoned for Sin. (40)

The Holy Spirit Is a Person. (57)

The Holy Spirit Is God. (58)

Humans Are Not Divine. (62)

Humans Are Fallen in Sin. (67)

Death Is Real. (76)

Hell Is Real. (78)

Occultism Is Prohibited. (98)

Spiritism Is Prohibited. (99)

Chanting Is Prohibited. (102)

Reincarnation Is False. (103)

Mysticism Is Unreliable. (104)

The Ascended Masters Are Demons in Disguise. (117)

17
Jehovah's Witnesses

THE WATCHTOWER SOCIETY WAS FOUNDED by Charles Taze Russell (1852–1916). Russell grew up in a Presbyterian family, and his mother encouraged him to consider the Christian ministry as a vocation. During his teen years, however, Charles left the Presbyterian church because he did not like their doctrines of predestination and eternal punishment. For a while he became a Congregationalist, but by the age of 17 he had become a full-fledged skeptic. Following this, he studied a variety of different religions, but he never found anything that satisfied him.

Soon enough, Charles came into contact with some Adventists who were excited about Bible prophecy. Charles also became excited, and this began his lifelong interest in Bible prophecy.

In 1879 Charles began publishing a new magazine entitled *Zion's Watch Tower and Herald of Christ's Presence*. This would eventually evolve into today's *Watchtower Magazine*. Congregations in various cities became committed to Russell's interpretation of prophecy.

In 1881 Russell established Zion's Watch Tower Tract Society in Pittsburgh, Pennsylvania. He recruited hundreds of evangelists who were committed to going door-to-door to distribute the literature published by the society. Russell later set up offices in New York.

By 1904 Russell had completed writing six volumes that came to be known as *Studies in the Scriptures*. Russell informed his followers that if they read these books alone, without even reading the Bible, they would have the light of the Scriptures. If, however, they read the Bible alone without reading his books, they would be in darkness within two years.

Judge Rutherford (1869–1942) took over the presidency of the Watchtower Society after Russell died. He developed the society into a tight-knit hierarchical organization. During his presidency, people started calling Watchtower members "Jehovah's Witnesses." Also during this time, Witnesses were instructed to go door-to-door and play phonograph recordings from Rutherford that concluded with an appeal to buy a Watchtower book.

Nathan Knorr (1905–1977) took over the presidency of the Watchtower after Rutherford died. He was a practical businessman and good administrator. Under his leadership, Jehovah's Witnesses were individually trained to make convincing presentations on the doorstep and to answer objections. A new Bible translation—the New World Translation—was also produced under his leadership.

Frederick Franz (1893–1992) became president after Knorr died. He became the premier theologian of the movement. Following his death, Milton Henschel—a third-generation Jehovah's Witness—became president. In 2000, Don Adam, a 50-year veteran of the Watchtower, became the president following Henschel's resignation.

Beliefs

The Watchtower Society. The Watchtower Society is the organization that governs Jehovah's Witnesses worldwide. Jehovah's Witnesses believe God personally set up this organization as his visible representative on earth. It is through this organization and no other that God allegedly teaches the Bible to humankind today. Without the Watchtower and its vast literature, people would be unable to ascertain the true meaning of Scripture.

The Jehovah's Witnesses' claim that the Watchtower Society is the sole possessor and propagator of God's truth is extremely exclusivistic. They believe other Christian organizations are deceptive and rooted in the work of the devil. Witnesses must obey the Watchtower as the voice of God. Not surprisingly, Watchtower literature is replete with admonitions to "dependent" Bible interpretation—that is, *dependent on the Watchtower Society.*[1]

If a Jehovah's Witness disobeys the instructions of the Watchtower Society, even on a relatively minor matter, the individual is "apostate," and the punishment is "disfellowshipping." Jehovah's Witnesses in good standing with the Watchtower are forbidden to interact with one who has been disfellowshipped. The only exception to this is if the disfellowshipped person is in one's immediate family, such as a husband or wife, in which case conducting "necessary business" with him or her is permissible. This fear of disfellowshipping is one of the Watchtower's most effective means of keeping individual Jehovah's Witnesses obedient to its teachings.

God's Name. Watchtower publications teach that God's true name is Jehovah. Superstitious Jewish scribes long ago allegedly removed this sacred name from the Bible. We need not worry, however, because the Watchtower's New World Translation has "faithfully" restored the divine name in the Old Testament where the Hebrew consonants YHWH appear. Moreover, the name Jehovah has been inserted in the New Testament in verses where the text refers to the Father (237 times from Matthew to Revelation). Of course, this contradicts the thousands of Greek New Testament manuscripts in our possession—some of which date from the second century.

Jehovah's Witnesses believe that a proper use of God's "correct" name is essential to one's salvation. Moreover, they believe that because they are the only group that consistently refers to God by His true name, Jehovah, they are the only true followers of God. All other so-called Christian denominations are part of a false, satanically inspired Christendom.

Jesus Christ. Jehovah's Witnesses believe Jesus was created as the archangel Michael billions of years ago. Michael (Jesus) was allegedly created first, and then God used him to create all other things in the universe. Jehovah's Witnesses concede that Jesus is a "mighty god" but deny he is God Almighty like Jehovah is.

Though Michael (Jesus) existed in his prehuman state for billions of years, at the appointed time he was born on earth as a human being—ceasing his existence as an angel. In order to ransom humankind from sin, Michael gave up his existence as a spirit creature (angel) when his life force was transferred into Mary's womb by Jehovah. This was not an incarnation (God in the flesh). Rather, Jesus became a perfect human. He also died as a mere human.

Jesus was crucified not on a cross but rather (allegedly) on a stake. The cross is considered a pagan religious symbol the church adopted when Satan took control of ecclesiastical authority in the early centuries of Christianity.[2]

When Jesus died, he became nonexistent and was raised (re-created) three days later as a spirit creature (that is, as Michael the Archangel). A physical resurrection did not occur. Jesus gave up his human life as a ransom sacrifice for the benefit of humankind. "Having given up his flesh for the life of the world, Christ could never take it again and become a man once more."[3]

To prove his resurrection to the disciples, Witnesses say Jesus "appeared to his disciples on different occasions in various fleshly bodies, just as angels had appeared to men of ancient times. Like those angels, he had the power to construct and to disintegrate those fleshly bodies at will, for the purpose of proving visibly that he had been resurrected."[4]

Consistent with Jesus' alleged spiritual resurrection is the teaching that a spiritual second coming of Christ occurred in 1914. Since then, he has been ruling as King on earth through the Watchtower Society.

The Holy Spirit. In Watchtower theology, the Holy Spirit is neither a person nor God. Rather, the Holy Spirit is God's impersonal "active force" for accomplishing his will in the world. Watchtower literature likens the Holy Spirit to electricity—"a force that can be adapted to perform a great variety of operations."[5] It was allegedly this powerful force of God that came upon Jesus in the form of a dove at his baptism—a force that enabled him to perform many miracles (Mark 1:10).

To prove the Watchtower position, members point out that Scripture portrays many people being "filled" by the Holy Spirit. Such an expression would be appropriate, we are told, only if the Holy Spirit were a force and not a person.[6] After all, how can one person "fill" thousands of people at the same time? A person cannot be split up in that way.

Besides, if the Holy Spirit *were* a person, it would have a name just as the Father and the Son do. We know from Scripture, the Watchtower says, that the Father's personal name is Jehovah. Likewise, the Son's personal name is Jesus. But nowhere in Scripture is a personal name ascribed to the Holy Spirit. Therefore, the Holy Spirit must not be a person like the Father and the Son.

The Trinity. Jehovah's Witnesses believe that if people were to read the Bible from cover to cover without any preconceived ideas, they would never arrive at a belief in the Trinity. Bible students would consistently find the belief that God is one. Witnesses argue that because God is not a God of disorder (1 Corinthians 14:33), Scripture could not possibly speak of a God impossible to understand by human reason. Moreover, the word "Trinity" is not in the Bible. Jehovah's Witnesses further argue that many centuries before the time of Christ, trinities of gods existed in ancient Babylonia, Egypt, and Assyria. The early Christian councils must have derived the doctrine from paganism.

Salvation. Though Jehovah's Witnesses often mention salvation by grace through faith in Christ, they actually believe in a works-oriented salvation. Salvation is impossible apart from total obedience to the Watchtower and vigorous participation in its various programs. The *Watchtower* says that "to get one's name written in that Book of Life will depend upon one's works."[7] Witnesses are to continually be "working hard for the reward of eternal life."[8] This hard work includes distributing Watchtower literature door-to-door.

Two Peoples of God. Watchtower theology recognizes two classes of saved people with two very different destinies and sets of privileges. These are the privileged Anointed Class and the lesser "other sheep." Jehovah's Witnesses believe only 144,000 Jehovah's Witnesses go to heaven, and these make up the Anointed Class (see Revelation 7:4 and 14:1-3). Only those who become "born again"—thereby becoming "sons" of God—can share in this heavenly kingdom (John 1:12-13; Romans 8:16-17; 1 Peter 1:3-4). These individuals look forward not to physical existence but to spiritual existence in heaven.

Jehovah's Witnesses who are not members of the Anointed Class look forward not to a heavenly destiny but to living eternally on an earthly paradise. They believe verses such as Psalm 37:9,11,29 indicate that God has forever given the earth to humankind for this purpose. Since the required number of 144,000 members for the Anointed Class became filled in 1935, all Jehovah's Witnesses since that year have looked forward to an earthly destiny.

No Conscious Existence After Death. Jehovah's Witnesses do not believe the human soul or spirit is distinct from the physical body. In their thinking, the "soul" refers not to an immaterial part of human beings that survives death but to the very life a person has. Every person is a "soul" not because he or she possesses an immaterial nature but because he or she is a living being (Genesis 2:7).

The doctrine of the soul explains what happens at death. Because all people inherited sin from Adam, they die and return to the dust just as animals do. They do not possess a spirit that goes on living as an intelligent personality after death. Their "spirit" is the "life-force" within them, and at death that life-force wanes.

Since at death human beings have no immaterial nature that survives, they are obviously not conscious of anything following death. "When a person is dead he is completely out of existence. He is not conscious of anything."[9] Even the righteous dead remain unconscious and inactive in the grave until the time of the future resurrection. Nor do people consciously suffer in hell. Satan, the father of lies, promoted this concept. Hell is redefined as the common grave of all humankind. The wicked are annihilated.

—— APOLOGETIC POWER POINTS ——

Jehovah Is Not God's Only Name. (21)

God Is a Trinity. (22)

The Trinity Is Not a Pagan Idea. (23)

Jesus Is God. (30)

Jesus Is Not Lesser than the Father. (32)

Jesus Was Not the Archangel Michael. (42)

The Incarnate Jesus Had Two Natures. (47)

Jesus Died on a Cross. (48)

Jesus Completed the Work of Salvation. (49)

Jesus Physically Rose from the Dead. (50)

Jesus Will Return at the Second Coming. (51)

The Holy Spirit Is a Person. (57)

The Holy Spirit Is God. (58)

Salvation Is by Grace Through Faith. (71)

Hell Is Real. (78)

There Is Conscious Existence After Death. (80)

Annihilationism Is False. (81)

There Are Not Two Peoples of God. (92)

False Prophets Are Recognizable. (96)

Setting Prophetic Dates Is Foolish. (97)

18
Kabbalism

KABBALISM IS A MYSTICAL JEWISH SECT that bases its views on the Kabbalah (also spelled Kabalah, Cabala, Cabbala, Cabbalah, Kabala, Kabbala, Qabbala, and Qabbalah). The entire religion hinges on a mystical interpretation of the Old Testament, holding that every word, letter, number, and even accent contains mysteries interpretable only by those who know the secret. This school of thought allegedly emerged among Jews in Babylonia and spread to Italy, Provence, and Spain between the sixth and thirteenth centuries AD. Some, however, claim that Kabbalism dates back to the first century, when some mystical Jews contemplated the divine throne ("chariot") described in Ezekiel 1.

This mystical tradition was allegedly handed down generation by generation to the present time. Christian apologist Elliot Miller makes this observation:

> The word "Cabala" means "to receive," and refers to heavenly revelation received by Jews and passed on to succeeding generations through oral tradition. At first it was used by the mainstream of Judaism, but eventually it became identified with those who believed that the Cabala was an esoteric, occultic tradition that explained the true meaning of the Hebrew Scriptures, which was kept hidden from the masses and only

made known to those who were spiritually ready to receive it.[1]

Beliefs

Occultic Interpretive Methods. Kabbalah uses an occultic method of interpreting Scripture. Kabbalah teaches that "Scripture is inspired, not only in its obvious interpretations, but even to the degree that, through the use of occult symbol interpretation, one could find hidden meanings in the very numerical and alphabetical interpretation of the texts."[2] So Kabbalists derive their doctrines through the Old Testament, albeit only after they apply occultic interpretative methods to it. *The Sorcerer's Handbook* tells us that "according to the Cabala, every letter in the Scriptures contains a mystery only to be solved by the initiated."[3] E.M. Storms tells us that "Cabalists declare that the Bible is incomprehensible without their Cabala!"[4] Storms gives this description:

> The Kabalah teaches that the Bible as a whole is an allegory. Permeated with sexual imagery, the Kabalah contains mystical rites and formulas. It intermingles sorcery and religion, providing the occultist with a great storehouse of magical words and symbols. Cabalists believe the hidden meanings of the Scriptures are unveiled by a specific means, including the manipulation of letters and numbers containing divine powers. The Cabala, comprised of magic, mysticism, and supernatural lore, was used for calling upon angels and demons![5]

Three Varieties. Kabbalists use three basic methods of esoterically interpreting the Scriptures—*gematria, notarikon,* and *themurah.* Kenneth Boa explains it this way:

Gematria is a method which works with the numerical values of the Hebrew letters. The letters of every Hebrew word can be added together in a variety of ways, and the numbers that result can be used to arrive at a "deeper" understanding of the things contained in the Old Testament. *Notarikon* is the system which forms new words or phrases out of the first or last letters of the words in a text. *Themurah,* a system of rearrangement and transposition of the letters of a word, was used to make new words from the original words. The Kabbalists took many different approaches to *themurah.* In one, the alphabet was divided into two or three equal parts and these parts were placed above each other. Letters in the same vertical column were then substituted for each other, and this was used as a code to form new words from the original words of Scripture.[6]

By using such esoteric methodology, Kabbalists derive hidden and allegorical meanings from the Old Testament Scriptures. Many Kabbalists have suggested that the Old Testament must be inspired precisely because of the complicated and intricate numerical relationships that can be observed within its pages.

No Uniform Meaning. Many Kabbalists, based on their subjective, mystical, and esoteric methodology, have come up with different and even contradictory meanings of Bible verses. This means that individual Old Testament verses may mean different things to different people. Verses have no final and definitive interpretation. Perhaps this is one reason one will not find specific "doctrinal statements" among Kabbalists.

Resources. Aside from the Torah, two resources are especially important to Kabbalists. One is the *Sepher Yetzirah*—"the Book of

Formation," which many Kabbalists believe originated with Abraham, though others believe it was written by Rabbi Aqiba between the sixth and ninth centuries. The second is the *Sepher ha Zohar*—"the Book of Splendor," written by Rabbi Moses de Leon in the thirteenth century. It is from these books that Kabbalists derive their mystical methodology. Based on these books, Kabbalists learn to experience a direct union with God. This is important, they say, because many Jews (such as Talmudists) seem stuck in dry formalism and externalism with no real sense of connection to the divine.

The Appeal. The appeal of Kabbalah is that it claims to bring personal empowerment, fulfillment, and improvement to people's lives. One Kabbalist made this assertion:

> According to Kabbalistic teachings, the universe operates according to certain supremely powerful principles. By learning to understand and act in accordance with these precepts, we will vastly improve our lives today, and ultimately we will achieve true fulfillment for ourselves and for all humanity. Just as basic physical laws such as gravity and magnetism exist independently of our will and awareness, the spiritual laws of the universe influence our lives every day and every moment. Kabbalah empowers us to understand and live in harmony with these laws—to use them for the benefit of ourselves and the world.[7]

The Close Connection to Freemasonry

There is a close connection between Kabbalism and Freemasonry. Masons are quite open about the connection. Albert Pike, for example, confesses that "the Kabbala is the key of the occult sciences."[8] He sees Kabbalism in Masonry at every turn, which is why he encourages the Mason to familiarize himself with Kabbalistic doctrine. He says that "Masonry is a search after Light. That search leads us directly…to the Kabalah. In that ancient and little understood medley of absurdity and philosophy, the Initiate will find the source of many doctrines."[9] He notes that "the Kabalistic doctrine," like Freemasonry, "incessantly tends toward spiritual perfection."[10]

Albert Mackey agrees:

> The Kabbala may be defined to be a system of philosophy which embraces certain mystical interpretations of Scripture, and metaphysical and spiritual beings…. Much use is made of it in the advanced [Masonic] degrees, and entire rites have been constructed on its principles. Hence it demands a place in any general work on Masonry.[11]

Still another Mason by the name of Vindex explains that Kabbalism has

> been called the parent of Freemasonry. The Kabbalists were a Jewish secret and mystical society, with their own symbolical interpretation of the scriptures and the Talmud, professing peculiar ideas about the nature of God, and had a great deal in common with the Gnostics of earlier days, who were also organized as a fraternity with secrets. The Kabbalists had great reverence for the Scripture, and yet they did not tie themselves to a literal or legalistic interpretation of them. They were certainly extremely devout, treasuring up their mystical lore as a possession of great value. They were syncretists in believing that at heart all the great religions are practically one, yet they

sought to find common ground for Jews, Christians, and Muslims.[12]

Kabbalism Goes Mainstream

Kabbalism has recently been heavily promoted by Hollywood celebrities, such as Madonna, Kate Capshaw (the actress-wife of Stephen Spielberg), Roseanne Barr, Jeff Goldblum, Naomi Campbell, and Liz Taylor. Madonna, Goldblum, and Campbell say they discovered their "inner light" at the Kabbalah Centre in Hollywood, California. Taylor says Kabbalism is "a light to lead me through the darkness." Barr says Kabbalism is the basis of "everything I believe."[13]

APOLOGETIC POWER POINTS

The Bible Is Inspired. (1)

Esotericism Is Illegitimate. (7)

Sound Hermeneutics Yields Proper Interpretation. (8)

Occultism Is Prohibited. (98)

Mysticism Is Unreliable. (104)

The World Religions Do Not Teach the Same Doctrines. (112)

19
The Masonic Lodge

MASONRY IS A CENTURIES-OLD FRATERNAL order and secret society that is deeply entrenched in symbolism, secret oaths, and secret rituals. Key themes include the universal fatherhood of God and the brotherhood of man.

The origin of Freemasonry is shrouded in deep mystery and wild legends. Some Masons claim Freemasonry goes back to the time of Adam and Eve, arguing that the fig leaves referenced in Genesis 3:7 were actually the first Masonic aprons (used in Masonic initiatory ceremonies). Others argue that Moses was a Grand Master who often marshaled the Israelites into a regular and general lodge while in the wilderness. Still others claim Freemasonry dates back to the time of Solomon, who utilized the skills of stonemasons when erecting the temple in Jerusalem. They say Solomon was Grand Master of the lodge at Jerusalem.

Contrary to such far-fetched claims, history reveals that Freemasonry formally began in London, England, in 1717, due to the efforts of James Anderson, George Payne, and Theopholis Desaguliers.[1] The earliest recorded minutes of a Masonic meeting date back to 1723. New lodges sprang up across England, Ireland, Scotland, Holland, Germany, France, and other European countries.

Freemasonry arrived on American soil by 1733, just 16 years after it first emerged in England. Throughout the 1800s, thousands of Masonic Lodges formed throughout the United States.

Understandably, Freemasonry grew to become a powerful influence in American religion, politics, and society. Today about half the Grand Lodges and two-thirds of the Freemasons in the world are in the United States.

Beliefs

Divergent Views. No single definition of Freemasonry will be acceptable to all Masons. Freemasonry has so many degrees and escalating levels of mysteries revealed to initiates that one person's Freemasonry may be quite different from someone else's. Low-level Masons may view Freemasonry as little more than a fraternal fellowship that provides business contacts and an enjoyable time. For others, particularly those in more advanced degrees, Freemasonry takes on religious significance and can even become a way of life.[2] Consequently, no one Mason speaks for another.[3]

Is Masonry a Religion? One of the more controversial aspects of Freemasonry relates to the question of whether it is a religion. Masons disagree amongst themselves on this issue.

Masonry does require belief in a deity and even teaches a concept of God.[4] Masonry also utilizes typical religious furniture and ceremonies. Within Masonic Lodges one will find altars, pulpits, "Worshipful Masters," rituals, prayers, pledges, sacred vows, sacred literature, hymns, and funeral services. Such factors constitute a strong argument that Freemasonry is a religion.

But most Masons deny that Freemasonry is a religion. They acknowledge that Freemasonry requires belief in a Supreme Deity, but they say the differences between Freemasonry and religion are far greater than any similarities that may exist. They point out that the term "religion" implies new revelation, a plan of salvation, a theology, a confession of faith, dogmas, sacraments, clergy, and ways of communicating with God. Freemasonry allegedly includes none of these things and is therefore not a religion but a philosophy of life.[5]

In Freemasonry, a person is free to follow his own personal religious beliefs—whether he is a Christian, a Jew, a Muslim, or a Hindu. "He may believe the teachings of any organized religion, or he may even have religious convictions that are his alone—as did Thomas Jefferson and John Locke—so long as he believes in a Supreme Being. On that basis, Masonry has welcomed Jews, Moslems, Sikhs, and others, all of whom take the oaths on their own Holy Books."[6] Freemasonry "teaches Masons that their daily life should reflect the principles of their own religion, whatever their religion might be."[7]

Rituals. The ritual for a new Masonic candidate is quite bizarre. The candidate is blindfolded, a noose is put around his neck, and he is brought to the outer door of the lodge, all of which symbolizes that he is in darkness and is in need of the light of Masonry. He is brought into the lodge room, bows before "the Worshipful Master," and says: "I am lost in darkness, and I am seeking the light of Freemasonry." He is instructed that he is entering into a secret organization and that he must keep the secrets of the lodge.

The candidate, still blindfolded, then kneels on his left knee, with his right leg in front of him in the angle of a square. Before him on the altar is the opened holy book of his faith (the Bible for Christians, the Koran for Muslims, and the Vedas for Hindus), with the compass and square on the open book. The candidate then places his left hand under the book, palm up, while his right hand is on top of the compass and square, palm downward. He then utters an oath in which he promises not to reveal the secrets of the lodge to anyone. At one point in the oath, he promises not to give away the secrets of the lodge, "binding myself under no less penalty than that of having my throat cut across, my tongue torn out by its roots, and my body buried in the rough sands of the sea."[8]

The candidate, following the oath, must kiss the holy book as a token of his sincerity. He is then asked what he desires most, to which the proper answer is "Light." At this response, lodge members promptly remove the blindfold and reveal the secrets of the Entered Apprentice. These include a secret handgrip and two hand signs.

Following this, the candidate receives a lambskin, an emblem of innocence "more ancient than the Golden Fleece or the Roman Eagle," more honorable a badge than any prince or potentate could bestow.[9] This emblem of innocence points to the purity of life necessary for one who seeks entrance into the celestial lodge above (heaven).

The Bible. Masons believe that even though the Bible is a significant book, it is not the exclusive Word of God. As one Mason put it, "Masonry as such refuses to distinguish, or to confine the divine revelation exclusively to the tenants or writings of any one particular faith, realizing that all contain elements of vital truth."[10]

All holy books are acceptable within the confines of any Masonic Lodge. All these books provide not just religious truth but moral truth and therefore constitute ethical guides by which to govern one's life. This is the important thing for the Mason.

God. Masons believe that Jews, Christians, Hindus, Muslims, and those of other faiths are all worshipping the same God using different names. God is "the nameless one of a hundred names."[11]

Freemasonry as an institution, however, does not affirm the Christian belief in the Trinity. Masons believe that if Freemasonry affirmed the Trinity, that would amount to sponsoring the Christian religion, since Christianity is the only religion that holds to this doctrine.[12]

The Royal Arch degree of the York Rite states that the real

name of God is Jabulon. This is a compound word derived from "Ja" (for Jehovah), joined with "Bel" or "Bul" (for Baal, the ancient Canaanite God), and "On" (for Osiris, the ancient Egyptian mystery god). "In this compound name an attempt is made to show by a coordination of divine names...the unity, identity, and harmony of the Hebrew, Assyrian and Egyptian god-ideas, and the harmony of the Royal Arch religion with these ancient religions."[13]

Jesus Christ. Masonry either denies or greatly downplays the deity of Christ. Christians within the Masonic Lodge may consider Jesus to be the divine Son of God, but they typically choose not to invoke his name when praying even if they believe he is divine. Masons are instructed that "prayers in the lodges should be closed with expressions such as 'in the Most Holy and Precious name we pray,' using no additional words which would be in conflict with the religious beliefs of those present at meetings."[14]

For the most part, Masons regard Jesus as a great moral teacher and ethical philosopher. He is in the same league with other great men like Socrates. He was a man who stood for virtue.

Although Masons admire Jesus, they reject any suggestion that he is the only way to God. They consider such an idea to be intolerant, and intolerance is not tolerated within Masonic Lodges.

Salvation. Masons deny the Christian doctrine of original sin and reject any suggestion that human beings are depraved. Rather, humans are just imperfect. They make mistakes. If a person works hard at keeping the principles and teachings of the Masonic Lodge—if he lives ethically—he will finally be ushered into the Celestial Lodge Above, where the Supreme Architect of the Universe resides. By ethical living, Masons can "mount by the theological ladder from the Lodge on earth to the Lodge in heaven."[15]

Occultism. Freemasonry has a strong connection with occultism, though perhaps some Masons—particularly Christian

Masons—may be unaware of this. Many Masons themselves acknowledge indebtedness to occultism. H.L. Haywood, for example, concedes that "all our historians, at least nearly all of them, agree that Freemasonry owes very much to certain occult societies or groups that flourished—often in secret—during the late Middle Ages."[16] One form of occultism particularly predominant in Freemasonry is Kabbalism, an occult art that some claim emerged among the Jewish people in the first century AD (see chapter 18, "Kabbalism").

Freemasonry is also closely connected to the mystery religions of paganism. Isis, Serapis, and Osiris are pagan deities affiliated with ancient Egyptian mystery religions that are mentioned regularly in Masonic literature. Albert Pike suggests that Masonry is "a successor of the mysteries," and is "identical with the ancient mysteries."[17] Vindex likewise says that Freemasonry is "the heir and legitimate successor of the ancient mysteries."[18]

APOLOGETIC POWER POINTS

The Bible Is Inspired. (1)

The Bible Should Not Be Added To. (2)

The Bible Is Authoritative. (6)

Esotericism Is Illegitimate. (7)

Sound Hermeneutics Yields Proper Interpretation. (8)

Other "Holy Books" Are Incompatible with the Bible. (11)

God Is a Trinity. (22)

God's Name Is Not Jabulon. (29)

Jesus Is God. (30)

Jesus Is the Son of God. (33)

Jesus Is the Only Way. (36)

Jesus Atoned for Sin. (40)

Jesus Was Not a Mere Moral Teacher. (41)

Christians Should Pray in Jesus' Name. (56)

Humans Are Fallen in Sin. (67)

All Humans Are Infected by Sin (Original Sin). (68)

The Law Cannot Save. (70)

Salvation Is by Grace Through Faith. (71)

Salvation Involves Justification. (72)

Occultism Is Prohibited. (98)

Mysticism Is Unreliable. (104)

Idolatry Is Prohibited. (107)

The World Religions Do Not Teach the Same
    Doctrines. (112)

20

The Nation of Islam

ONE OF THE MORE CONTROVERSIAL and intriguing religious groups to emerge on the American landscape is the Nation of Islam. In this group we find extravagant claims regarding spaceships, the sudden disappearance of a top leader, murder, racial conflict, a bizarre explanation regarding where white people came from, a continual emphasis on black empowerment, and much more. Understandably, this group has regularly been in the popular media. Current membership is difficult to verify but is probably between 20,000 and 100,000, and 80 percent of the membership is male. Significantly, however, Louis Farrakhan's "Million Man March" drew more than 800,000 people in Washington, D.C., in 1995. The movement clearly has influence far beyond its membership figures.

The Nation of Islam began in 1930 in the ghettos of Detroit, Michigan. The group did not emerge in a vacuum; the plight of African Americans during this time provided fertile soil for its emergence and growth. Blatant racism was sweeping across the country. The Ku Klux Klan was alive, well, and active. Blacks often found themselves living in overcrowded slum conditions. Many could not find a job. Those who found a job often suffered discrimination in the workplace, earning far less than their white counterparts. Meanwhile, white police appeared on television roughing up blacks suspected of violating the law. Race riots erupted.

Enter Wallace Fard Muhammad. Fard, believed to have been an orthodox Muslim from Mecca (the capital city of the Islamic religion), appeared in Detroit in 1930 and sought to be a black-supremacy savior to African Americans. His goal was to liberate his people from the whites—"blue-eyed devils"—and restore their position of dignity and primacy in the world. He came with a mission to teach blacks the truth about whites. "He instructed blacks to prepare for the battle of Armageddon, which he interpreted to mean the final confrontation between blacks and whites."[1] He established a mosque in Detroit, and in just a few years he had a following of 8000. That number grew by the day.

Elijah Muhammad. One of Fard's early converts was Robert Poole, born of a Baptist minister in Sandersville, Georgia, in 1898. He moved to Detroit and became a devoted follower of Fard, changing his name to Elijah Muhammad. He soon became Fard's Chief Minister. When Fard suddenly and mysteriously disappeared in the summer of 1934, Elijah Muhammad was immediately named his successor in leading the Nation of Islam. Following Fard's disappearance, Elijah Muhammad proclaimed, "We believe that Allah (God) appeared in the Person of Master W. Fard Muhammad, July, 1930—the long awaited 'Messiah' of the Christians and the 'Mahdi' of the Muslims."[2] He suggested that Fard's disappearance was due to his ascension into heaven, from which he will one day return at Armageddon to proclaim the black man's victory over whites.

Under Elijah Muhammad's leadership, which lasted some 41 years, the movement grew substantially, establishing mosques in major cities with black populations. The Nation of Islam gave blacks "a new sense of dignity, a conviction that they are more than the equals of the white man and are destined to rule the earth."[3]

Malcolm X. Perhaps the most famous figure to emerge in the Nation of Islam was Malcolm X, formerly known as Malcolm

Little. Malcolm was the son of a Baptist minister, born in Lansing, Michigan. His was not an easy life. At an early age, young Malcolm came face-to-face with the harshest form of racism: the Ku Klux Klan, with their white robes on, burned his family's house to the ground. Soon thereafter, his father was found dead. Malcolm would never forget these events. In the years that followed, he continued to experience racism and spent a decade in prison for his own criminal acts.

Malcolm converted to the Nation of Islam in 1948, after his brothers shared the teachings of Elijah Muhammad with him. Once he was released from prison, he relocated to Detroit and became a disciple and exponent of the Nation of Islam. He changed his name to Malcolm X. He attained national prominence as a dynamic speaker and became a cultural hero among African Americans. As a result of his dynamic missionary efforts, the membership of the Nation of Islam skyrocketed.

Eventually, however, Malcolm X became disillusioned with the Nation of Islam. He became aware that Elijah Muhammad had impregnated two of his young secretaries.[4] Moreover, Malcolm discovered that the teachings of the Nation of Islam departed from traditional Islam. For example, Islam teaches that Allah is the only true God, whereas the Nation of Islam allows for many gods and claims that Fard himself was an incarnation of Allah. Malcolm moved increasingly toward traditional Islam and even participated in a pilgrimage to Mecca in 1964. Soon after he returned to the United States, during a speech he was giving in Harlem, New York, he was gunned down. This widely reported assassination took place on February 1, 1965. Just earlier, as a result of Malcolm X distancing himself from the Nation of Islam, Elijah Muhammad commented: "It's time to close that nigger's eyes."[5] No one knows, however, who was responsible for Malcolm X's death.

Wallace Al-Din. Upon the death of Elijah Muhammad in 1975, his son Wallace Deen Muhammad became his successor. Wallace moved the Nation of Islam back into the fold of traditional Islam in the late 1970s. Wallace also led the group away from its radical racism and began teaching racial harmony, no longer viewing whites as a race of devils. He also repudiated Fard's alleged deification. The organization was renamed the American Muslim Mission.

Louis Abdul Farrakhan. Louis Farrakhan, among others, was not happy about Wallace's changes. He and other Nation of Islam members split off from Wallace's group and re-founded the Nation of Islam, maintaining allegiance to the teachings of Elijah Muhammad. Farrakhan assumed leadership of the group.

Farrakhan had been a recruit of Malcolm X in 1955. He served under Malcolm for a time before becoming minister of a mosque in Boston, Massachusetts. An eloquent man, he eventually became the national spokesman for Elijah Muhammad and rose to great notoriety as a result of his fiery sermons (he was twice featured on the cover of *Time* magazine). Among his teachings were warnings to his followers that the Jews are "our enemies" and that they should make every effort to avoid the "evil and filth of the white race."[6]

Beliefs

The Bible. The Nation of Islam teaches that the Bible is not trustworthy, for white people have tampered with it. It is a poison book.[7]

God. Elijah Muhammad flatly denied the doctrine of the trinity:

> The Christians refer to God as a "Mystery" and a
> "Spirit" and divide Him into thirds. One part they call

the Father, another part the Son, and the third part they call the Holy Ghost—which makes the three, one. This is contrary to both nature and mathematics. The law of mathematics will not allow us to put three into one.[8]

Apparently the Nation of Islam recognizes many gods of varying degrees. Elijah Muhammad once proclaimed that "the Black Man's Gods, according to the history Allah taught me, have all been the wisest."[9] A council of 24 scientist-gods write human history. Jerry Buckner notes that "one of them acts as God, while the others do the work of getting the future together for the Nation."[10]

One of these 24 gods, named Yakub, rebelled against Allah and the council, and committed the horrible crime of creating the white race—a race of devils—through a perverse breeding experiment that removed not only their color but also their moral virtues. At some point the whites tried to reverse-breed themselves back into the black race, but this effort only succeeded in producing gorillas.[11]

Even African Americans are gods in Nation of Islam theology. Speaking to his (black) reader, Elijah Muhammad said: "You are walking around looking for a God to bow to and worship. You are the God!"[12] Blacks as individuals and as a whole are divine. "Allah is all of us...He is rooted in all of us. Every righteous person is a god. We are all god. When we say 'Allah' we mean every righteous person."[13]

Wallace Fard, the founder of the Nation of Islam, was supposedly the Supreme God or Supreme Allah, who came from Mecca in 1930. As a Supreme God, Fard has "appeared among us with the same infinite wisdom to bring about a complete change."[14] The reason he is called "supreme" is that he is wiser than all.

No god, however, is eternal. "There are not any gods who live forever."[15] The black God who created the universe does not exist today; at some point he died.

Jesus Christ. Jesus was not virgin-born, was not God in human flesh, and was not the Son of God. Nor was he the equal of the Father. He was merely a man and a prophet of God. He was not crucified on a cross but rather died by being stabbed in the heart in Jerusalem by a police officer seeking a reward from Jewish authorities. He did not rise from the dead.

Humanity. Black people, the original inhabitants of earth, are divine and righteous by nature. They are gods in Nation of Islam theology. The evil scientist-god Yakub created the whites as a race of devils. The whites connived and conquered nations, making slaves of the black people and imposed on them an inferior religion—Christianity. Allah, for his own purposes, allowed white domination for 6000 years. Now the time has come for the Nation of Islam to regain ascendancy.

Sin and Salvation. The Savior of African Americans was born in 1877. His name was Wallace Fard. "Salvation" is interpreted in a temporal sense—that is, salvation from conditions of oppression. Salvation is achieved in the realization that the true God is the black man and the true devil is the white man. White people cannot be saved. White people will eventually be destroyed by a great spaceship that carries out Allah's judgment.

Heaven and the Afterlife. There is no afterlife. Elijah Muhammad said: "I have no alternative than to tell you that there is not any life beyond the grave. There is no justice in the sweet bye and bye. Immortality is NOW, HERE."[16] Therefore, whatever justice is attained by African Americans must be accomplished in this life.

APOLOGETIC POWER POINTS

The Bible Is Inspired. (1)

The Bible Is Reliable. (3)

The Bible Is Authoritative. (6)

God's Attributes Reveal His Nature. (18)

God Is a Trinity. (22)

Polytheism Is False. (27)

Jesus Is God. (30)

Jesus Is Not Lesser than the Father. (32)

Jesus Is the Son of God. (33)

The Incarnate Jesus Had Two Natures. (47)

Jesus Died on a Cross. (48)

Jesus Will Return at the Second Coming. (51)

Humans Are Not Divine. (62)

God Created All Races. (64)

Humans Are Fallen in Sin. (67)

Salvation Is by Grace Through Faith. (71)

Heaven Is Real. (77)

Hell Is Real. (78)

All People Will Face Judgment. (83)

21

The New Age Movement

THE NEW AGE MOVEMENT IS A loosely structured network of individuals and organizations who share a common vision of a New Age of enlightenment and harmony (the "Age of Aquarius") and who subscribe to a common set of religious and philosophical beliefs. This common set of beliefs is based on *monism* (all is one), *pantheism* (all is God), and *mysticism* (the experience of oneness with the divine).[1]

Because it is so broad and organizationally diffuse, we cannot categorize the New Age movement as a cult. Cults are exclusivistic groups made up of individuals who subscribe to a uniform set of beliefs and operate in a rigidly defined organizational structure. Movements have an element of unity but are multifaceted, including a variety of individuals and groups (including cults) whose beliefs, practices, and emphases are distinctive and diverse. This is the case with the New Age movement.

At least five primary factors contributed to the emergence of the New Age movement:

1. *Nineteenth-Century Transcendentalism.* This school of thought, heavily dependent on Eastern scriptures (such as the Hindu Vedas), emphasized intuition as a means of ascertaining truth, held that all religions contain God's truth, and said the goal of religion was conscious union with the divine.

126

2. *Revival of the Occult.* Occultism experienced a revival in the emergence of such groups as the Theosophical Society (1875), the Anthroposophical Society (1912), the Arcane School (1923), and the I AM movement (1930s). Many modern New Agers draw from one or more of these occultic groups.

3. *The Failure of Secular Humanism.* Human reason has not been able to solve all of humankind's problems. A heavy emphasis on secularized reason weakened society's sense of the divine. New Agers seek a return to the divine and the sacred in all things.

4. *The Counterculture of the 1960s.* In the 1960s many people reacted against the West's traditional way of doing things. People were open to new ideas—religious and otherwise. The counterculture became saturated with fringe ideas, including antimaterialism, utopianism, interest in the occult, and a rejection of traditional morality. This contributed to the emergence of the New Age movement.

5. *The Eastern Tidal Wave of the 1960s.* A tidal wave of Eastern ideas swept over the United States in the 1960s. People became interested in Transcendental Meditation, reincarnation, chanting, visualization, and the idea that all reality was divine or sacred. These ideas are pivotal to the New Age movement.

Beliefs

Eclecticism. New Agers feel free to draw ideas from all kinds of sources—holy books (including the Bible and the Hindu Vedas), psychics and channelers, and spirit guides that people meet during deep meditation.

Religious Syncretism. New Agers combine and synthesize religious and philosophical teachings into their mystical worldview. They mix ideas from Jesus, Buddha, Krishna, Zoroaster, alleged space brothers aboard UFOs, and so-called Ascended Masters who live on planet Venus.

Monism. Monism—from the Greek word *monos,* meaning "one"—is the idea that all is one in the universe. God, humanity, and the world of nature are viewed as waves in one big cosmic ocean.

Transformation. Personal transformation takes place when a human being recognizes his or her oneness with all things in the universe. Planetary transformation takes place when a critical mass of human beings come into this same awareness.

Ethics. New Age ethics are relativistic. An example is Values Clarification, a New Age curriculum that has penetrated public schools. Values Clarification instruction helps students discover their own values. The idea is that values are not to be imposed from without (such as from Scripture or from parents) but must be discovered within. The underlying assumption is that truths or values are not absolute.

Meditation. The practice of deep meditation leads to a "non-dualistic state of mind, in which the distinction between subject and object having disappeared and the practitioner having become one with 'god' or 'the absolute,' conventions like time and space are transcended...until finally that stage is reached which religions refer to as salvation, liberation, or complete enlightenment."[2]

Visualization. New Agers believe they can use visualization to accomplish "mind over matter." David Gershon and Gail Straub say this in their bestselling New Age book *Empowerment: The Art of Creating Your Life as You Want It:* "Your thoughts are always creating your reality—it's up to you to take charge of your

thoughts and consciously create a reality that is fulfilling."[3]
Devotees to Seth (an alleged spirit entity that speaks through
channelers) said, "We literally create our reality through the
beliefs we hold, so by changing those beliefs, we can change
reality."[4]

The Bible. New Agers believe the Bible is one of many holy
books communicating revelation from God. They advocate an
esoteric method of reading the Bible—that is, they seek hidden,
secret, or inner spiritual meanings of Bible verses, especially in
the teachings of Jesus. For example, David Spangler believes that
when Jesus said, "Seek first his kingdom and his righteousness"
(Matthew 6:33), he was teaching his disciples to seek "the state of
identification with one's true individuality, the source within, the
Divine center, that I AM THAT I AM."[5]

God. New Agers espouse pantheism—the view that God is all
and all is God. In pantheism, all reality is infused with divinity.
The God of pantheism is an impersonal, amoral "it" as opposed
to the personal, moral "he" of Christianity. The distinction
between the Creator and the creation is completely obliterated in
this view.[6]

Jesus Christ. New Agers distinguish between Jesus and the
Christ. "Jesus" refers to a mere human vessel, while "the Christ"—
variously defined—is divine. Some New Agers see the Christ as a
cosmic, divine entity that dwelt in Jesus' body for a time. Others
see the Christ as an office or a function. Here are three representative New Age views:

- David Spangler says Jesus "attuned" to the cosmic Christ
  and that the Christ descended upon the human Jesus at
  his baptism.[7]

- Levi Dowling says that Jesus underwent seven degrees of

initiation (an occultic ceremony) in Egypt, the seventh degree being the Christ.[8]

• Elizabeth Clare Prophet says Jesus traveled to India as a child and learned from Hindu gurus, and this eventually led to his Christhood.[9]

This human Jesus, who somehow became the Christ, was one of many enlightened "way-showers" for humanity. *The Aquarian Gospel of Jesus the Christ* quotes Jesus saying, "I am your brother man just come to show the way to God."[10] David Spangler said, "Jesus was one of a line of spiritual teachers, a line that continues today."[11]

Humanity. New Agers, based on their acceptance of monism and pantheism, view human beings as divine.[12] Human beings therefore have unlimited potential. *The Aquarian Gospel of Jesus the Christ* quotes the New Age rendition of Jesus as saying, "I came to show the possibilities of man; what I have done all men may do, and what I am all men shall be."[13] This Jesus said, "What I can do all men can do. Go preach the gospel of the omnipotence of Man."[14]

Sin and Salvation. To New Agers, everything is God, so sin cannot exist. Without sin, any talk of salvation becomes meaningless. This means Jesus did not die on the cross for humankind's sin. Many New Agers say Jesus died to balance world karma so the world would not self-destruct.

Humankind's only problem is its ignorance of divinity.[15] Since this is humankind's only problem, the solution is enlightenment. New Agers refer to this enlightenment, or change of consciousness, as attunement, personal transformation, self-realization, or God-realization.

End Times. New Agers hold to different interpretations regarding the second coming of Christ. Some, such as Benjamin

Creme, believe that prophecies of the second coming are fulfilled in the coming of a specific individual named Maitreya. This individual will allegedly take the primary role of leadership in the New Age. Maitreya, says Creme, is the leader of the "Planetary Hierarchy"—a group of exalted Ascended Masters who guide humankind's spiritual evolution. Maitreya has allegedly been living incognito among human beings since 1977, when his consciousness entered a specially created human-like body of manifestation, the *Mayavirupa*. In the near future, Maitreya will allegedly manifest himself to all humanity. He will usher in a new era of peace and happiness. He will solve all the world's problems.

Other New Agers believe that biblical references to the second coming refer not to the coming of a single individual (Maitreya) but rather to the coming of the cosmic Christ spirit on all of humanity. This is the view of New Agers such as David Spangler and George Trevelyan. Spangler says, "the second coming is occurring now in the hearts and minds of millions of individuals of all faiths as they come to realize this spiritual presence within themselves and each other."[16] He says "the second coming of the Christ in our age will be fundamentally, most importantly, a mass coming. It will be the manifestation of a consciousness within the multitudes."[17]

APOLOGETIC POWER POINTS

Esotericism Is Illegitimate. (7)

Sound Hermeneutics Yields Proper Interpretation. (8)

Other "Holy Books" Are Incompatible with the Bible. (11)

God Is Personal. (12)

Pantheism Is False. (26)

Jesus Is the Christ. (34)

Jesus Is the Only Way. (36)

Jesus Atoned for Sin. (40)

Jesus Did Not Go East. (46)

The Incarnate Jesus Had Two Natures. (47)

Jesus Will Return at the Second Coming. (51)

Man Is a Creature. (60)

Humans Are Not Divine. (62)

Humans Are Fallen in Sin. (67)

Salvation Is by Grace Through Faith. (71)

Occultism Is Prohibited. (98)

Spiritism Is Prohibited. (99)

Astrology Is Prohibited. (100)

Reincarnation Is False. (103)

Mysticism Is Unreliable. (104)

Visualization Can Be Dangerous. (105)

Altered States of Consciousness Are Dangerous. (106)

Eastern Meditation Is Prohibited. (108)

Relativism Is Illogical. (109)

The World Religions Do Not Teach the Same
    Doctrines. (112)

The Space Brothers Are Demons in Disguise. (116)

The Ascended Masters Are Demons in Disguise. (117)

22

The New Thought Movement

PHINEAS PARKHURST QUIMBY WAS BORN in New Lebanon, New Hampshire, in 1802. As a boy, he was trained as a clock maker and had a knack for mechanics. As an adult, he developed a knack for metaphysics. Ultimately, he is the father of all the Mind Science cults.

Quimby would often use his metaphysical techniques to heal people whether they could pay him or not. He eventually committed his theories to writing, producing ten volumes of manuscripts in which he discussed religion, disease, spiritualism, clairvoyance, science, error, and truth. As a whole, however, his writings have never been formally published.

Quimby's metaphysics spawned several important movements, including Christian Science, Religious Science, and the Unity School of Christianity. He did not create an organization himself, but individuals he helped adopted his ideas and passed them on to others, adding to or modifying them along the way. The term "New Thought" is a way of describing some of the metaphysical groups that emerged from his thinking.

The New Thought movement developed slowly during the nineteenth century after Quimby's death in 1866, but the New Thought label stuck because of its optimistic ring. New Thought author Horatio Dresser commented on this:

> The "old thought" was undeniably pessimistic, it dwelt

on sin, emphasized the darkness and misery of the world, the distress and the suffering. The new dwelt on life and light, pointing the way to the mastery of all sorrow and suffering. This optimism has since been one of the most characteristic features of New Thought.[1]

Beliefs

Healing. Quimby espoused the metaphysical idea that the source of physical healing lies in the mind. He was convinced that physical diseases were caused by wrong thinking or false beliefs. If we eliminate false beliefs, we remove the chief culprit for disease and enjoy a healthy body.

The Law of Attraction. New Thought proponents subscribe to the "law of attraction."[2] This law says that just as like attracts like, so our thoughts can attract the things they want or expect. Negative thoughts attract dismal circumstances; positive thoughts attract more desirable circumstances. Our thoughts can be either creative or destructive. New Thought sets out to teach people how to use their thoughts creatively.

A Unity of Religions. New Thought proponents espouse a unity of religions. Popular New Thought champion Emma Hopkins makes this claim:

> The remarkable analogies of the Christian Bible, and Hindu Sacred Books, Egyptian Ancient Teachings, Persian Bible, Chinese Great Learning, Oriental Yohar, Saga, and many others, show that the whole world has had life teachings so wonderfully identical as to make them all subjects for respectful attention and investigation by the thoughtful of our age.[3]

God. New Thought espouses a monistic, pantheistic God. In his *In Tune with the Infinite,* New Thought author Ralph Waldo Trine asserts that the great central fact of the universe is the "Spirit of Infinite Life and Power that is back of all, that animates all, that manifests itself in and through all; that self-existent principle of life from which all has come, and not only from which all has come, but from which all is continually coming."[4]

Humankind. This understanding of God leads to the conclusion that human beings are divine. Trine says that "in essence, the life of God and the life of man are identically the same, and so are one. They differ not in essence, in quality; they differ in degree."[5] Human beings therefore have unlimited potential. By using the principles of New Thought this unlimited potential becomes readily attainable.

Sin and Salvation. Sin in the sense of "moral offense against God" does not exist in New Thought theology. Rather, to sin is to succumb to the illusory world of matter, which is the source of all sickness and death. Right thinking is the cure for the New Thought version of sin. Salvation is a release from ignorance concerning oneness with God. Being "born again" refers to being born anew in one's consciousness. "You are constantly being born again as you develop in your awareness of the Christ within."[6]

Spirit and Matter in New Thought. Like many occultists, New Thought proponents say that the spiritual world is related to the material world in terms of cause and effect: "Within every physical planet is a corresponding ethereal planet, or soul world, as within and above every physical organism is a corresponding ethereal organism, or soul body, of which the physical is but the external counterpart and materialized expression."[7]

This cause and effect relationship is governed by the "law of correspondence." New Thought critic Dean Halverson explains that according to this law, "the outer reality mirrors the inner reality, the physical universe corresponds to and is caused by the spiritual universe."[8] This is noticeably similar to the views of Anthroposophy founder Rudolf Steiner and New Age writers David Spangler and George Trevelyan.

Jesus Christ. The Christ of New Thought—an outgrowth of Quimby's metaphysics—is not a person but an impersonal divine nature or principle. Jesus, a mere human, embodied or appropriated the Christ-principle as no human had before. "Not that He as a man was any better," said Quimby, "but He was the embodiment of a higher Wisdom, more so than any man who has ever lived."[9] He fully realized his Christ nature. But Jesus was not a savior to humankind; he was merely a way-shower. All humanity can embody the Christ-principle by following Jesus' example.[10]

New Thought proponents reinterpret the teachings of Jesus to fit their metaphysical theology. The vine and branch analogy in John 15 is an example: "Thus we have the figure of the vine as the symbol of all effective life in the Spirit, all true discipleship and service. The Christ is here a principle such that it can abide in all who are faithful to the precepts and the love set before the disciples as an ideal."[11]

No Death. In New Thought theology there is no death. "So-called death is an entry into the fourth dimension of life, and our journey is from glory to glory, from wisdom to wisdom, ever onward upward and Godward, for there is no end to the glory which is man."[12]

—— APOLOGETIC POWER POINTS ——

Esotericism Is Illegitimate. (7)

Sound Hermeneutics Yields Proper Interpretation. (8)

Other "Holy Books" Are Incompatible with the Bible. (11)

Pantheism Is False. (26)

Jesus Is God. (30)

Jesus Is the Christ. (34)

Jesus Is the Savior. (35)

Jesus Atoned for Sin. (40)

Humans Are Not Divine. (62)

Humans Are Fallen in Sin. (67)

Salvation Is by Grace Through Faith. (71)

Death Is Real. (76)

Heaven Is Real. (77)

Hell Is Real. (78)

Occultism Is Prohibited. (98)

Visualization Can Be Dangerous. (105)

The World Religions Do Not Teach the Same
Doctrines. (112)

Healing Is Subject to God's Will. (118)

23

Nichiren Shoshu Buddhism

NICHIREN SHOSHU BUDDHISM EMERGED out of the teachings of Japanese monk Nichiren Daishonin, also known as Zennichi-maro (1222–1282), who claimed to set forth the *true* form of Buddhism. Nichiren studied at various Buddhist temples and concluded after a prolonged time of meditation that all other Buddhist sects in Japan had misunderstood the truth. He was quite outspoken in his condemnation of these sects and the Japanese government that supported them. One historian commented that "he blamed the social unrest of the period on the erroneous religious beliefs of the nation and proclaimed that the salvation of the Japanese nation depended on devotion to the truth contained in the *Lotus Sutra*."[1] Nichiren believed that the Buddha gave the *Lotus Sutra* to supersede all his other teachings and that it constitutes the very essence of Buddhism. He also believed that reciting the chant *Namu-my-ho-renge-kyo* (see below) embodied the essence of this sutra.[2]

Nichiren Buddhism existed as a small sect from the time of Nichiren's death in 1282 to the mid-twentieth century. At that time, the Nichiren *Shoshu* Buddhist sect emerged and greatly surpassed Nichiren Buddhism in popularity and importance. The lay organization for Nichiren Shoshu Buddhism, called *Soka Gakkai* ("Value Creation Society"), was founded in 1930 by Tsunesaburo Makiguchi. From 1960 to 1990, this organization, under the leadership of Daisaku Ikeda, was responsible for the incredible growth of Nichiren Shoshu Buddhism. This form of Buddhism now has 17 million members in 117 nations.[3] An estimated 500,000 people in the United States are associated with the movement.

What is the appeal? Nichiren Shoshu Buddhism helps worshippers attain "absolute and unwavering good fortune whereby all the people are able to fundamentally overcome the basic universal sufferings of being born, of old age, sickness and death as well as doubts and disillusionments that plague mankind."[4] Indeed, "every believer, without exception, will be able to purify one's life, maintain both spiritual and physical health, bring joy to one's family, enrich one's life, and above all, transform all of one's misfortunes into good fortune, and thereby achieve true happiness."[5] By practicing Nichiren Shoshu Buddhism, "one's individual wishes are answered and the happiness of one's family is granted. More importantly, and on a much larger scale, countless people are emancipated from their sufferings."[6] Among converts to Nichiren Shoshu Buddhism today are celebrities Tina Turner and Herbie Hancock.

Beliefs

The Exaltation of Nichiren. Members of this sect greatly exalt Nichiren Daishonin. They believe he was an incarnation of a bodhisattva named Jogyo. (A bodhisattva is a divine individual who has earned the right to enter into Nirvana or into illumination, but instead voluntarily turns back from that state in order to aid humanity to reach that same state.) They feel he arose to teach the truth in an age of spiritual darkness. Among the "truths" revealed by Nichiren is the worship of the Gohonzon.

Worship of the Gohonzon. The Gohonzon is a "small altar that houses a piece of paper used as a *mandala* (a visual object upon which to meditate)."[7] This paper contains the words to a sacred chant, as well as the names of Nichiren and various Buddhist gods mentioned in the *Lotus Sutra*.

Daimoku. Another "truth" communicated through Nichiren involves *Daimoku*, a prayer of praise in which the worshipper chants the words *Namu-my-ho-renge-kyo*, meaning, "Hail to the wonderful truth of the *Lotus Sutra*."[8] Chanting these words for a prolonged time results in a union of the worshipper with the Buddha. As one continues to chant, one attains enlightenment and harmony with the flow of life in the universe. John Ankerberg and John Weldon explain:

> By chanting "Nam-my-ho-renge-kyo" (the magical invocation believed to summarize and internalize the essence of the *Lotus Sutra*), one's individual nature is brought into harmony with the "essential life" of the universe. Eventually, the highest expression of essential life, the Buddha nature, which is dormant in the inner self, is brought to the surface. The individual nature thus becomes united to the Buddha nature, the result (allegedly) being new spiritual power, self-renewal, greater wisdom, more vitality and, not the least, material wealth.[9]

God. Nichiren Shoshu Buddhism has no concept of a personal God but rather espouses what may be considered a form of pantheism. The Gohonzon is a representation of this pantheistic deity and itself functions like a God among proponents of Nichiren Shoshu Buddhism. It is a visible manifestation of the pantheistic God. Walter Martin notes that Nichiren Shoshu Buddhism ascribes attributes to the Gohonzon that other people ascribe to God:

- It is the savior of humankind.
- It is the source of all divine help.
- The believer has faith in the Gohonzon.
- It is the only source of eternal good fortune.
- One must render it full devotion.
- It is the source of happiness.
- It is the ultimate source of the universe.
- It purifies believers.
- It forgives sin and answers prayer.
- It is omnipotent.
- The Dai Gohonzon anxiously awaits the world's worship and holds the key to world peace and happiness.[10]

Jesus Christ. Jesus is not God in human flesh, nor did he die for the sins of humankind on the cross. Rather, he was more or less an enlightened man who sought to aid others in attaining enlightenment. Nichiren, not Jesus, is the savior of humankind.

Salvation. Salvation from ignorance, unhappiness, and suffering is rooted in the *Daimoku*. More specifically, chanting *Namu-my-ho-renge-kyo* brings enlightenment, removes the penalty of bad karma, and keeps one in harmony with the flow of life in the universe. The chant, supposedly a repository of magical power, brings about material blessings and increased happiness. Nichiren Shoshu Buddhist leader Daisaku Ikeda said this form of Buddhism will "save the whole world through the attainment of each individual's happiness in life."[11]

——— APOLOGETIC POWER POINTS ———

God Is Personal. (12)

God Alone Is to Be Worshipped. (25)

Pantheism Is False. (26)

Polytheism Is False. (27)

Jesus Is the Savior. (35)

Jesus Atoned for Sin. (40)

Salvation Is by Grace Through Faith. (71)

Chanting Is Prohibited. (102)

Reincarnation Is False. (103)

Eastern Meditation Is Prohibited. (108)

Healing Is Subject to God's Will. (118)

24

Occultism

THE WORD "OCCULT" COMES FROM the Latin word *occultus* and literally means "hidden," "secret," or "concealed." The term refers to hidden or secret knowledge, "to that which is beyond the range of ordinary human knowledge; to mysterious or concealed phenomena; to inexplicable events. It is frequently used in reference to certain practices (occult 'arts') which include divination, fortune telling, spiritism (necromancy), and magic."[1]

These occult arts have three primary characteristics: (1) They disclose information unavailable to humans through normal means (that is, through the five senses); (2) they place people in contact with supernatural powers, paranormal entities, or demonic forces; and (3) they sometimes seek to empower one to manipulate or influence other people into certain actions.[2]

Occultism takes many forms but often includes such practices as trance states, séances, clairvoyance, spiritism (also called channeling), automatic handwriting, peering into crystals, levitation, and out-of-body experiences. Let us briefly consider each of these.

Definitions

A *trance state* involves an altered state of consciousness, a mental state other than normal waking consciousness that ranges from a mild sense of the transcendent to a deep trance. In such a state, one often has a sense of oneness with all things and a sense of harmony with the universe. Trances open the way to mystical experiences with spiritual forces (demons).

A *séance* is a meeting of people, often around a table, who attempt to communicate with the spirit world or with souls of departed people through a medium. Mediums often use the assistance of a "guide," a Ouija board, and/or automatic handwriting. A guide is a spirit present during a séance that offers advice and guidance—often considered to be a guru or priest from centuries past. A Ouija board is a game board containing numbers and letters with a pointer that a "visiting spirit" can use to communicate a message from the spirit world by guiding the hand of the medium. ("Automatic handwriting" is defined below.)

Clairvoyance is the mental "seeing" of physical objects or events at a distance by psychic means. It involves the ability to perceive things beyond physical reality. Sometimes the term refers to the psychic ability to "see" and describe future events.

Spiritism, also called *channeling,* is "the practice of attempting communication with departed human or extra-human intelligences (usually nonphysical) through the agency of a human medium, with the intent of receiving paranormal information and/or having direct experience of metaphysical realities."[3] However, some spiritists are not involved in communication with spirit entities but rather claim the ability to read the Akashic Records. The Akashic Records are allegedly an energy field that surrounds the earth and psychically records all events in earth's history. Some psychics claim they can "read" the Akashic Records and thereby provide secret information about the past.

Automatic handwriting is a phenomenon in spiritualism in which a medium writes words without apparent awareness. The source of such writing is believed to be a dead person's spirit or a paranormal entity. An example is the book *A Course in Miracles,* written by Helen Schucman, as guided by a spirit entity named Jesus. This spirit guided Schucman's hand in all that she wrote.

Peering into crystals (or a crystal ball) is a form of divination or fortune telling that involves seeking paranormal information or knowledge of the future by means of a crystal. "Gazing into the glass, the clairvoyant enters into a trance-like state and is able to view future events."[4]

Levitation occurs when an inanimate object is suspended in the air with no apparent means of support. An example of this phenomenon involves séances in which the spiritualist's table reportedly lifts off the ground, indicating the presence of spirit beings or paranormal entities.

Out-of-body experiences, also called *astral projection*, involves the body remaining stationary while one's soul or spirit allegedly leaves the body and travels around to different locations—even (occultists claim) into outer space. Occultists often speak of a thin gray cord that remains connected between one's soul and the body (at the naval).

Ancient Divination

The use of divination is nothing new, for it existed even in Bible times. People of pagan nations often engaged in various forms of divination in order to determine the future or to determine the will of the gods. Sometimes these ancient occultists would seek communication with the dead through spiritists or mediums and try to obtain paranormal information (Deuteronomy 18:11; 1 Samuel 28:3,9). Others would engage in witchcraft to extract information from a pagan god (Numbers 22:7; 23:23; Joshua 13:22).

Some in ancient times conjured spells (Deuteronomy 18:11) or practiced sorcery (Exodus 22:18; Deuteronomy 18:10). Others interpreted omens (Genesis 30:27; 44:5). Some in Babylon observed and interpreted the stars (astrology) because they believed the stars were connected to the pagan gods (Daniel 1:20;

2:2,10,27; 4:7; 5:7,11,15). Still others practiced soothsaying by, for example, examining the liver of a dead animal that had been sacrificed. They would interpret any abnormalities in the liver as a possible indication of some aspect of the will of the gods.

Popular Manifestations of Modern Occultism

Occultism has penetrated Western culture in many ways. To illustrate, I will briefly describe three: near-death experiences, the UFO movement, and New Age energetic medicine.

Near-Death Experiences. Many researchers have noted a clear connection between near-death experiences and occultism. John Weldon and John Ankerberg, for example, tell us that "in large measure the NDE [near-death experience] is merely one form of the occult out-of-body experience (OBE)."[5] Moreover, "both the NDE and OBE have many other similarities including…spiritistic contacts, worldview changes, and development of psychic powers."[6]

In keeping with this, near-death researcher Kenneth Ring commented that "I could not help noticing the frequency with which psychic events were spontaneously reported by NDErs and how often these experiences were said to have occurred following the NDE.…Many NDErs simply claimed that their psychic sensitivities have developed strikingly since their NDE."[7]

What kinds of psychic phenomena are we talking about? Some people experience astral travel or out-of-body experiences—that is, their soul leaves their body and travels around the so-called astral realm. Some people develop clairvoyance—the ability to perceive things that are outside the natural range of human senses. Some people develop telepathic abilities—that is, abilities to mystically communicate by means of thoughts alone. Many people report coming into contact with spirit guides.

The UFO Movement. Christian UFO researchers have noted

that individuals who claim to be contacted by (or become abducted by) UFOs often have a strong prior involvement in some form of occultism. Brooks Alexander of the Spiritual Counterfeits Project notes that "many of the reported cases show some kind of occult involvement prior to initial UFO contact."[8] John Weldon and Zola Levitt likewise note that "UFO contactees often have a history of psychic abilities or an interest in the occult."[9]

David Wimbish has suggested that interest in UFOs can actually draw one *into* the occult: "Many UFO investigators have followed a path that has taken them directly into the world of the occult. They believe they are rediscovering ancient spiritual truths and uncovering new realities about the universe. It's more likely that they are getting involved with some ancient deceptions."[10] Indeed, the UFO phenomenon "has led many to experiment with astral projection, to believe in reincarnation, and to get involved in other practices that directly oppose the historic teachings of the Christian church."[11]

Jacques Vallee, well-known French UFO investigator, made the following comments regarding the occult connection to UFO phenomena: "A few investigators…have suggested both in public statements and in private conversations with me that there may be a link between UFO events and 'occult' phenomena….At first view, the very suggestion of such a link is disturbing to a scientist. However, the phenomena reported by UFO witnesses involve poltergeist effects, levitation, psychic control, healing, and out-of-body experiences."[12]

New Age Energetic Medicine. The New Age model of holistic health is heavily based on a conception of energy, not matter. The editors of the *New Age Journal* give this report:

All of the healing systems that can be called "holistic" share a common belief in the universe as a unified field of energy that produces all form and substance....This vital force, which supports and sustains life, has been given many names. The Chinese call it *"chi'i,"* the Hindus call it *"prana,"* the Hebrews call it *"ruach,"* and the American Indians name it "the Great Spirit."[13]

This energy is not a visible, measurable, scientifically explainable energy. Rather, New Agers speak of a "cosmic" or "universal" energy—a "life force"—based on their monistic (all is one) and pantheistic (all is God) worldview. To enhance the flow of "healing energy" in the body, one must allegedly attune to it and realize one's unity with all things. Becoming "one" with this universal energy ("God") yields health. (Whoever heard of a sick god?) One must also "smooth out" any energy blockages that may develop within the body. One will then be healthy. Many New Age health therapies are based on this premise.

An example is the "therapeutic touch." This is a therapy in which the practitioner places his or her hands two or three inches above the patient's body, palms down, and moves the hands up and down the body in search of energy imbalances. What is actually "touched" is a person's "energy field" around the body. By using circular sweeping motions, the patient's blocked energy is "decongested." This allegedly yields health for the patient. The healer also seeks to transfer healing energy into the body of the patient, yielding health.

An undeniable and very strong connection exists between the "life force" of energetic medicine and occultism. New Age critic Elliot Miller points this out:

> Wherever it has appeared—in ancient paganism, modern occultism, or parapsychological research— this "life force" has been accompanied by altered states

of consciousness, psychic phenomena, and contact with spirits. Additionally, those who are capable of perceiving, and adept at manipulating, this force invariably are shamans (e.g., witch doctors), "sensitives," or psychics, thoroughly immersed in the pagan/occult world.[14]

Many holistic health therapies seek to enhance the flow of "healing energy" in the body. Unfortunately, by engaging in such holistic practices, many people have fallen headlong into New Age occultism. Miller warns, "My wide-ranging research of occultism emboldens me to suggest that this energy is part and parcel of the occult—where the occult appears, it can be found; where it is found, the occult will inevitably appear."[15]

Reader, beware! Western society is drenched in whitewashed occultism.

APOLOGETIC POWER POINTS

Satan Is a Fallen Angel. (84)

Satan's Titles Reveal His Nature. (85)

Fallen Angels Hurt Believers. (86)

Christians Should Test the Spirits. (89)

Occultism Is Prohibited. (98)

Spiritism Is Prohibited. (99)

Witchcraft Is Prohibited. (101)

Reincarnation Is False. (103)

Mysticism Is Unreliable. (104)

Altered States of Consciousness Are Dangerous. (106)

Eastern Meditation Is Prohibited. (108)

25

Oneness Pentecostalism

ONENESS PENTECOSTALISM EMERGED out of Assemblies of God churches in the early 1900s.[1] A minority of pastors affiliated with this Christian denomination began teaching that God manifests himself in three different modes (not persons): the Father, the Son, and the Holy Spirit. The one true God who manifests himself this way is Jesus. These pastors also taught that baptism must be in the name of Jesus only, not in the name of the Father, the Son, and the Holy Spirit (see Acts 2:38).[2]

The larger corpus of Assemblies of God pastors took a stand against such teachings, and at a denominational council in 1916, they strongly affirmed belief in the Trinity. This action led to the withdrawal of 156 out of 585 pastors (and their congregations).[3]

Over the following years a number of small denominations emerged among the Oneness pastors who withdrew from the Assemblies of God. A number of splits and mergers took place, the ultimate result being the formation of the largest of the Oneness Pentecostal groups: the United Pentecostal Church International (UPCI). Today there are over five million advocates of Oneness theology in the world, with about one million of these living in the United States.[4] Approximately 75 percent of Oneness Pentecostals are affiliated with the UPCI, embracing some 3800 churches in the United States.[5]

Beliefs

Jesus Is the Father, Son, and Holy Spirit. A distinctive of

Oneness Pentecostalism is that they consider Jesus to be the one true God. He himself is the Father, the Son, and the Holy Spirit. These three are simply different roles that Jesus plays on different occasions.

Oneness Pentecostals point to verses in the Bible that show that God is absolutely one (for example, Deuteronomy 6:4; Isaiah 42:8; 43:10-11; 44:6; 1 Corinthians 8:4-6; Ephesians 4:4-6; 1 Timothy 2:5). They reason that because only one true God exists, and because the New Testament teaches that Jesus is God (John 8:58; Colossians 2:9; Titus 2:13-14), Jesus must be the one true God of which Scripture speaks. Therefore, Jesus is the Father, the Son, and the Holy Spirit.[6]

Oneness Pentecostals cite biblical passages that they believe prove Jesus is the Father. Isaiah 9:6 refers to Jesus as "Mighty God, Everlasting Father."[7] Jesus in John 10:30 affirms that "I and the Father are one," thus establishing their common identity.[8] As well, Jesus indicated that if anyone saw him, they actually saw the Father (John 14:7-11).

In Romans 1:7, the apostle Paul writes, "Grace and peace to you from God our Father *and* from the Lord Jesus Christ" (italics added). Oneness teachers argue that the Greek word for "and" *(kai)* should be translated as "even," so that the phrase should read, "God our Father, *even* the Lord Jesus Christ."[9] Seen in this light, Jesus must be one and the same as the Father.

Oneness Pentecostals also cite biblical verses that support their view that Jesus is the Holy Spirit. Second Corinthians 3:17 (NASB) is an example: "Now the Lord is the Spirit, and where the Spirit of the Lord is, there is liberty." They believe this is an explicit reference to the Lord Jesus being the Holy Spirit.

They also interpret Matthew 28:19 in conjunction with Acts 2:38. In Matthew 28:19 (NASB) Jesus said to the disciples, "Go therefore and make disciples of all the nations, baptizing them in the *name* of the Father and the Son and the Holy Spirit" (italics added). Yet, in Acts 2:38, Jesus' followers are instructed to baptize "in the *name* of Jesus" (italics added). This must mean that "in the name of the Father and the Son and the Holy Spirit" is the same as "in the name of Jesus." Therefore, Jesus is the Father, the Son, and the Holy Spirit.

If Jesus is the Father, the Son, and the Holy Spirit, as Oneness Pentecostals believe, then how are we to understand these various roles of Jesus? Generally speaking, the term "Father" refers to Jesus' deity, the term "Son" refers to Jesus in his humanity or in the incarnate state, and the term "Holy Spirit" refers to God imparting himself to humankind in various ways.

Though quite confusing, Oneness theology teaches that Jesus is both the Father who sent his Son and the Son who obeyed the Father. He was the Son who prayed to the Father and at the same time was the Father who answered the Son's prayers. Yet Jesus was and is just one person.

The Trinity Is a False Doctrine. Oneness Pentecostals believe Scripture militates against the doctrine of the Trinity. They argue that the word "Trinity" is not in the Bible and that Scripture speaks of only one God (Deuteronomy 6:4; 1 Timothy 2:5). They concede that Scripture calls the Father God (Malachi 2:10), the Son God (John 1:1), and the Holy Spirit God (Acts 5:3-4), but their conclusion is that Jesus is the one God who is the Father, the Son, and the Holy Spirit.

In Bible passages where three persons seem to be present, such as the baptism account of Jesus in Matthew 3:16-17, Oneness Pentecostals argue that different modes of Jesus are being manifest. At the same time, Jesus was the Son who was being baptized, he was the Father who spoke from heaven, and he was the Holy Spirit who descended on the Son.[10]

Moreover, Oneness Pentecostals argue, if Jesus were the

second person of the Trinity, how could he pray to the first person of the Trinity without "undeifying" himself? A truly divine person does not need to pray, for he needs no help. Only human beings need help and need to pray. Therefore the Son is the human nature of Jesus, who prayed to the eternal divine spirit (the Father).[11]

Still further, Oneness Pentecostals argue that the New Testament makes certain statements about the Son that could not be true of someone who was fully God. An example is Mark 13:32, where we are told that the Son does not know the day or hour of the second coming. If the Son were truly divine, he would be omniscient like the Father.

Yet another problem for the doctrine of the Trinity, Oneness Pentecostals say, is that some Bible passages mention the Father and Son, but not the Holy Spirit. An example of this is 1 John 1:3, where we read that "our fellowship is with the Father and with his Son, Jesus Christ" (see also 1 Corinthians 1:3; 2 Corinthians 1:2). Why isn't the Holy Spirit mentioned? If the Holy Spirit were the third person of a Trinity, would he not be mentioned alongside the Father and the Son?

Finally, Oneness Pentecostals appeal to history. Like the Jehovah's Witnesses, they argue that the doctrine of the Trinity is rooted in the ancient paganism of the Babylonians and Assyrians. Since these pagan nations believed in a form of the Trinity, the doctrine could not be a part of true Christianity.

Salvation Does Not Come Easy. Oneness Pentecostals teach that people must meet a number of conditions in order to be finally saved. Faith in Christ is necessary, but so is repentance, water baptism by immersion in the name of Jesus only (and not in the name of the Father, the Son, and the Holy Spirit), baptism in the Holy Spirit as evidenced by speaking in tongues, and continued obedience to the burdensome holiness code of Oneness Pentecostalism.

APOLOGETIC POWER POINTS

Sound Hermeneutics Yields Proper Interpretation. (8)

God Is a Trinity. (22)

The Trinity Is Not a Pagan Idea. (23)

Modalism Is False. (24)

Jesus Is God. (30)

Jesus Is the Son of God. (33)

Jesus Is Not the Father. (44)

Jesus Is Not the Holy Spirit. (45)

The Incarnate Jesus Had Two Natures. (47)

Jesus' Praying Is Not Incompatible with His Deity. (54)

The Holy Spirit Is a Person. (57)

The Holy Spirit Is God. (58)

The Law Cannot Save. (70)

Salvation Is by Grace Through Faith. (71)

Salvation Involves Justification. (72)

Tongues Is Not Necessary for Salvation. (74)

Baptism Is Not Necessary for Salvation. (75)

Baptism Is Trinitarian. (93)

26

The Raelian Movement

THE RAELIAN MOVEMENT IS "an atheist, non-profit, spiritual organization; 'atheist' because it demystifies the old concept of god, 'spiritual' because it links us with our creators and infinity, and 'non-profit' because no member gets paid any salary."[1] The movement was founded in 1973 by a French race car driver and journalist named Claude Vorilhon. He claims he founded the movement after encountering space aliens while walking through a volcanic mountain range in France.[2] The aliens changed his name to "Rael."

The backdrop to this encounter allegedly goes back much further. According to Raelian literature, Rael (Vorilhon) was born as a hybrid being with a human mother but an alien father. Following the explosion of the atomic bomb in Hiroshima in 1945, advanced alien scientists known as the Elohim selected Marie Colette Vorilhon to be his mother. On December 25, 1945, the Elohim took her inside a spacecraft and inseminated her. They then erased the experience from her memory so as not to psychologically unbalance her. Rael was born from this union on September 30, 1946.

Vorilhon had his first alien encounter when he was an adult. He describes the aliens as four feet tall with long dark hair, almond shaped eyes, and olive skin.[3] These beings, according to Rael, entrusted him with a message. Out of all the human beings on earth, Rael was the one chosen to spread "the greatest message ever revealed to humanity," and he was to be an apostle of a new world order. The message entrusted to him answered the existential questions that have plagued human beings since the beginning of humankind's existence: *Who am I? Where did I come from? Why am I here?* "This message is the final chapter of all the world religions, it is the key which enables everyone to understand that what we thought was god is in fact people just like us but more advanced, who love us very much and have been waiting for us to reach a stage where we can finally understand them."[4]

Rael subsequently wrote *The Message Given to Me by Extraterrestrials*, which is claimed to be a world bestseller and is translated into 22 languages. The Raelians presently boast 60,000 members in 84 countries.[5] The movement has more than a dozen offices throughout the world—including ones in Japan, Africa, Switzerland, Mexico, Canada, and three in the United States: Los Angeles, Las Vegas, and Miami.[6]

Beliefs

The Origin of Life on Earth. The aliens told Rael that humans were "implanted" on the earth by advanced extraterrestrial scientists known as the Elohim. Rael claims that the plural word *Elohim* means "Those who came from the sky." These Elohim allegedly scientifically created humanity from inert chemicals using DNA in their laboratories. This is what the book of Genesis was *really* talking about in its early chapters. Genesis is simply a written account of how aliens from another planet created life on earth.

The alien that appeared to Rael told him that "we were the ones who made all life on earth; you mistook us for Gods. We were at the origin of your main religions. Now that you are mature enough to understand this, we would like to enter official contact."[7] We are told that the Elohim

> maintained contact with us via prophets including Buddha, Moses, Jesus, and Mohammed, all specially chosen and educated by them. The role of the prophets was to progressively educate humanity through the messages they taught, each time adapted to the culture and level of understanding at the time. They were also to leave traces of the Elohim so that we would be able to recognize them as our creators and fellow human beings when we had advanced enough scientifically to understand them.[8]

Rael's Task. Rael says he is the last of 40 prophets—each of whom was crossbred between the Elohim and human women. As a prophet, Rael's task is to warn humankind that since the explosion of the first atomic bomb in 1945, humanity has been in the "Age of Apocalypse." We humans now have a huge collective choice to make. We can destroy ourselves with nuclear bombs, or we can make a leap into planetary consciousness that will then qualify us to receive the scientific knowledge of our space forefathers.

An Embassy in Jerusalem. In the not-too-distant future, a descent of UFOs will reveal the Elohim as well as the 39 previous immortal prophets—including Jesus, Buddha, Mohammed, and the Mormon prophet Joseph Smith. Rael has been assigned to build an embassy in Jerusalem by the year 2025 where the creators (the Elohim) can live and hand down to human beings their scientific heritage.

The Necessity of Neutrality. Why is an embassy necessary for the alien visitors? Raelian literature tells us that "without the neutrality of an embassy, free air space and an official welcome, an unannounced and undesired landing would have enormous political, economic, and social repercussions with disastrous consequences worldwide."[9] Moreover, the alien visitors do not wish "to endorse any government, religion, or ideology other than that of the Raelian Philosophy, by contacting any other institution first. Thus they will only come when we build their embassy, such is their love and respect for us."[10]

The Secret of Eternal Life. The aliens will also deliver to us the secret of eternal life, which is cloning. "Cloning is the secret of eternal life. Cloning will make the life of people better by curing genetic diseases."[11] This hope of "eternal life" involves a peculiar ritual. Researcher Susan Jean Palmer explains it this way:

> Denying the existence of God or the soul, Rael presents as the only hope of immortality a regeneration through science, and to this end members participate in four annual festivals so that the Elohim can fly overhead and register the Raelians' DNA codes on their machines. This initiation ritual, called "the transmission of the cellular plan," promises a kind of immortality through cloning. New initiates sign a contract which permits a mortician to cut out a piece of bone in their forehead (the "third eye") which is stored in ice awaiting the descent of the Elohim.[12]

APOLOGETIC POWER POINTS

Other "Holy Books" Are Incompatible with the Bible. (11)

God Is the Creator. (19)

God Is Elohim. (20)

Atheism Is False. (28)

Jesus Is God. (30)

Jesus Is the Savior. (35)

Jesus Is the Only Way. (36)

Jesus Is Unique. (37)

False Prophets Are Recognizable. (96)

The World Religions Do Not Teach the Same Doctrines. (112)

The Space Brothers Are Demons in Disguise. (116)

27

Religious Science

THE UNITED CHURCH OF RELIGIOUS Science (hereafter Religious Science) is an offshoot of the New Thought movement—a movement that emerged out of the teachings of Phineas P. Quimby (1802–1866) (see chapter 22, "The New Thought Movement"). Religious Science was founded by "Dr." Ernest Holmes, who wrote *The Science of Mind* in 1926. This book became the standard textbook for the movement. In it, Holmes syncretized the metaphysical ideas he sifted from New Thought with psychology, philosophy, Theosophy, psychic phenomena, hypnotism, the writings of transcendentalist Ralph Waldo Emerson, and the various world religions. Holmes once said, "I didn't like any of the religions I was acquainted with, and so I made up one that I did like."[1]

Religious Science experienced rapid growth due to the endorsements it received from several famous people. Norman Vincent Peale said: "Only those who knew me as a boy can fully appreciate what Ernest Holmes did for me. Why, he made me a positive thinker."[2] Among those who have been on the board of directors at the Holmes Center for Research in Holistic Healing are Robert Young (of *Father Knows Best* fame), Norman Cousins (editor of the *Saturday Review*), and Maurice Starts (former United States secretary of commerce).

Beliefs

Eclectic. Religious Science is well known for its eclecticism. In his book *What Religious Science Teaches*, Holmes exclaims, "It has been well said that 'religions are many,' but Religion is one....Faith is One. Truth is One. There is One Reality at the heart of all religions, whether their name be Hindu, Mohammedan, Christian or Jewish."[3]

Holmes derived his doctrines from a vast array of religious writings, including the Koran (Islam), the Bhagavad-Gita, Vedas, and Upanishads (Hinduism), the Apocrypha, the Talmud (Judaism), the Kabbalah (Jewish mysticism), the Egyptian Book of the Dead, and the Christian Bible. As to why Holmes sought spiritual "truth" from such a wide variety of sources, he gave this explanation:

> The Christian Bible, perhaps the greatest book ever written, truly points a way to eternal values. But there are many other bibles, all of which, taken together, weave the story of spiritual truth into a unified pattern....It is unreasonable to suppose that any one person, or race, encompasses all truth, and alone can reveal the way of life to others....Religious Science reads every man's Bible and learns the truths therein contained....Without criticism, without judgment, but by true discrimination, that which is true and provable may be discovered and put to practical use.[4]

God. Holmes espouses a God who is both *impersonal* (he often calls God "The Thing Itself," "Principle," and "Neutral Force") and *pantheistic* ("God is everything").[5] Holmes speaks of each person of the Trinity in impersonal terms. He says "the Father [is] the supreme creative Principle...and means Absolute Being."[6] "The entire manifestation of the infinite in any and all planes, levels, states of consciousness, or manifestations, constitutes the Son."[7]

"The Holy Ghost signifies the feminine aspect of the Divine Trinity. It represents the divine activity of the higher mental plane."[8]

Humanity. Consistent with his metaphysical roots, Holmes believes human beings are part of the divine essence and that humankind's problem is not sin but ignorance of his union with the divine: "I have always taught that there is no sin but ignorance."[9] He argues that "there is something Divine about us which we have overlooked. There is more to us than we realize....Man, the real man, is birthless, deathless, changeless; and God, as man, in man, IS man."[10]

"But if we are Divine beings," Holmes asks, "why is it that we appear to be so limited, so forlorn, so poor; so miserable, sick, and unhappy? The answer is that we are ignorant of our own nature, and also ignorant of the Law of God which governs all things."[11]

Salvation. Religious Science teaches that the solution to humankind's dilemma is enlightenment: "True salvation comes only through true enlightenment, through a more conscious and a more complete union of our lives with the Invisible."[12] Those who become enlightened become the Christ: "When any individual recognizes his true union with the Infinite, he automatically becomes the Christ."[13]

Eventually, Holmes says, all human beings will become enlightened: "We believe the ultimate goal of life to be a complete emancipation from all discord of every nature, and that this goal is sure to be attained by all."[14] Moreover, "in the long run, each will fully express his divinity, for good will come at last alike to all."[15]

Jesus Christ. Holmes' Christology is similar to other New Thought groups that separate the human Jesus from the impersonal Christ. Holmes believes that "Jesus was a man, a human being,"[16] and that he "never thought of himself as different from others."[17]

Holmes defines the Christ (as opposed to the human Jesus) by using standard metaphysical jargon: "Christ is the unseen principle in Man....Christ is the reality of every man, this true inner self."[18] Moreover, "Christ is the Universal idea...the Higher Self."[19]

At some point in Jesus' earthly life, this impersonal Christ—or divine idea—came upon him. Holmes tells us that "as Jesus, the man, gave way to the Divine Idea, the human took on the Christ Spirit and became the voice of God to humanity."[20]

That Holmes did not consider Jesus unique is clear in the following statement from his book *The Science of Mind*:

> Jesus is the name of a man. Christ means the Universal Principle of Divine Sonship....Jesus became increasingly the Christ as his mentality increasingly perceived the relationship of the man Jesus to the Christ principle, which is inherent in all people. This Christ has come in certain measures of power throughout the ages to different ones and still does come and is ever inherent within each one of us. Christ is a Universal Presence....There is no one particular man predestined to become the Christ. We must understand the Christ is not a person, but a Principle....Fortunately, we do not have to contemplate Jesus as being "unique and different," for the Bible makes it more than plain that he was a man like as we are.[21]

Holmes concludes, "Every man is a potential Christ. From the least to the greatest the same life runs through all, threading itself into the patterns of our individuality. He is 'over all, in all and through all.'"[22]

—— APOLOGETIC POWER POINTS ——

The Bible Is Authoritative. (6)

Esotericism Is Illegitimate. (7)

Sound Hermeneutics Yields Proper Interpretation. (8)

Other "Holy Books" Are Incompatible with the Bible. (11)

God Is Personal. (12)

God Is a Trinity. (22)

Pantheism Is False. (26)

Jesus Is the Christ. (34)

Jesus Is Unique. (37)

Jesus Atoned for Sin. (40)

The Holy Spirit Is a Person. (57)

The Holy Spirit Is God. (58)

Humans Are Not Divine. (62)

Humans Are Fallen in Sin. (67)

Salvation Is by Grace Through Faith. (71)

Death Is Real. (76)

Occultism Is Prohibited. (98)

The World Religions Do Not Teach the Same
   Doctrines. (112)

28

The Rosicrucian Fellowship

THE ROSICRUCIAN FELLOWSHIP IS A worldwide mystical brotherhood, encompassing a number of factions, that passes on to members an esoteric wisdom allegedly handed down, generation by generation, from ancient times. This ancient wisdom—an eclectic mix of Christianity, Hinduism, Buddhism, Judaism, pagan mythology, and occultism—allegedly enables people to find needed answers within themselves.[1] Through Rosicrucianism, people can allegedly gain applicable knowledge of metaphysics, mysticism, philosophy, psychology, parapsychology, and science.

What is the appeal? Rosicrucian literature is alluring:

> Imagine having the ability to actualize your highest potential in all areas of life including family and social relationships, career, health, and personal development. Imagine developing greater creativity and discipline to overcome life's problems. Imagine setting a new course for your future; one that promises to be more in line with who you really are and more fulfilling than anything you have previously experienced.[2]

Rosicrucianism claims to be able to fulfill these needs in a way unlike any other organization or religion. Through Rosicrucianism, people can allegedly achieve their highest potential on all levels of being—the physical, mental, psychic, and spiritual.[3] Through Rosicrucianism, people can attain "cosmic consciousness."

The term "Rosicrucian" derives from its symbol: a rose (*Rosi*) and a cross (*crucian*). The cross intertwined with roses is said to symbolize humankind's evolutionary development into God (past, present, and future).

Rosicrucian literature claims many famous people have joined the group through the years, including such luminaries as Leonardo da Vinci (1452–1519), Francis Bacon (1561–1626), Jacob Boehme (1575–1624), René Descartes (1596–1650), Blaise Pascal (1623–1662), Benjamin Franklin (1706–1790), Thomas Jefferson (1743–1826), and Claude Debussy (1862–1918).[4] I, however, have not seen any indisputable historical proof that any of the above figures were members. Regardless, the Rosicrucians now have about a hundred lodges in the United States, 26 in France, 21 in Brazil, and a lesser number in Nigeria, Canada, Mexico, England, Venezuela, and Australia.[5] More than a quarter of a million people are Rosicrucianists.[6] Their main textbook is Max Heindel's *Rosicrucian Cosmo-Conception.*

Rosicrucianism claims not to be a religion, even though it does set forth well-defined views of the Bible, God, Jesus, salvation, and other religious issues. The group claims to attract people of a variety of religions. One need not leave one's present church or change any religious beliefs in order to join.[7] (The folly of this statement will become clear in the discussion of their beliefs.)

Making definitive statements about the origin of the Rosicrucians is difficult for it is shrouded in legend and lore. Some have claimed the organization ultimately goes back to an Egyptian Pharaoh in the fourteenth century BC who met with students in the Great Pyramid and passed on to them occultic revelations he had received. Others believe it goes back to a German scholar named Christian Rosenkreuz (1378–1434), an occultist who allegedly had a mystical experience in which spirit masters conveyed to him the mysteries of the universe along with revelations regarding a new phase of Christianity that would keep pace with the normal progress of evolution. Still others believe it goes back to fiction novelist Johann Valentin Andrea (1586–1654), whose satirical fiction piece featured a character named Rosenkreuz who discovered hidden secrets, and this fiction was mistakenly taken to be fact.[8]

Members of AMORC (Ancient Mystical Order Rosae Crucis) continue to argue that Rosicrucianism began with the ancient Pharaohs of Egypt. They say their movement

> can be traced from its beginnings in the mystery schools of ancient Egypt founded by Pharaoh Thutmose III (1500 to 1477 BC), and more particularly from his grandson Pharaoh Amenhotep IV (also known as Akhenaton)—through to the Greek philosophers such as Thales and Pythagoras, the Roman philosopher Plotinus, and others, who journeyed to Egypt and were initiated into the mystery schools—through to the symbolism hidden in the love songs of Troubadours, the formularies of Alchemists, the symbolical system known as the Qabala, and the rituals of Orders of Knighthood during the dark and dangerous times of medieval Europe.[9]

No historical evidence exists for such claims. The *Encyclopedia Britannica* gives us this insight:

> The earliest extant document that mentions the order is the *Fama Fraternitatis* ("Account of the Brotherhood"), first published in 1614, which may have given the movement its initial impetus. The *Fama* recounts the journeys of Christian Rosenkreuz, the reputed

founder of Rosicrucianism, who was allegedly born in 1378 and lived for 106 years. He is now generally regarded to have been a symbolic rather than a real character, whose story provided a legendary explanation of the order's origin. According to the *Fama*, Rosenkreuz acquired secret wisdom on trips to Egypt, Damascus, Damcar in Arabia, and Fès in Morocco, which he subsequently imparted to three others after his return to Germany.[10]

Whatever the case, the fellowship ultimately made its way to America in 1694 when a Rosicrucian colony was established in Philadelphia by Johann Kelpius (1673–1708).

Beliefs

The Bible. Rosicrucians use the Bible, but they do not interpret it literally. Instead, they look for an esoteric or hidden meaning of each Scripture verse. Another oft-used "holy book" is *The Egyptian Book of the Dead*.

God. Rosicrucianism holds to a pantheistic concept of God. God is all and all is God. He is an impersonal being and an unknowable essence. This impersonal deity is composed of seven spirits that manifest themselves as a "triune godhead."[11] The Father is the first aspect of God; Jesus is the second aspect; the Holy Spirit is the third aspect. "The seven spirits before the throne….collectively, they are God, and make up the triune godhead."[12]

Jesus Christ. Jesus was not God in human flesh, nor was he the only begotten Son of God. Rosicrucianists make a distinction between the human Jesus and the evolving divine Christ spirit. The Christ spirit allegedly took up habitation in the human Jesus. Jesus was a "great thinker" in the same league as

Plato, Muhammad, Buddha, and Lao-Tse. Along with other great religious leaders, Jesus came to facilitate spiritual evolution.

Humankind. Since all is God (pantheism), humanity too is God, or is at least evolving toward godhood. Rosicrucianism also teaches that humans of different color developed in different epochs:

> We find that there have been various epochs or great stages of unfoldment in the earth's history, and that the Negro was the humanity of the third of these epochs, the Lemurian. The whole human race of that time was black-skinned. Then came a time, called the Atlantean Epoch, when humanity was red, yellow, except one race which was white.[13]

Salvation. Jesus Christ did not atone for human sin at the cross. There is no need for atonement. After all, the symbol of Rosicrucianism—a cross intertwined with roses—represents humankind's ability to evolve into God.

How does this evolution take place? Rosicrucianism teaches that each human being must be reincarnated numerous times on earth. During each lifetime, he or she increasingly progresses by self-effort until eventually he or she can be absorbed back into the pantheistic "God."

Occultism. Rosicrucian enthusiasts practice a variety of forms of occultism, including astrology, astral projection, trance meditation, mental telepathy, aura reading, and alchemy.

APOLOGETIC POWER POINTS

Esotericism Is Illegitimate. (7)

Sound Hermeneutics Yields Proper Interpretation. (8)

God Is Personal. (12)

God Is a Trinity. (22)

Pantheism Is False. (26)

Jesus Is God. (30)

Jesus Is the Son of God. (33)

Jesus Is the Christ. (34)

Jesus Atoned for Sin. (40)

Jesus Was Not a Mere Moral Teacher. (41)

God Created All Races. (64)

Salvation Is by Grace Through Faith. (71)

Occultism Is Prohibited. (98)

Astrology Is Prohibited. (100)

Reincarnation Is False. (103)

Mysticism Is Unreliable. (104)

Altered States of Consciousness Are Dangerous. (106)

Idolatry Is Prohibited. (107)

Eastern Meditation Is Prohibited. (108)

29

Satanism

SATANISM INVOLVES THE INVOCATION, exaltation, and even worship of Satan. Satan is variously defined.[1] Some view him as the devil. Others view him as a supernatural person, a deity, a natural force of some kind, an innate force within human beings, or perhaps just "self" (that is, one's *own* self).[2] Some Satanists believe what the Bible says about Satan (including the fact that he will end up in the lake of fire) but still give allegiance to him, knowing that they too will suffer eternal punishment.

Some Satanists believe God and Satan are equal and opposite forces, both being viable options for attaining one's goals in life. Others—perhaps the majority—use the word "Satan" to metaphorically symbolize their rejection of Christianity, which they view as a powerless and ineffective religion.[3] This last group of Satanists rejects belief in a personal God and a personal Satan, focusing their exclusive attention on the gratification of self. Satan symbolizes one's fleshly desires. These Satanists reject the Christian view that such desires should be suppressed. They are hedonists in the fullest sense of the term. They hold greed, pride, and lust as satanic virtues.

Satanists are diverse but fit into these categories:

- *Traditional Satanists* are highly secretive, are members of a satanic group, and engage in satanic rituals, such as taking communion using animal blood or urine in place of wine.

- *Self-styled Satanists* are often alienated teenagers who have trouble socializing. They perform satanic rituals for empowerment and to attain money, popularity, romance, and sex.[4]

- *Religious Satanists* join satanic churches and seek self-gratification, placing a high premium on greed, pride, envy, anger, gluttony, lust, and sloth.

- *Dabbler Satanists* are generally young people not totally committed to Satan who experiment and dabble in satanic literature and rituals, satanic rock music, occultic games, and horror movies.[5]

- *Outlaw Satanists* are generally socially alienated people who not only worship the devil but also engage in drug use, vandalism, and violence.

- *Psychotic Satanists* are mentally deranged, claim to hear voices, and often say that Satan has instructed them to engage in some violent and destructive act (such as murdering someone).[6]

Though Satanists are diverse, Satanism actually involves a relatively small group of people. The best guesstimate is that fewer than 6000 Satanists are alive today. An exact figure is difficult because many Satanists are clandestine.

The secrecy in Satanism makes a detailed chronological history difficult to construct. However, two of the most significant personalities who have contributed to the emergence of modern Satanism are Aleister Crowley and Anton LaVey.

Aleister Crowley (1875–1947). Aleister Crowley was raised by Christian parents who took him to church, but he rejected his parents' faith, opting instead for occultism and magic to attain personal empowerment. Crowley was thoroughly self-focused and engaged in a life of depravity, including homosexuality, group sex, and sex with animals. He claims various encounters with demonic spirits as he engaged in sex rituals. He even says he had sex with some of these depraved spirits.[7] Based on revelations from spirits, Crowley wrote books that became instrumental in the emergence of modern Satanism.

Anton LaVey (b. 1930). Anton LaVey spurned Christianity because of the hypocrisy he witnessed among Christians. He concluded that Christianity was an irrelevant religion, and he wanted nothing to do with it.

Through the effort of LaVey and his wife, the Church of Satan slowly evolved throughout the 1950s. The church began in their home, with nonconformists visiting to listen to LaVey's occultic lectures and watch him perform magic.[8] Their collective goal was to invoke the dark force of nature metaphorically known as Satan.[9] LaVey eventually formulated a satanic creed, entitled "The Nine Satanic Statements":

1. Satan represents indulgence instead of abstinence.

2. Satan represents vital existence instead of spiritual pipe dreams.

3. Satan represents undefiled wisdom instead of hypocritical self-deceit.

4. Satan represents kindness to those who deserve it instead of love wasted on ingrates.

5. Satan represents vengeance instead of turning the other cheek.

6. Satan represents responsibility to the responsible instead of concern for psychic vampires.

7. Satan represents man as just another animal—sometimes

better, more often worse than those that walk on all fours—who, because of his "divine spiritual and intellectual development," has become the most vicious animal of all.

8. Satan represents all the so-called sins, as they all lead to physical, mental, or emotional gratification.

9. Satan has been the best friend the church has ever had, as he has kept it in business all these years.[10]

Beliefs

The following synopsis is representative of what many Satanists believe in regard to the Bible, God, Jesus, humankind, sin, salvation, rituals, and the afterlife.

The Bible. Satanists view the Bible as a book of fables and full of contradictions. They say it enslaves and oppresses people, thwarting any sense of independence and individuality. Satanists refuse submission to it (they refuse submission to *any* holy book). In place of the Bible is *The Satanic Bible*, written by Anton LaVey. This book claims no final authority but rather is just a guide.

God. Satanists differ in their understanding of God. Many do not believe in God, holding instead that man is his own deity.[11] Others believe that both God and the devil eternally exist, equal in power, and that Satan may eventually conquer God. Still others view God as a force in the realm of nature that can be harnessed by satanic rituals.

Jesus. Satanists differ in their understanding of Jesus. Some believe he existed but was an embarrassing failure—a wimp with no spine, always talking about meaningless things like love and forgiveness. Others deny that Jesus ever existed and claim he is a popular myth that has no historical basis.

Humankind. Humankind is supreme. Many Satanists are

unrestrained hedonists who seek self-fulfillment, self-indulgence, and self-exaltation. Even if self-gratification infringes upon or harms another human being, it is still good.

Sin and Salvation. Satanists believe human beings are not fallen in sin and therefore do not need to be saved. They believe Christianity invented sin so it could "stay in business."[12] Jesus was certainly no Savior. Satanists consider the idea that he died on the cross to redeem humankind to be an outrageous myth. Instead of focusing attention on being "saved," Satanists focus on self-indulgence in the present life.

Rituals. Satanists perform a variety of perverted rituals. Some are sexual, involving sexual intercourse, homosexual acts, oral copulation, or masturbation. Others involve slashing various parts of the body to inflict pain, allegedly raising sexual ecstasy to increasing heights. Still others engage in animal sacrifices so that the Satanist can harness the "life force" released in the vicinity of the dead animal. All such rituals have the goal of empowering the one performing the ritual. Some who believe in a personal devil think such sacrifices move the devil to grant their desires.

The Black Mass is probably the most controversial of satanic rituals. This perverted ritual involves suspending a crucifix upside down, reciting the Lord's Prayer backward, and engaging in depraved sexual acts with a naked woman on an altar.

The Afterlife. Satanists understand the afterlife variously. Some deny the afterlife exists, suggesting that since this life is all we have, we should "live it up." Others believe in reincarnation, looking forward to unending lifetimes to indulge carnal appetites. Still others believe Satan will overcome God in the end, and the afterlife will involve serving Satan in his kingdom of hell. Still others believe that both Satan and all Satanists will be judged by God and suffer eternal torment. They nevertheless choose to serve Satan in this life because of their hatred of the Christian God and because they enjoy the sensual pleasures of this life.

——— APOLOGETIC POWER POINTS ———

The Bible Is Reliable. (3)

Bible "Contradictions" Are Easily Explained. (5)

The Bible Is Authoritative. (6)

God Is Personal. (12)

God Is All-Powerful. (16)

God Alone Is to Be Worshipped. (25)

Jesus Is God. (30)

Jesus Is the Savior. (35)

Jesus Atoned for Sin. (40)

Jesus Was Not Spineless (55)

Man Is a Creature. (60)

Humans Are Fallen in Sin. (67)

All Humans Are Infected by Sin (Original Sin). (68)

Heaven Is Real. (77)

Hell Is Real. (78)

All People Will Face Judgment (83)

Satan Is a Fallen Angel. (84)

Satan's Titles Reveal His Nature. (85)

Fallen Angels Hurt Believers. (86)

There Are Six Judgments Against Satan. (88)

Occultism Is Prohibited. (98)

Reincarnation Is False. (103)

Sexual Immorality Is Prohibited. (113)

30

Self-Realization Fellowship

SELF-REALIZATION FELLOWSHIP (SRF) is a worldwide organization, headquartered in Los Angeles, California, whose goal is to spread the spiritual and "scientific" teachings of its founder-guru, Paramahansa Yogananda (1893–1952). SRF, founded in 1920, publishes Yogananda's writings, lectures, and recorded talks, as well as oversees temples, retreats, meditation centers, and monastic communities affiliated with the organization. At present almost 500 meditation centers in 54 countries are affiliated with SRF. At these centers, followers meet to hear readings from Yogananda, engage in meditation and devotional chanting, and participate in spiritual fellowship.

SRF is presently headed by the Reverend Mother Sri Daya Mata, one of Yogananda's earliest disciples and one of the first women in religious history to head a worldwide religious movement. She has maintained a low profile through the years, quietly but effectively promoting the teachings and practices of Yogananda.

SRF has clearly delineated its aims and ideals based on the teachings of Yogananda:[1]

- To teach scientific techniques that enable one to attain direct personal experience of God.

- To teach that humankind's purpose is to evolve from mortal consciousness into God consciousness.

- To reveal the harmony and oneness of original Christianity as taught by Jesus and the original yoga as taught by Bhagavan Krishna.

- To facilitate the liberation of human beings from three-fold suffering: physical disease, mental inharmonies, and spiritual ignorance.

- To demonstrate that the mind is superior to the body and that the soul is superior to the mind.

- To unite science and religion.

- To advocate cultural and spiritual understanding between East and West.

Paramahansa Yogananda was born Mukunda Lal Ghosh on January 5, 1893, in Gorakhpur, India. Even as a child, Mukunda was highly advanced as a spiritual person. At age 17, he became a disciple of the revered Swami Sri Yukteswar Giri. He eventually took vows as a monk in India's Swami Order and received the name Yogananda. (This is a compound name: *Ananda* means "bliss" and *yoga* means "through divine union." Hence, Yogananda means "bliss through divine union.")[2]

In 1920 Yogananda was invited to speak at an international congress of religious leaders in Boston. He spoke on "The Science of Religion." That same year he founded the Self-Realization Fellowship to disseminate his brand of yoga. In 1925, the international headquarters for the group was established in Los Angeles, California. Yogananda traveled widely, speaking to large capacity audiences, enthralling them with his powerful delivery of Hindu "truths." He emphasized the underlying unity of the world's religions and taught people how to have a direct personal experience with God via Kriya Yoga. His notoriety steadily increased, and in 1927 he was invited to the White House by President Calvin Coolidge.

In 1935 Swami Sri Yukteswar (Yogananda's former guru) bestowed on him India's highest title, *Paramahansa*. This title means "supreme swan" and signifies one who manifests a supreme state of unbroken communion with God.

In 1946 Paramahansa Yogananda published his life story, *Autobiography of a Yogi*, which became a huge bestseller and continues to sell to the present day. It contains accounts of Yogananda's mystical and miraculous experiences as well as his ecstatic visions of Hindu saints.

On March 7, 1952, Yogananda entered *mahasamadhi*, a term referring to an enlightened master exiting the physical body at death. Following his death, his body allegedly did not suffer decay. An alleged notarized statement from the director of Forest Lawn Memorial Park testified, "No physical disintegration was visible in his body even twenty days after death."[3]

Beliefs

Kriya Yoga. Paramahansa Yogananda taught Kriya Yoga as a means of reaching "self-realization." This form of yoga involves

> scientific techniques of concentration and meditation that lead to the direct personal experience of God. These yoga methods quiet body and mind, and make it possible to withdraw one's energy and attention from the usual turbulence of thoughts, emotions, and sensory perceptions. In the clarity of that inner stillness, one comes to experience a deepening interior peace and awareness of God's presence.[4]

Through Kriya Yoga, one can allegedly achieve balanced physical, mental, emotional, and spiritual well-being. This type of yoga "reinforces and revitalizes subtle currents of life energy in the body, enabling the normal activities of heart and lungs to slow down naturally. As a result, the consciousness is drawn to higher levels of perception, gradually bringing about an inner awakening more blissful and more deeply satisfying than any of the experiences that the mind or the senses or the ordinary human emotions can give."[5] By the time Yogananda died in 1952, he had initiated some 100,000 people into Kriya Yoga.

God. Self-Realization Fellowship espouses a pantheistic concept of God—what Hindus call Brahman. God is "the only Real Substance." He is the "all in all in the universe."[6]

Humankind. Since all is God, humankind's true essence is divine. "In reality, God and man are one, and the separation is only apparent."[7]

Jesus Christ. Since all is God, Jesus too was God. But he was not God in a unique sense. Jesus was basically an enlightened yogi who achieved Christ consciousness through self-mastery.[8]

Salvation. In salvation, people shed ignorance and attain self-realization. Self-realization involves the recognition of one's divine nature. Paramahansa Yogananda said, "We are all part of the One Spirit. When you experience the true meaning of religion, which is to know God, you will realize that He is your Self, and that He exists equally and impartially in all beings."[9] Self-realization thus involves the recognition that one is now in possession of divinity and need not seek it. God's omnipresence is said to be *our* omnipresence, and the recognition of this fact is "self-realization."

APOLOGETIC POWER POINTS

Other "Holy Books" Are Incompatible with the Bible. (11)

God Is Personal. (12)

Jesus Is God. (30)

Jesus Is the Savior. (35)

Jesus Is the Only Way. (36)

Jesus Is Unique. (37)

Jesus Atoned for Sin. (40)

Humans Are Not Divine. (62)

Humans Are Fallen in Sin. (67)

Salvation Is by Grace Through Faith. (71)

Chanting Is Prohibited. (102)

Mysticism Is Unreliable. (104)

Altered States of Consciousness Are Dangerous. (106)

Eastern Meditation Is Prohibited. (108)

The World Religions Do Not Teach the Same
    Doctrines. (112)

31

Spiritism

SPIRITISM IS "THE PRACTICE OF ATTEMPTING communication with departed human or extra-human intelligences (usually non-physical) through the agency of a human medium, with the intent of receiving paranormal information and/or having direct experience of metaphysical realities."[1] The practice has become popular in recent years. Forty-two percent of American adults believe they have been in contact with someone who has died, and 14 percent endorse the work of spirit mediums or channelers.[2]

The "spiritualist movement" (involving spiritism) emerged in 1848 at the home of farmer John Fox in Hydesville, New York.[3] Fox's daughters—Margaret (1836–1893), Leah (1814–1890), and Catherine (1841–1892)—claimed to hear rapping sounds in the house and believed the sounds were a form of communication from spirits. The sisters became highly influential in the spiritualist movement. Not quite three decades later, spiritism received a shot in the arm from spiritualist Helena Petrovna Blavatsky, one of the founders of the Theosophical Society, in 1875 (see chapter 33). The Arcane School, founded in 1923, promoted spiritism, as did the I AM movement, which emerged in the early 1930s (see chapters 4 and 16).

Today, people call spiritism "channeling." A channeler is a person who yields control of his or her perceptual and cognitive capacities to a spiritual entity or force with the intent of receiving paranormal information. Channeling can be described as "voluntary possession."[4] Jane Roberts (d. 1983), who channeled an entity named Seth, had much to do with the current rise of interest in channeling. Her books on Seth have attracted millions of readers. Millions of other Americans have been introduced to channeling through the bestselling books of Shirley MacLaine.

Kevin Ryerson, one of today's best known New Age channelers (he is Shirley MacLaine's channeler), wrote a book entitled *Spirit Communication*. MacLaine praised this book as the "most comprehensive book on the phenomenon of channeling I've read."

A look at this book provides an overview of what channeling is all about. Ryerson compares channeling to a radio broadcast. If two stations are competing for the same frequency, by slightly adjusting the dial one channel can be tuned down and the other will come in more clearly. "Kevin Ryerson," he tells us, is the channel that gets tuned down; this allows the other channel (spirit entities) to come through. Ryerson provides readers with guidelines to "adjust the tuning" so that they—like he—can become channelers.[5]

Ryerson believes that the personalities or entities that speak through him during channeling sessions are people he has known in his past lives (through reincarnation). He also believes that *he himself* has been a spirit guide who has spoken through channelers when he was in a discarnate state (in between reincarnations). The "spirit entities" who speak through Ryerson bear testimony to common New Age themes: You are God, you have unlimited potential, you create your own reality, death and hell do not exist.

Ryerson denies the possibility of demon possession: "I personally believe there's a psychic lock on the frequency or vibration of each person's physical body that only we, ourselves, can match. It would be impossible for someone else to 'inhabit' our vibration."[6] Besides, says Ryerson, "I trust the transformative process of the inner divine...I believe that God acts as our personal body-guard."[7]

Other channelers claim to receive "revelations" not from spirit entities but from the Akashic Records. In this view, the physical earth is surrounded by an immense spiritual field known as Akasha on which is impressed—like a celestial tape recording—every impulse of human thought, will, and emotion. These records therefore constitute a complete record of human history. Some New Age seers claim the ability to "read" the Akashic Records.

An example of this is Civil War army chaplain Levi Dowling (1844–1911), who transcribed *The Aquarian Gospel of Jesus the Christ* from the Akashic Records. The title page of this gospel bears theses words: "Transcribed from the Book of God's Remembrances, Known as the Akashic Records." Levi's transcriptions from the Akashic Records took place between two and six o'clock every morning for several months. He considered his gospel to be higher scriptures than the New Testament and even assigned verse numbers like the Bible.

Beliefs

The following spiritistic "revelations" from Levi Dowling's *Aquarian Gospel* are representative of the revelations other spiritists and channelers receive:

Jesus Was a Way-Shower. Dowling's *Aquarian Gospel* portrays Jesus as saying, "All the people were entranced, and would have worshipped Jesus as a God; but Jesus said, I am your brother, man, just come to show the way to God; you shall not worship man; praise God, the Holy One."[8] Jesus also allegedly said, "I come to be a pattern for the sons of men."[9] Jesus thus never claimed to be uniquely God; he was merely a human being who showed others how to attain what he attained.

God. Dowling's *Aquarian Gospel* portrays Jesus as saying, "With much delight I speak to you concerning life—the brotherhood of life. The universal God is one, yet he is more than one; all things are God; all things are one."[10] The reference to "the brotherhood of life" reminds one of the New Age emphasis on the interrelatedness and interdependency of all things in the universe.

Humanity. Dowling's *Aquarian Gospel* portrays Jesus as saying, "Because I have the power to do these things is nothing strange. All men may gain the power to do these things; but they must conquer all the passions of the lower self; and they can conquer if they will." Jesus said, "So man is God on earth, and he who honors God must honor man; for God and man are one, as father and the child are one."[11]

Jesus also taught that God is *within* man. According to Levi, Jesus said, "Men carry with them all the time the secret place where they may meet their God. It matters not where men abide, on mountain top, in deepest vale, in marts of trade, or in the quiet home; they may at once, at any time, fling wide the door, and find the Silence, find the house of God; it is within the soul." Jesus said, "Your human will must be absorbed by the divine; then you will come into a consciousness of holiness."[12]

World Religions. Dowling's *Aquarian Gospel* portrays Jesus as saying, "The nations of the earth see God from different points of view, and so he does not seem the same to everyone....You Brahmans call him Parabrahm; in Egypt he is Thoth; and Zeus is his name in Greece; Jehovah is his Hebrew name."[13] Though different names are used of God in the various world religions, they are all referring to the same deity.

Heaven and Hell. Dowling's *Aquarian Gospel* portrays Jesus as teaching that heaven or hell do not exist literally: "My brother, man, your thoughts are wrong; your heaven is not far away; and it is not a place of metes and bounds, is not a country to be reached; it is a state of mind. God never made a heaven for man; he never made a hell; we are creators and we make our own."[14]

APOLOGETIC POWER POINTS

The Bible Should Not Be Added To. (2)

The Bible Is Authoritative. (6)

Other "Holy Books" Are Incompatible with the Bible. (11)

God Is Personal. (12)

Pantheism Is False. (26)

Jesus Is God. (30)

Jesus Is the Savior. (35)

Jesus Is the Only Way. (36)

Jesus Is Unique. (37)

Jesus Atoned for Sin. (40)

Humans Are Not Divine. (62)

Humans Are Fallen in Sin. (67)

Death Is Real. (76)

Heaven Is Real. (77)

Hell Is Real. (78)

Unbelievers Can Be Demon Possessed. (87)

Occultism Is Prohibited. (98)

Spiritism Is Prohibited. (99)

Reincarnation Is False. (103)

Mysticism Is Unreliable. (104)

Altered States of Consciousness Are Dangerous. (106)

The World Religions Do Not Teach the Same Doctrines. (112)

32
Swedenborgianism

SWEDENBORGIANISM, ALSO KNOWN AS the Church of the New Jerusalem, is a religious group that emerged out of the teachings of Emanuel Swedenborg (1688–1772), a scientist, mystic, and religious philosopher. Swedenborg was the son of a revered Lutheran minister in Sweden. He was educated at the University of Uppsala and in his early years was entirely dedicated to scientific endeavors. He excelled in many areas, including mathematics, geology, chemistry, physics, mineralogy, astronomy, and anatomy.[1] He is credited with a number of mechanical inventions. He also published the first scientific journal in Sweden, *Daedalus Hyperboreus.*

By the time Swedenborg reached the age of 52, he began to have a change of heart regarding what he wanted to do with the rest of his life. He switched interests from science to theology. He was not satisfied, however, to become a part of what he considered to be the cold formalism of traditional Christianity (the state church his father ministered in). He wanted something deeper, more alive, more mystical.

Swedenborg eventually became convinced that he had received a divine calling to derive deeper, hidden, esoteric meanings from the biblical text. He claimed to have "systematically opened his consciousness to inner influences."[2] He recalls the vision he had:

> He said that He was the Lord God, the Creator and

Redeemer of the world, and that He had chosen me to declare to men the spiritual contents of Scripture; and that He Himself would declare to me what I should write on this subject.

Then, on the same night, the world of spirits, hell, and heaven were opened to me will full conviction. I recognized there many acquaintances of every condition in life. And from that day on I gave up all practice of worldly letters and devoted my labor to spiritual things.

I have written entire pages, and the spirits did not dictate the words, but absolutely guided my hand, so that it was they who were doing the writing.[3]

During this time, Swedenborg became involved in various forms of occultism, including spiritism and astral travel (out-of-body experiences). While in the spirit realm, he claimed he had conversations with many religious luminaries of the past, including the Apostle Paul, Saint Augustine, Martin Luther, and John Calvin. These conversations served to confirm his divine calling to derive esoteric meanings buried in the text of Scripture.

Swedenborg did not intend to formally establish a church or a sect. However, his theological writings—including 30 volumes between 1749 and 1771—eventually became the basis of a new spiritual movement. Fifteen years after his death, a Swedenborgian society formed in London, and this organization eventually spawned a convention of Swedenborgian churches.[4]

By the late 1700s, Swedenborgianism reached the shores of the United States. A Swedenborg society was organized in Baltimore, Maryland, in 1792, and a general convention was established in 1817 in Philadelphia, Pennsylvania. The movement grew from there.

Swedenborg enthusiasts claim that a number of famous personalities were affiliated with their church: Johnny Appleseed often handed out Swedenborgian publications. Ralph Waldo Emerson allegedly utilized Swedenborg's work in his writings. Other literary artists influenced by Swedenborgianism include William Blake, Edgar Allan Poe, and Samuel Taylor Coleridge. Helen Keller is said to have been an advocate of Swedenborgianism.[5]

The Swedenborgian church claims its present international membership is about 50,000.[6]

Beliefs

The Bible. Swedenborg believed the text of Scripture had a natural meaning—a *plain meaning*. He also believed it contained a corresponding *spiritual meaning* (or esoteric meaning) that scholars could not derive by normal hermeneutics (principles of interpretation). Only Swedenborg himself had learned about such things from the encounters he had with famous religious personalities in the spirit realm.[7] Swedenborg's interpretations therefore became a higher authority than the biblical text itself. His followers consider his writings to be scripture.

Swedenborg did not accept all biblical books because he did not believe they all have a corresponding spiritual sense. He accepted Genesis, Exodus, Leviticus, Numbers, Deuteronomy, Joshua, Judges, 1 and 2 Samuel, 1 and 2 Kings, Psalms, Isaiah, Jeremiah, Lamentations, Ezekiel, Daniel, Hosea, Joel, Amos, Obadiah, Jonah, Micah, Nahum, Habakkuk, Zephaniah, Haggai, Zechariah, Malachi, Matthew, Mark, Luke, John, and Revelation.[8]

Swedenborg's spiritual interpretations of biblical books includes a creative doctrine of the second coming. Swedenborgianism teaches that "the Second Coming is not an actual physical appearance of the Lord, but rather His return in spirit and truth that is being effected as a present reality....The information revealed to Swedenborg, he felt, is a continually-occurring Second Coming in that the new information enables a new perception of the Word of God."[9]

God. Swedenborg denied the doctrine of the Trinity, as Christians traditionally understand it, and considered it a perversion of the truth. In Swedenborg's view, the Father, Son, and Holy Spirit are just modes of manifestation of God. "These three, the Father, the Son, and the Holy Spirit, are the three essentials of the one God, which make one, like the soul, the body, and operation in man."[10] Indeed, "the Christian Trinity of Father, Son, and Holy Spirit are aspects of God just as soul, body, and activities are aspects of each one of us."[11] The Father is God in his essence. The Son is God as manifest among human beings in the flesh. The Holy Spirit is God as a life-giving influence.

Swedenborgians claim to worship a God of unconditional love who seeks to give warmth and light to worshippers. They consider love to be the very essence of God.

Jesus Christ. Jesus Christ was a manifestation of God. Through Jesus, "humanity was given an overt expression of God's reality in human terms."[12] Christ did not come to redeem us from original sin. He did not come to appease an angry God at the cross. "Rather, His mission was that of revealing the nature and reality of the spiritual life, and to provide a living example of it."[13]

Humanity. Swedenborgianism teaches that "people are spirits clothed with material bodies. At death our material body is put aside and we continue living in the spiritual world in our inner, spiritual body, according to the kind of life we have chosen while here on earth."[14] What Swedenborg means by this is that human beings are destined to become angels or evil spirits in the afterlife, according to the kind of life they have chosen while here on earth (that is, according to how righteous or evil they were). "If our love is solely selfish in this life, we will later abide with others of selfish motives. Just as we choose our own company and values in this life, in the afterlife we choose our destiny."[15] Swedenborg learned all this after having conversations with angels in the spirit realm.

Swedenborg taught that angels do not have physical bodies, but they retain the physical likeness of their human state with faces, eyes, ears, bodies, and the like. Because of this, Swedenborg believed that men and women can continue to engage in sexual relations in the afterlife.[16]

Salvation. The basic problem of human beings is that they have lost the ability to do good. They have misused free will and diverted love from God to their own egos. Because of what Christ accomplished—resisting every possible temptation, thereby breaking the power of temptation—he delivered human beings from the domination of evil. He restored their capacity to do good and resist evil. Human beings must now trust in the Redeemer and perpetually *choose* to do good and resist evil.

APOLOGETIC POWER POINTS

Esotericism Is Illegitimate. (7)

Sound Hermeneutics Yields Proper Interpretation. (8)

God's Attributes Reveal His Nature. (18)

God Is a Trinity. (22)

Modalism Is False. (24)

Jesus Is God. (30)

Jesus Is the Savior. (35)

Jesus Atoned for Sin. (40)

Jesus Completed the Work of Salvation. (49)

Jesus Will Return at the Second Coming. (51)

The Holy Spirit Is a Person. (57)

The Holy Spirit Is God. (58)

Man Is Both Material and Immaterial. (61)

Humans Do Not Become Angels. (63)

Humans Are Fallen in Sin. (67)

All Humans Are Infected by Sin (Original Sin). (68)

Salvation Is by Grace Through Faith. (71)

Salvation Involves Justification. (72)

All People Will Be Resurrected. (82)

Occultism Is Prohibited. (98)

Spiritism Is Prohibited. (99)

Mysticism Is Unreliable. (104)

33

Theosophy

OCCULTISTS HELENA PETROVNA BLAVATSKY (1831–1891) and Henry Steel Olcott (1832–1907), who married after encountering each other in the United States, began the Theosophical Society in 1875. "Theosophy" comes from the Greek word *theosophia,* which means "divine wisdom." Blavatsky wrote several important books about this alleged divine wisdom, including *The Secret Doctrine* and *The Key to Theosophy.*

Theosophy grew quickly because of the rich soil in which it was planted. The ground had been fertilized with nineteenth-century transcendentalism, especially as represented in the written works of Ralph Waldo Emerson (1803–1882). Among other things, Emerson elevated intuition over the senses as the means of finding truth, he believed in a dichotomy between the natural and spiritual worlds, he said the goal of religion was the conscious union of man with God, he said that God could reveal himself through man's intuitions, and he believed that God had given revelation in all the religions. All these ideas may be found in Theosophy.

The soil also was fertilized with the philosophy of Emmanuel Swedenborg (see chapter 32). Swedenborg (1688–1772) believed that one should seek a spiritual or intuitive meaning of Bible verses instead of the literal meaning. Readers can use spiritual or intuitive meanings to make the Bible say whatever they want it to say. This laid the groundwork for Theosophical Esoteric

Christianity, a distorted form of Christianity that bases its occult, mystical theology on inner or hidden meanings of Bible verses.

The soil also was fertilized by an influx of Hindu monism, especially from the *Upanishads*, the *Bhagavad-Gita*, and the *Vishnu Purana* from India—all of which helped set aside the idea of a theistic God. Monism is a metaphysical theory that all of reality is a unified whole. Everything in the universe is composed of the same substance. Man, God, and the world of nature are all one.

Further, the soil was fertilized by deism, which in the seventeenth and eighteenth centuries espoused the idea of an absentee God who originally created the world but has since remained distant and remote from it. This school of thought weakened confidence in doctrinal theology and promoted the idea of an impersonal God.

Sprinkle on this soil a little ancient Gnosticism (which says that God manifests himself to finite man through descending emanations, the highest of which is the Christ), third-century neoplatonism (a forerunner of modern Western mysticism), and some spiritism (which emerged in the mid-eighteenth century with the famous Fox sisters), and you have a cultural milieu that has continued as a part of Western society to the present day. This was the fertile soil in which Theosophy grew.

Blavatsky emphasized three essential goals of the Theosophical Society: (1) to form the nucleus of a universal brotherhood of humanity without distinction of race, color, or creed; (2) to promote the study of the scriptures of the world's religions and to vindicate the importance of old Asiatic literature, namely, of the Brahmanical, Buddhist, and Zoroastrian philosophies; and (3) to investigate the hidden mysteries of nature as well as the psychic and spiritual powers latent in human beings.

At present, Theosophy has penetrated some 60 countries in the world.

Beliefs

World Religions. Theosophy seeks to encompass all religions and claims to possess the "central truth" common to all religions. C.W. Leadbeater writes this in *A Textbook of Theosophy*:

> All religions, at the time of their first presentation to the world, have contained a definite statement of the Truth, and in its fundamentals this Truth has been always the same. The presentations of it have varied because of differences in the races to whom it was offered. The conditions of civilization and the degree of evolution obtained by various races have made it desirable to present this one Truth in diverse forms. But the inner Truth is always the same.[1]

Scripture. One cannot read the various scriptures of the world religions *in a literal fashion* and conclude that they are teaching the same truth. Theosophists are thus careful to emphasize that all the scriptures of the world religions contain both an *exoteric* (outer) meaning and an *esoteric* (inner) meaning. Esoteric methodology uncovers the secret, hidden, and "inner" meanings of the Scriptures. Theosophists use such esoteric methodology to show that the world religions teach the same basic thing.

God. Blavatsky, when asked whether or not she believed in the God of the Bible, answered, "We reject the idea of a personal, or an extra-cosmic and anthropomorphic God, who is but the gigantic shadow of man, and not of man at his best, either. The God of theology, we say—and prove it—is a bundle of contradictions and a logical impossibility. Therefore, we will have nothing to do with him."[2] Blavatsky affirmed belief in "a Universal Divine Principle, the root of ALL, from which all precedes, and within which all shall be absorbed at the end of the great cycle of Being."³ The god of Theosophy is an impersonal, pantheistic, divine being.

Humanity. Human beings will one day be absorbed into the great cycle of Being (the Absolute, or God). Blavatsky taught that each human being evolves through seven planes of existence (including the physical plane, the astral plane, and the mental plane). Each plane a person evolves through brings him or her ever closer to union with the Absolute (God). Theosophists reason that this process can take a very long time and requires innumerable reincarnations.

According to revelations Blavatsky claims to have received via spiritistic contact with Ascended Masters, not only individual human beings but the human race *as a whole* evolves. So far this evolution has produced three races: the *Lemurian* race, the *Atlantean* race, and the *Aryan* race. Each of these, which Theosophists call "rootraces," is divided into "subraces." Humankind is now allegedly about to enter the sixth subrace of the third (Aryan) rootrace.

The Christ. Theosophy teaches that at the beginning of each subrace, the Supreme World Teacher (the Christ, the bestower of divine wisdom) enters the body of a human disciple in order to assist and guide the spiritual evolution of humankind. Each "incarnation" reveals more to human beings about God than the previous one. The five incarnations of Christ in the five subraces of the Aryan rootrace have been Buddha (in India), Hermes (in Egypt), Zoroaster (in Persia), Orpheus (in Greece), and Jesus (at the River Jordan, where the Christ came upon Jesus at his baptism).⁴

Jesus supposedly volunteered his body for use by the Christ. Annie Besant, who took over Theosophical leadership when Blavatsky died, said, "For Him [the Christ] was needed an earthly tabernacle, a human form, the body of a man. The man Jesus yielded himself a willing sacrifice, 'offered himself without spot' to the Lord of Love, who took unto Himself that pure form as tabernacle, and dwelt therein for three years of mortal life."[5]

Sin and Salvation. Theosophists reject any suggestion that Jesus died on the cross to pay for the sins of humanity. "Sin" is interpreted in terms of irresponsibility. Hell is interpreted as a myth. Theosophists believe human beings can save themselves through continual reincarnations. This spiritual evolution leads human beings increasingly away from the physical plane and increasingly nearer to spiritual planes of existence. Because of this process, every human being—regardless of race or religion—is a potential Christ.

Human beings who continue to evolve through reincarnation eventually become Ascended Masters. This is a group of historical persons who have finished their earthly evolutions and have moved on to higher planes of existence. They now voluntarily seek to help lesser-evolved human beings reach their exalted level. Eventually all will be absorbed into God.

The Next Incarnation of the Christ. Because Theosophists believe the fifth subrace of the Aryan rootrace is about to give way to the sixth subrace, they believe another incarnation of the Christ is imminent. This will be the sixth appearance of the Christ in the Aryan rootrace, so Theosophists do not call it the second coming.

Annie Besant first announced the coming of this Messiah in 1906. Her aim was to groom Jiddu Krishnamurti for the role of World Teacher or Messiah. In 1925 she claimed for this young Indian man the title of "Messianic Leader and Reincarnation of the World Teacher." By 1929, however, Krishnamurti became convinced it was all a mistake. On November 20 of that year, he "refused to receive further adoration [saying frankly], 'I am not an actor; I refuse to wear the robes of a Messiah; so I am again free of all possessions.'"[6] Theosophy's Christ remains to appear.

APOLOGETIC POWER POINTS

The Bible Should Not Be Added To. (2)

The Bible Is Reliable. (3)

The Bible Is Authoritative. (6)

Esotericism Is Illegitimate. (7)

Sound Hermeneutics Yields Proper Interpretation. (8)

Other "Holy Books" Are Incompatible with the Bible. (11)

God Is Personal. (12)

Pantheism Is False. (26)

Jesus Is God. (30)

Jesus Is the Christ. (34)

Jesus Is the Only Way. (36)

Jesus Atoned for Sin. (40)

The Incarnate Jesus Had Two Natures. (47)

Jesus Will Return at the Second Coming. (51)

Humans Are Not Divine. (62)

Humans Are Fallen in Sin. (67)

Salvation Is by Grace Through Faith. (71)

Occultism Is Prohibited. (98)

Spiritism Is Prohibited. (99)

Reincarnation Is False. (103)

Mysticism Is Unreliable. (104)

The World Religions Do Not Teach the Same
   Doctrines. (112)

The Ascended Masters Are Demons in Disguise. (117)

34

Transcendental Meditation

MAHARISHI MAHESH YOGI WAS ONE of the most influential gurus to arrive on the scene during the mid-1960s. He taught his followers Transcendental Meditation (TM). More than a million Americans have now been initiated into TM. One observer said that "what McDonald's has done for the hamburger, Transcendental Meditation has done for Eastern mysticism."[1] TM has succeeded in making Eastern mysticism acceptable, fashionable, and desirable to the American public. It has penetrated virtually every major city in the United States, with hundreds of TM centers promoting the practice. About 6000 doctors in the United States practice TM or recommend it to their patients, and TM chapters meet on about 95 percent of all public university campuses.

Maharishi Mahesh Yogi was born in India in 1911. During the 1940s, he met and became a disciple of Swami Brahmananda Saraswati ("Guru Dev"). From this guru, he learned a meditation technique that would eventually become the foundation of TM.

Before Guru Dev died, he asked Maharishi to develop and spread his meditation technique in the West.[2] After a few years of seclusion in the Himalayas, during which time he meditated, Maharishi resolved to change the world. He soon decided to head for the West, where efficient transportation and communication would enable him to quickly spread his message.

Upon his arrival in the United States in 1959, he met with

little success, primarily because his meditative technique—called the Spiritual Regeneration Movement—had a Hindu religious nature, which did not go over well in a predominantly Christian country. After a number of name changes over the next decade, he finally settled on "Transcendental Meditation."

The technique itself employs mantras (holy words that are repeated), breathing exercises, and focusing attention on an object, all to clear the mind of all distractions. One eventually reaches what is called an "altered state of consciousness"—a mental state other than normal waking consciousness that ranges from a mild sense of transcendence to a deep trance. In such a state, one has a sense of oneness with all things and a sense of harmony with the universe.

Beliefs

God. In keeping with its Hindu roots, TM holds to a pantheistic view of God. God is described as "the one eternal unmanifested absolute Being [that] manifests itself in many forms."[3] All things in the universe are viewed as a manifestation of the impersonal being of God.

Sin. Humans are not sinful or fallen but rather have become separated from their true being. Humanity's big problem is ignorance of divinity. Every human being is a manifestation of the impersonal being of God but has forgotten this reality.

Reincarnation. TM teaches that people are reincarnated through countless lifetimes. The process of reincarnation continues until the soul has reached a state of perfection and merges back with its source (God, or the Universal Soul).

All of this is based on the law of karma. Karma refers to the debt a soul accumulates because of good or bad actions committed during one's life (or past lives). The word "karma" comes from a root meaning "to do or act"; karma thus involves the idea that every action yields a consequence. If one accumulates good karma, he or she will allegedly be reincarnated in a desirable state in the next life. If one accumulates bad karma, he or she will be reincarnated in a less desirable state in the next life. Eventually, over many lifetimes, karma can allegedly rid a person of all selfish desires.

TMs inherited its belief in reincarnation from Hinduism, and Hindu history reveals some interesting facts about the emergence of the doctrine. As Indian society evolved, it began to be segregated into classes, and the system of classification was known as *Varian* (which means color). These classes included the Brahmins (priests), Kshatriyas (warriors or rulers), Vaishyas (merchants), and Sudras (laborers/servants). Lowest of all were the "untouchables," who were forbidden contact with the other groups because they were regarded as impure. Eventually this evolved into the present caste system that is predominant in India. The breaking down of society into various classes or castes is based on Hinduism's belief in reincarnation. One's social status in life is dictated by the law of karma. Build up good karma, and you increase your status in the next life. Build up bad karma, and you will find yourself born in a lower caste.

In Hinduism, the continual cycle of death and rebirth is known as *samsara* (transmigration).[4] Samsara literally means "to wander across." Scholar Lewis M. Hopfe tells us that "Indian religions believe that the life force of an individual does not die with the death of the body. Instead it 'wanders across.' The life force moves on to another time and body where it continues to live."[5] Scholar John H. Hick explains that "at death, this physical body dies and the soul survives as a mental entity called the 'subtle body' *(lingua sharira)*.…This subtle body is the continuous element throughout the reincarnation process until salvation occurs. The soul, as the subtle body, bears the karma of its past lives."[6] The idea is that one's thoughts, words, and deeds have definite ethical consequences and determine one's lot in the next life. One's state in the present life hinges entirely on the karma built up in a previous life.

In this view, when a person dies, his so-called "subtle body" makes "karmic calculations" and then attaches itself to a developing embryo. If the person has been virtuous, the subtle body enters a "pleasant womb" and is born in a better socioreligious class. If the person has lived a corrupt life, the subtle body enters a "foul and stinking womb" and is born in a lower class, or perhaps as a vegetable or mineral.

Salvation. One obtains salvation by practicing TM, which enables one to "remember" or realize one's union with God. TM claims that by reaching a state of bliss-consciousness, or happiness through meditation, human beings can free themselves from an endless cycle of reincarnations.

Through TM, one's consciousness is eventually completely absorbed into Brahman. "One sees that there is no difference between myself, other selves, and the material world. It is all one."[7] If one manages to achieve this "unity consciousness," he is freed from the endless cycle of successive reincarnations.

The Mainstreaming of Transcendental Meditation

Like some other religious groups, TM has achieved considerable publicity by affiliating with major celebrities. Through the years, such luminaries as the Beatles, the Beach Boys, the Rolling Stones, and Mia Farrow have practiced TM, all providing worldwide press coverage. In the early 1960s, TM was red hot in popularity (at one point Maharishi was taking in $20 million per year), but it began to decline in the late 1960s. The movement revived in the 1970s, however, when the meditation technique was marketed as a "scientifically proven" means of obtaining inner peace and tranquility. This "scientific" technique even made its way into public schools.

Many Americans were interested in TM because they were told they could practice the technique without fear of violating their own religious beliefs. Many fell for the idea that TM was a nonreligious meditation technique rooted in science.

TM again declined in popularity in the late 1970s, this time due to the ruling of United States courts that TM was indeed religious in nature. Three key factors support this court ruling:

- TM is rooted in the Hindu Vedas (scriptures).

- The Sanskrit words given to TM initiates to use as mantras are actually names of Hindu gods and are intended to invoke these gods from the spirit world.

- The Sanskrit hymn that is recited during TM sessions involves the worship of Hindu deities.[8]

Understandably, once the religious nature of TM became public knowledge, many were angry that they had been deceived, and they promptly exited the movement. Further, TM was no longer welcome in public schools (federal aid was cut off). Still, about a million people in the United States regularly practice TM.

APOLOGETIC POWER POINTS

God Is Personal. (12)

Pantheism Is False. (26)

Polytheism Is False. (27)

Jesus Is the Only Way. (36)

Jesus Atoned for Sin. (40)

Man Is a Creature. (60)

Humans Are Not Divine. (62)

Humans Are Fallen in Sin. (67)

Salvation Is by Grace Through Faith. (71)

Heaven Is Real. (77)

Hell Is Real. (78)

Reincarnation Is False. (103)

Mysticism Is Unreliable. (104)

Altered States of Consciousness Are Dangerous. (106)

Idolatry Is Prohibited. (107)

Eastern Meditation Is Prohibited. (108)

35

The Unarius Academy of Science

AMONG THE STRANGEST OF THE popular UFO cults of our day is the Unarius Academy of Science. "Unarius" stands for UNiversal ARticulate Interdimensional Understanding of Science, and was founded in 1954 by the late Ernest and Ruth Norman.[1] According to members of the Unarius Academy of Science, UFO starships will one day touch down on earth. More than 60 acres of land have been purchased in the mountains of San Diego, California, to accommodate the landings. Understandably, Unarius has been the subject of numerous news reports in the print and broadcast media.

Ernest and Ruth Norman had a long history of occultic involvement. They met in 1954 at a psychic convention. Prior to this time, Ernest had worked in spiritualist churches (that is, churches that engaged in *spiritism*—communicating with the dead). Ernest did a psychic reading the first time he met Ruth and claimed that in a previous incarnation she had been the pharaoh's daughter who rescued Moses in the bulrushes. Ernest later claimed that they were also Jesus and Mary Magdalene in a previous incarnation.[2]

Using clairvoyance, Earnest claimed to receive psychic "transmissions" from Mars and Venus. Subsequent transmissions revealed to him that other "spiritual planets" included Eros,

Orion, Muse, Elysium, and Hermes. These transmissions indicated that advanced learning centers existed on these planets, with Ascended Masters living there who would transmit knowledge to psychic adepts like Ernest. One unique teaching of Unarius is that students who are asleep may have out-of-body experiences and "astral travel" to these centers where the great Masters teach.[3]

Beliefs

Golden Age Imminent. Based on the transmissions received by Ernest, Unarius members believe that the imminent alien landing will usher in a utopia—a golden age of "logic and reason." These space brothers will bring with them higher knowledge and various gifts of technology. Unique to Unarius is the suggestion that these starships will land *on top of each other*, forming a saucer tower of sorts. These saucers, each from one of 33 other worlds, will invite humans to join their Interplanetary Confederation.

The flying saucers described by the Unarius Academy of Science are five miles in diameter. According to Unarius literature, each of these ships will bring 1000 scientists to the earth—a total of 33,000 interplanetary scientists. These scientists will all work for the betterment of humankind.

Technology Will Solve All Problems. Each level of the multilevel saucer tower will be devoted to a different field of science. The incredible technology brought by these alien scientists will serve to solve all of humankind's economic and social problems. This means that earthlings will no longer have to spend their time earning a living. They will be able to devote themselves to education and serving man. A new form of learning will use technocaps that people can wear in order to read "a book a night."[4]

Atlantis Recovered. Prior to landing in San Diego, the alien starships will allegedly land in the Bermuda Triangle on a sub-merged but soon-to-rise land mass that once was home to Atlantis:

> The ships are expected to land first in the Bermuda Triangle. One of their first benevolent acts will be to recover the libraries of Atlantis and Lemuria. The contents of these libraries, said to be on thin metal plates somewhere in the debris of the sunken continents, will be given back to the Earth people. The Space Brothers have plans to train technicians with this knowledge in order to build crystal and gold computers and other wondrous technology.[5]

Atlantis, of course, is the legendary lost continent that supposedly sank as a result of a natural disaster. Occultic literature is brimming with references to Atlantis, with constant mention of the extremely advanced and enlightened society that once lived there. Some occultists, particularly those in the New Age movement, have speculated that this "lost culture" was actually a group of alien beings.

Perfect Peace and Harmony. When the alien space brothers arrive, they will teach human beings the way to perfect peace and harmony. "They will speak from their experiences to end hatred and disease."[6] Wars and suffering will cease. "It will be proof for the skeptics. It will be rapturous, and it will be heavenly."[7]

Healing for Everyone. Unarius literature claims these alien scientists will build a magnificent university and medical center that will be open to all people without charge. The space brothers will provide humans with advanced healing machines. These machines will examine the *past lives* of people in order to bring healing in the present:

The hospital will be able to heal mental as well as physical diseases with the help of the "psychic anatomy viewer." According to Unarian science, information about past lives leads to healing. As such, the "psychic anatomy viewer" will X-ray the "electronic body," a term used to describe the past-life karma as it is held in the electromagnetic memory of the body. This machine will reveal any "malformations" and the exact time they occurred in a past life. With this information, a person is then thought to be able to release his or her problem.

For example, if a person injured another during battle in a past life on Atlantis, the guilt would still be found in the "electronic body." According to Unarius, this might cause any number of illnesses which would heal upon receipt of this datum. This "psychic anatomy viewer" is expected to empty all hospitals, prisons, and asylums. Drug abuse and alcoholism will be unheard of in the age the new science will create.[8]

Therapy Available. Meanwhile, until the aliens arrive, past-life therapy is offered at the Unarius New World Teaching Center. "For more severe or critical cases," we are told, "'Akashic' readings are available to help the individual discover the originating cause for his mental or physical block."[9] Occultists believe that the physical earth is surrounded by an immense spiritual field known as "Akasha" on which is impressed—like a celestial tape recording—every impulse of human thought, will, and emotion. It constitutes a complete record of human history. Unarius psychotherapists claim the ability to read the Akashic Records to derive important information for treating their clients' past hurts.

Presently 90,000 people are on the mailing list for Unarius

books and literature.[10] The center's video programs have aired since 1978 on 25 cable stations throughout the United States. Proponents claim that about 500,000 people worldwide have received the Unarius message.[11]

――――― APOLOGETIC POWER POINTS ―――――

Occultism Is Prohibited. (98)

Spiritism Is Prohibited. (99)

Reincarnation Is False. (103)

Mysticism Is Unreliable. (104)

The Space Brothers Are Demons in Disguise. (116)

The Ascended Masters Are Demons in Disguise. (117)

Healing Is Subject to God's Will. (118)

36

The Unification Church

THE UNIFICATION CHURCH WAS founded by the Reverend Sun Myung Moon, born in Korea in January, 1920. As a teenager, Moon claims Jesus appeared to him and asked him to complete the work of redemption that he began 2000 years ago. Moon accepted the call, realizing that Korea was the new Israel, the nation God chose for the Lord of the Second Advent (that is, Moon).[1]

Satan allegedly tried to thwart Moon from his messianic mission by tempting him to sin, but Moon was victorious over the devil. This victory, Moon says, qualified him to be the Messiah. Meanwhile, Moon claims he received revelations from Moses, the Buddha, and even God himself.

In the mid-1940s, Moon preached against communism in Korea and suffered great resistance from government authorities. He compared his sufferings to those of Christ in New Testament times. His delusions of grandeur escalated with each passing year.

Moon started to gather a small following in the 1950s and founded a small church. It was then that followers started calling him "reverend," not because he had attended seminary or had been ordained but because they considered him their pastor.

Moon soon relocated to Seoul, the capital of South Korea, where he established a church called the Holy Spirit Association for the Unification of World Christianity. The church became more popularly known as the Unification Church. Why "Unification"? Moon did not intend establish a new denomination but wanted his church to be the foundation for unity for all Christian denominations. His membership grew, but so did the opposition.

In 1957 Moon published *Divine Principle*, based on revelations he claimed to have received over many years. This book constitutes the basic teachings of the Unification Church. The church has published several editions of this book, with doctrinal changes made in each.

The Unification Church penetrated the United States in the late 1950s. Not until the 1970s, however, did Moon and his church begin attracting attention. At that time, headlines ran across the country about Moon and the mass marriages he arranged. In one ceremony in 1975, Moon married 1800 couples from 25 countries. He was suddenly on the evening news everywhere. He also made headlines when he chose to publicly support Richard Nixon during the Watergate scandal.[2] His invitation to the White House by Nixon was heavily reported.

During the 1970s, mainstream Christians categorized the Unification Church as a cult. They made allegations of brainwashing and financial fraud, and they challenged hints from Moon that he was the new Messiah, the Lord of the Second Advent. Christians did not react well to the idea that Jesus did not complete the work of redemption.[3] Moon responded by saying that just as Jesus was persecuted in the first century by religious leaders, so he was being persecuted by religious leaders in his day.

Beliefs

The Bible. Unification teaches that human history includes three ages: the Old Testament age, for which God gave humanity the Law of Moses; the New Testament age, for which God gave humanity the teachings of Christ; and the Completed Testament age, for which God has given Reverend Moon's book, *Divine*

Principle. This final revelation takes precedence over the Old and New Testaments. Those who reject Moon's revelation go to hell.

Moonies argue that the Bible itself refers to Moon. They cite John 16:12-13, where Jesus speaks of the Spirit of truth: "I have much more to say to you, more than you can now bear. But when he, the Spirit of truth, comes, he will guide you into all truth. He will not speak on his own; he will speak only what he hears, and he will tell you what is yet to come." Moon's revelations are allegedly communicating new truth.

God. Moonies deny the Trinity as traditionally understood by historic Christianity. Moon says that God's original intention was to form a Trinity with himself, Adam, and Eve. But Adam and Eve's fall into sin foiled this Trinity. Tragically, a Satanic trinity was formed with Satan, Adam, and Eve. Later, however, Jesus was able to perfect himself spiritually, and a spiritual Trinity was formed with God, Jesus, and the Holy Spirit. A future physical Trinity will involve God, the Lord of the Second Advent (Moon), and the Lord of the Second Advent's wife. When this last Trinity is formed, the kingdom of heaven will be established on earth.

Humankind's Fall. The Unification Church teaches that there was a twofold fall of human beings—a *spiritual* fall and a *physical* fall. The spiritual fall took place as a result of Eve giving in to Lucifer's sexual seduction. Eve and Lucifer had an illicit (spiritual) sexual relationship. They committed fornication by means of their spirit bodies in the spirit world. This caused a spiritual fall to come upon the human race. From this moment forward, the spiritual nature of human beings was corrupted and had a propensity to do evil.

When Eve realized she had deviated from God's plan, she sought to set things right in a misguided fashion by *physically* seducing Adam.[4] Neither Adam nor Eve, however, were yet spiritually mature enough to engage in physical sex, and Eve's plan backfired. This sexual union constituted yet another deviation from God's perfect plan and represented the *physical* fall of humanity. Adam and Eve's sin was therefore sexual in nature. Original sin involves a tainted blood lineage that goes back to Eve's illegitimate sexual liaison with Satan and her premature physical seduction of Adam.

Humankind's Redemption. Because humanity fell both spiritually and physically, human beings must be redeemed spiritually and physically. According to Moon's *Divine Principle*, Jesus' basic purpose was to marry and bear children so he and his wife would become "True Parents" of a perfect humanity, giving rise to the kingdom of God on earth. In doing this, he would redeem humanity both spiritually and physically. However, Jesus failed to complete his task. Jesus at the cross allegedly accomplished the *spiritual* redemption of humankind, but he failed to accomplish humankind's *physical* redemption. (That is, he failed to get married and give birth to a perfect humanity.)

Because Jesus failed to accomplish physical redemption, the Lord of the Second Advent (Moon) must do so. Unificationists say the new Messiah will first perfect himself by defeating the devil and removing himself from Satan's lineage. He will then perfect his family by marrying and having children. Following this, he will perfect Korea (the nation chosen for the Second Advent) by defeating communism. Finally, he will perfect the world in the sense that all religions will be unified under the Lord of the Second Advent, communism will be defeated, and all nations will be united into one kingdom on earth, centered on God.

Jesus Christ. Jesus is not eternal deity. The early church is responsible for fabricating his eternal deity. Jesus did, however, attain a *lesser* degree of deity in view of his spiritual perfection. But this deity is not equal to that of the Father. That Jesus was not absolute deity is evident in the facts that Jesus was tempted by the devil, he prayed to the Father, and he was nailed to a cross.

Moonies say Jesus did not physically rise from the dead. Rather, at the resurrection, Jesus became "transcendent" of the material world. After all, John 20:19 indicates that Jesus could suddenly appear in a room without having gone through a door.

Human Destiny. Moon teaches that those who reject him as the Lord of the Second Advent will go to hell. Yet it is only a temporary abode. People in hell will eventually see the truth and be delivered from hell. Ultimately, all people will be redeemed. Moonies believe that eventually all human beings will become divine beings.

APOLOGETIC POWER POINTS

The Bible Should Not Be Added To. (2)

The Bible Is Authoritative. (6)

God Is a Trinity. (22)

Jesus Is God. (30)

Jesus Is Not Lesser than the Father. (32)

Jesus Atoned for Sin. (40)

Jesus Completed the Work of Salvation. (49)

Jesus Physically Resurrected. (50)

Jesus Will Return at the Second Coming. (51)

Jesus' Death Does Not Detract from His Deity. (52)

Jesus' Temptation Is Not Incompatible with His Deity. (53)

Jesus' Praying Is Not Incompatible with His Deity. (54)

The Spirit of Truth Is the Holy Spirit. (59)

Humans Are Not Divine. (62)

Humans Are Fallen in Sin. (67)

All Humans Are Infected by Sin (Original Sin). (68)

The Fall Was Not Sexual. (69)

Universalism Is a False Doctrine. (73)

Hell Is Real. (78)

Spiritism Is Prohibited. (99)

Sexual Immorality Is Prohibited. (113)

37

Unitarian Universalism

MANY FAMOUS PEOPLE IN UNITED STATES history have been Unitarian Universalists, including five presidents, famous authors such as Henry Wadsworth Longfellow, Ralph Waldo Emerson, Henry David Thoreau, and Charles Dickens, eight U.S. Supreme Court justices, famous women such as Florence Nightingale and Susan B. Anthony, and various other famous folks like Charles Darwin, Alexander Graham Bell, and Paul Revere.[1] Presently more than 1000 Unitarian Universalist congregations exist around the world.[2]

The Unitarian Universalist Association was founded in 1961 as a result of a merger of the American Unitarian Association (incorporated in 1825) and the Universalist Church of America (incorporated in 1793).[3] Prior to this time, the Unitarians and Universalists were separate traditions.

Unitarians are so named because they deny the doctrine of the Trinity. The Unitarian movement rose to prominence during the sixteenth century and spread through Europe to England and later to America.

Universalists are so named because they believe in the salvation of all human beings. They do not believe in the doctrines of hell or eternal punishment because they feel such doctrines are incompatible with a loving God. Universalist teachings spread from England to America in the eighteenth century.

Both these schools of thought became hugely influential in

the eighteenth century during the Age of Reason (the Enlightenment period). They held similar views on a number of issues. Both rejected Calvinistic predestination, the total depravity of humankind, and eternal damnation.[4] Both groups believed human beings had the potential for good or evil but that in the end, all people would be saved. No one will suffer for eternity in hell. Because of such similarities, their merger in 1961 made good sense.

Beliefs

Diversity. A great diversity of beliefs exists among Unitarian Universalists. One reason for this is that Unitarian Universalists base their individual beliefs on their own experiences rather than on a particular holy book. One will find New Agers, neopagan goddess worshippers, humanists, atheists, agnostics, liberal Jews, and liberal Christians within the fold of Unitarian Universalism. They are not committed to any one religious system of thought. There are no creeds or confessions of faith one must subscribe to. Creeds are viewed as a hindrance, for they imply that religious beliefs are concrete and final. Unitarian Universalists believe religious ideas should be open to growth.

Unitarian Universalists do not criticize each other's particular religious viewpoints. One is free to explore whatever religious path one chooses, without fear of being infringed upon by someone else. Each person in the group places personal reason and conscience in top authority, and each decides what religious viewpoint he or she wants to subscribe to. "We believe in the authority of reason and conscience. The ultimate arbiter in religion is not a church, a document, or an official, but the personal choice and decision of the individual."[5]

Understandably, Unitarian Universalists consider tolerance a virtue and exclusivism a vice. Their philosophy "excludes all exclusiveness."[6] No absolute truth can be true for all people in all times in all places. No religion has a corner on truth. For this reason, they honor all religions for the truth they espouse. Any religion, Unitarian Universalists say, can lead one to have a meaningful life and provide a foundation of ethics upon which to build one's life.[7]

I will summarize in a generalized way how many Unitarian Universalists view doctrines such as the Bible, God, Jesus, humankind, sin, and salvation.

The Bible. Unitarians generally do not hold the Bible in high regard. They acknowledge some inspiring thoughts in it, but most view it as a fallible human book that is "very imperfect" and that can hardly contain the actual words of Jesus. They consider the Gospels to be heavily influenced by the theological biases of the Gospel writers. The Bible as a whole is unscientific, mythological (and thus not to be interpreted literally), full of primitive ideas, permeated with ethical barbarisms, and loaded with excessively strict rules. The Bible is certainly not unique or exclusive, for the Hindu Vedas and Muslim Koran are just as valid.[8]

God. Unitarian Universalists interpret God in various ways, though they are unanimous in rejecting the idea of a Trinity. Members are free to hold whatever view of God that is most meaningful to them. Some do not believe in God at all (atheists). Some believe that all is God (pantheists). Some believe in the Mother Goddess (neopagans). Some believe in many gods (polytheists). Some believe in a "higher power," roughly equated with God (New Agers). Some believe in an evolving and changing God (process theologians). Still others believe in some kind of personal God who does not generally intervene in the affairs of human beings (deists).

Jesus Christ. Unitarian Universalists see Jesus as a good moral teacher and positive influence. He is one of many great holy men who came to show us how to live better lives and how to show love. He is respected and admired for his good example and his values, but he is not worshipped as God. He was not virgin-born, nor did he rise from the dead. He did not perform any genuine miracles, for science clearly disproves such claims. Nor did Jesus die for the sins of humankind. People needed no such sacrifice because they did not inherit original sin.

Humankind. Unitarian Universalists believe human beings are not fallen in sin. One can attend a Unitarian Universalist church a long time and never hear the word "sin." When the word "sin" is used, it does not signify a moral offense against a holy God but rather something akin to a simple mistake.

Human beings are therefore essentially good and have great potential. This is one reason Unitarian Universalism is popular among humanists. Church services emphasize that humankind is capable of solving any problem or crisis it confronts. No supernatural help is needed.

Salvation. Unitarian Universalists interpret salvation in various ways. Some speak of salvation as cultural reconstruction—that is, we save the world by making it a better place to live. Others speak of salvation as deliverance from social evils (such as racism). Still others speak of salvation as personal character improvement. Still others interpret salvation as having a sudden epiphany of the wonder of life around us—an awakening to the goodness of the world.

The Afterlife. Most Unitarian Universalists do not recognize an afterlife where people continue to exist following death. Rather, death is the final end of one's existence. In view of this, Unitarian Universalists choose to spend their time on making the most of the present moment. Contrary to the Bible's admonition to set our minds on things above (Colossians 3:2), they focus on the here and now. Because of the reality of our impending deaths, we should live life to the fullest. We have no eternal life, but the hope for "immortality" expresses itself in the positive effect one has had on others throughout life. We live on in the memories of those whom we have touched.

—— APOLOGETIC POWER POINTS ——

The Bible Is Inspired. (1)

The Bible Is Reliable. (3)

The Gospel Writers Were Reliable. (4)

The Bible Is Authoritative. (6)

Sound Hermeneutics Yields Proper Interpretation. (8)

Other "Holy Books" Are Incompatible with the Bible. (11)

God's Attributes Reveal His Nature. (18)

God Is a Trinity. (22)

Pantheism Is False. (26)

Polytheism Is False. (27)

Atheism Is False. (28)

Jesus Is God. (30)

Jesus Performed Miracles. (39)

Jesus Atoned for Sin. (40)

Jesus Was Not a Mere Moral Teacher. (41)

Jesus Physically Rose from the Dead. (50)

Humans Are Fallen in Sin. (67)

All Humans Are Infected by Sin (Original Sin). (68)

Universalism Is False. (73)

Heaven Is Real. (77)

Hell Is Real. (78)

All People Will Face Judgment. (83)

Witchcraft Is Prohibited. (101)

Relativism Is Illogical. (109)

Science Does Not Disprove the Bible. (111)

38

The Unity School of Christianity

CHARLES AND MYRTLE FILLMORE founded the Unity School of Christianity (hereafter Unity), the largest offshoot of the New Thought movement (see chapter 22), in 1891. Their backgrounds provided fertile soil for the development of Unity's theology. Myrtle became interested in transcendental philosophy at an early age and was admittedly eclectic in her theology, pulling "truth" from a wide variety of religious groups.[1] As a youth, Charles dabbled in spiritualism, and as an adult, he studied Hinduism, Buddhism, Rosicrucianism, and Theosophy. All these elements would later show their influence in Unity's theology, especially in the doctrines of God and Jesus Christ.

Charles Fillmore, answering some critics who charged that Unity was a cult, explained the significance of the name Unity this way:

> We have borrowed the best from all religions, that is the reason we are called Unity....Unity is not a sect, not a separation of people into an exclusive group of know-it-alls. Unity is the Truth that is taught in all religions, simplified and systemized so that anyone can understand and apply it. Students of Unity do not find it necessary to sever their church affiliations.[2]

The reason the Fillmores did not encourage their students to sever their church affiliations is that "we see the good in all religions and we want everyone to feel free to find the Truth for himself wherever he may be led to find it."[3] Many Unity proponents are members of mainline denominational churches, but membership also includes spiritists, occultists, Eastern mystics, and New Agers. Members do not see any conflict with this broad membership because they consider Unity less of a church and more of a school or educational institution where the "truth of the ages" can be sought.

Because of Unity's eclecticism, Charles Fillmore tried to avoid developing a statement of faith. Even when the "Unity Statement of Faith" was eventually produced, it contained the following qualification: "We are hereby giving warning that we shall not be bound to this tentative statement of what Unity believes. We may change our mind tomorrow on some of the points, and if we do, we shall feel free to make a new statement."[4]

Beliefs

The Bible. Unity proponents believe the Bible is the greatest and most spiritual of all the scriptures, but they also hold that "other Scriptures, such as the Zend Avesta, and the Upanishads, as well as the teachings of Buddha, the Koran, and the Tao of Lao-tse and the writings of Confucius, contain expressions of eminent spiritual truths."[5] Adherents interpret the Bible esoterically.

God. Unity holds to a pantheistic concept of God. Charles Fillmore said that "each rock, tree, animal, everything visible, is a manifestation of the one spirit-god, differing only in degree of manifestation."[6] Fillmore's view of God is an example of multilevel pantheism, a form of pantheism that surfaces often in New Age circles. Multilevel pantheism recognizes different (or multi) levels of manifestation of God in the universe. A rock would be a very low-level manifestation of God. An animal would be a higher manifestation of God. A human being would be an even higher manifestation of God.

Fillmore generally perceived God as impersonal, as evidenced in his concept of the Trinity: "The Father is Principle, the Son is that Principle revealed in creative plan, the Holy Spirit is the executive power of both Father and Son carrying out the creative plan."[7] Unity teaches that "God is not a...person, having life, intelligence, love, power. God is that invisible, intangible, but very real something we call life."[8]

Reincarnation. Unity is distinguished from mainstream New Thought groups by its doctrine of reincarnation. The "Unity Statement of Faith" tells us, "We believe that dissolution of spirit, soul and body, caused by death, is annulled by rebirth of the same spirit and soul in another body here on earth. We believe the repeated incarnations of man to be a merciful provision of our loving Father to the end that all may have opportunity to attain immortality through regeneration, as did Jesus."[9]

Unity's concept of reincarnation is different, however, from that of traditional Hinduism. This becomes evident in Unity's rejection of the Hindu "law of karma." According to Unity, Christ has set humanity free from the wheel of karma. Charles Fillmore argued that "the regenerative work of Christ released man from the karmic wheel and prepared him for new life, a series of new lives, in fact, which might be looked upon as vehicles for the attainment of the perfect, deathless body."[10] Unity teaches that reincarnation is God's means of restoring humankind to a deathless state.

Salvation and Jesus Christ. In Unity, salvation is attained by "at-one-ment" with God—a reuniting of human consciousness with God-consciousness: "The atonement is the union of man with God the Father, in Christ. Stating it in terms of mind, we should say that the Atonement is the At-one-ment or agreement of reconciliation of man's mind with Divine Mind through the superconsciousness of Christ's mind."[11]

Jesus attained this at-one-ment with the Divine Mind. Indeed, all humanity can:

> The difference between Jesus and us is not one of inherent spiritual capacity, but in difference of demonstration of it. Jesus was potentially perfect, and He expressed that perfection; we are potentially perfect, [but] we have not yet expressed it....Jesus attained a divine awareness and unfoldment without parallel in this period of the world's history.[12]

Unity thus exhorts followers to "follow into this perfect state and become like Him [Jesus], for in each of us is the Christ, the only begotten Son. We can, through Jesus Christ, our Redeemer and example, bring forth the Christ within us."[13]

An outgrowth of this concept of the Christ is Unity's view of the second coming. The "Unity Statement of Faith" affirms that "the second coming of Jesus Christ is now being fulfilled....His spirit is quickening the whole world."[14] This view is noticeably similar to that of New Age writers David Spangler and George Trevelyan, who define the second coming as the incarnation of the Christ in all humanity.

APOLOGETIC POWER POINTS

Esotericism Is Illegitimate. (7)

Sound Hermeneutics Yields Proper Interpretation. (8)

Other "Holy Books" Are Incompatible with the Bible. (11)

God Is Personal. (12)

God Is a Trinity. (22)

Pantheism Is False. (26)

Jesus Is God. (30)

Jesus Is the Christ. (34)

Jesus Is the Only Way. (36)

Jesus Is Unique. (37)

Jesus Atoned for Sin. (40)

Jesus Will Return at the Second Coming. (51)

Humans Are Not Divine. (62)

Salvation Is by Grace Through Faith. (71)

Death Is Real. (76)

Occultism Is Prohibited. (98)

Spiritism Is Prohibited. (99)

Reincarnation Is False. (103)

Mysticism Is Unreliable. (104)

Relativism Is Illogical. (109)

The World Religions Do Not Teach the Same Doctrines. (112)

39

The Way International

Victor Paul Wierwille (1916–1985) founded the Way International—an alleged restoration of first-century Christianity. Wierwille earned a degree from Princeton Theological Seminary. He also claimed to have a doctorate, but this degree was from a diploma mill called Pikes Peak Bible Seminary.[1] Unaware of this, his followers regularly referred to him as "Doctor."

Following his education, Wierwille served for a time as a pastor of the Evangelical and Reformed Church (also known as the United Church of Christ) in Van Wert, Ohio. During these years, he was conflicted because of the contradictory views of doctrine he encountered when reading various theologians. He eventually resigned this position under suspicious circumstances, apparently to avoid being fired.

During this time, Wierwille claimed that as he witnessed the lives of Christians and even ministers around him, he could find no evidence anywhere of the abundant life that Jesus spoke of in John 10:10. This caused him to engage in a search for how a person could attain this kind of life.[2]

Soon enough, Wierwille claimed to have received a divine call from God to preach the truth. "God spoke to me audibly, just like I'm talking to you now. He said He would teach me the Word as it had not been known since the first century, if I would teach it to others."[3]

The Way—a name taken from the book of Acts, in which

Christians were referred to as followers of "the way" (Acts 9:2)—began not as a church, denomination, or religious sect but as a research organization. Wierwille set up camp for the organization at his family's 150-acre ranch in New Knoxville, Ohio, in 1967. The goal of the organization was to set "before men and women of all ages the inherent accuracy of the Word of God (the Bible) so that everyone who so desires may know the power of God in his life."[4] The structure of the national organization was based on the metaphor of a tree: "Each statewide unit is a limb, each city unit a branch, each household fellowship group a twig, each believer a leaf."[5]

The organization was able to effectively tap in to the ever-growing Jesus movement of the 1960s. Under Wierwille's leadership, The Way experienced exponential growth and eventually became a multimillion-dollar empire. During the organization's peak, some 35,000 people were active followers, but more than 100,000 people in all 50 states and 40 foreign countries had taken the Way's famous course, "Power for Abundant Living." This course guaranteed "to answer 95% of your questions about the Bible and about everything else."[6]

L. Craig Martindale became the new president of the organization in 1982 when Wierwille was fighting for his life with cancer. Wierwille finally died in 1985, and membership soon plummeted. Disillusioned members made charges of mismanagement of funds, accused the late Wierwille of plagiarism (of E.W. Bullinger, J.E. Stiles, E.W. Kenyon, and others), and made charges of adultery and promiscuous sex against the highest levels of ministry leadership. Further, the organization was accused of authoritarianism regarding its unbending enforcement of tithing requirements. Trouble continued to escalate with charges of homosexuality in the movement. Understandably, the drop in membership was paralleled by a drop in ministry finances, forcing the organization to sell off some of its assets. A number of splinter groups have emerged as refuges for former Way members.[7]

Beliefs

The Bible. Wierwille believed that the four Gospels were part of the Old Testament. He said the New Testament epistles are the only books of doctrine that are applicable to the present age. Because God's voice came to Wierwille, Wierwille's interpretation of the Bible is authoritative.

God. Members of the Way believe in only one God (the Father). The Father is the divine Creator of all things, including Jesus Christ and the Holy Spirit. There is no Trinity. The doctrine of the Trinity is rooted in paganism and was introduced into Christianity in the third and fourth centuries by pagan converts to Christianity.[8]

Jesus Christ. Jesus is not the second person of the Trinity, nor is He absolute deity. Wierwille's most famous book was *Jesus Christ Is Not God*, in which he argued that "Jesus Christ is not God, but the Son of God....Jesus Christ was not literally with God in the beginning; neither does he have all the assets of God."[9] We read that "God is eternal whereas Jesus was born."[10] "Jesus Christ's existence began when he was conceived by God's creating the soul-life of Jesus in Mary."[11] He was a sinless man because he was conceived by the Holy Spirit, but he is not to be worshipped.[12]

The Holy Spirit. Wierwille drew a distinction between the Holy Spirit (with capital letters) and the holy spirit (with lowercase letters). The Holy Spirit (with capital letters) is another name for the Father and is God. The holy spirit (with lowercase letters) is the gift—an inanimate, impersonal force—that the Holy Spirit (the Father) gives to individual Christians to empower them.[13]

This distinction is important, we are told, for "many confuse the Giver, Holy Spirit, with the gift, holy spirit."[14]

Human Beings. Wierwille taught that "man was originally body (physical) and soul (breath of life) and spirit (that part of man that communicates with God)."[15] When Adam fell in sin, however, he lost his spirit. Human beings thus now have a body and a soul (much like the animals) but no spirit. "The spirit disappeared....Their entire spiritual connection with God was lost. From that very day Adam and Eve were just body and soul—as any other animal."[16] Only when a person is born again by believing in Jesus does he receive holy spirit, which is the power for abundant living, enabling the believer to attain sinless perfection, perfect health, happiness, and success.

Salvation. Since the time of Adam, all human beings have been born dead in trespasses and sin. To be saved, one must believe in Jesus Christ, physically and vocally confess one's faith before others, and then speak in tongues as a proof of being filled with holy spirit.[17] Based on his understanding of Acts 2:2 (which makes reference to a "violent wind"), Wierwille taught that the gift of speaking in tongues must be received by believers inhaling the holy spirit through deep breathing.[18]

Physical Healing. Physical healing is believed to be part of the redemption we have received in Christ. "Christ has redeemed us, not only from some of the things mentioned in the curse, but from all of them, which includes sickness and disease."[19] "When we have salvation, we have wholeness, even physical wholeness, if we simply accept it."[20] This teaching, of course, was undermined when Wierwille was diagnosed with cancer and died.

Tithing. Followers are required to give a minimum 10 percent tithe of their gross income. This minimum required amount can be supplemented by "abundant sharing" donations beyond the 10 percent.

Water Baptism. Wierwille taught that water baptism was for ancient Israel and not for New Testament believers.

Afterlife. The Way teaches that when people die, they "fall asleep" in the sense that they are no longer consciously existent until they are "awakened" in the future resurrection to face judgment. Believers will experience eternal life. Unbelievers will meet a second and final death (extinction).

APOLOGETIC POWER POINTS

Sound Hermeneutics Yields Proper Interpretation. (8)

God Is a Trinity. (22)

The Trinity Is Not a Pagan Idea. (23)

Jesus Is God. (30)

Jesus Is Not Lesser than the Father. (32)

Jesus Is the Son of God. (33)

Jesus Was Sinless. (38)

The Incarnate Jesus Had Two Natures. (47)

The Holy Spirit Is a Person. (57)

The Holy Spirit Is God. (58)

Man Is Both Material and Immaterial. (61)

Humans Are Fallen in Sin. (67)

All Humans Are Infected by Sin (Original Sin). (68)

Salvation Is by Grace Through Faith. (71)

Salvation Involves Justification. (72)

Tongues Is Not Necessary for Salvation. (74)

Hell Is Real. (78)

There Is Conscious Existence After Death. (80)

Annihilationism Is False. (81)

All People Will be Resurrected. (82)

All People Will Face Judgment (83)

Christians Should Tithe as They Are Able. (91)

Sexual Immorality Is Prohibited. (113)

Homosexuality Is Prohibited. (115)

Healing Is Subject to God's Will. (118)

40

Wicca / Witchcraft

WICCA, OR WITCHCRAFT, HAS BECOME extremely popular in our day. Among the hottest-selling books of all time are those in the Harry Potter series. *Sabrina the Teenage Witch* has been a popular television show, a series that has now spawned some 45 books. Adults also have their pick of books on witchcraft, including *Wicca: A Guide for the Solitary Practitioner* by Scott Cunningham, *The Craft: A Witch's Book of Shadows* by Dorothy Morrison, and *The Element Encyclopedia of 5000 Spells: The Ultimate Reference Book for the Magical Arts* by Judika Illes.

Several individuals have made significant contributions to the emergence of modern witchcraft. Gerald Gardner (1884–1964) wrote two extremely important books: *Witchcraft Today* (1954) and *The Meaning of Witchcraft* (1959). Gardner, a longtime proponent of the occult, formulated his religious views based on the Mother Goddess and has influenced most of the other Wiccan leaders who have written books on the subject. For example, Sybil Leek (1923–1983), heavily dependent on Gardner (though with some modifications), wrote quite a few books on witchcraft and popularized the craft in the United States in the late 1960s. As well, Raymond and Rosemary Buckland, who personally studied under Gardner, wrote many books and helped bring witchcraft to the mainstream in America in the 1960s and beyond.[1]

Beliefs

Misconceptions Not Appreciated. Many people, Christians

included, have misconceptions about witchcraft, and witches do not appreciate being misrepresented.

- Many people have wrongly concluded that the term "witch" refers only to female members of the religion. The truth is that "witch" can refer to both females and males.

- Others have wrongly concluded that witchcraft is another word for Satanism. Most witches do not even believe in Satan.

- Still others have said that witchcraft is just another name for occultism. Witches utilize various forms of occultism, but occultism is a general term that encompasses far more than what witches believe and practice.[2]

Diversity. One of the difficulties in talking about witches—even just *defining* witches—is that they are so diverse. Witches do not subscribe to one creedal statement.[3] They do not use one definitive textbook. Witches come in many different shapes and colors, and for this reason, a statement that is true about one witch may not necessarily be true of another witch. In this chapter, I will include commonalities that are representative of many witches.

Toleration. Witches pride themselves in being religiously tolerant. No one witch speaks for all other witches. *The Encyclopedia of Witches and Witchcraft* tells us that "there is no central authority or liturgy; various traditions have their own rituals, philosophy, and beliefs. Some have added elements from Eastern, Native American Indian, aboriginal and shamanic systems; others have injected politics into their traditions. New ritual, songs, chants, and poetry are continually created."[4]

Because witches express a diversity of beliefs on various issues, tolerance is a Wiccan virtue. Each person is autonomous, free to decide what he or she wants to believe religiously. No one has an exclusive corner on the truth, and no religion can claim to be in sole possession of the truth.[5] Witches strenuously avoid forcing a religious dogma on another person.[6]

Personal Experience. Witches base their beliefs on personal experience. Experience is the final arbiter regarding what one decides to accept as true. Truth is therefore subjective—something to be intuited. If something *feels* right, then it *is* right.

Truth. Therefore witches have a relativistic view of truth. You can have your truth and I can have my truth. What is right for me may not necessarily be right for you, and vice versa. No absolute rights or wrongs exist. The governing principle of what is right seems to be whatever works for a particular person.

Nature Exalted. Witches have a high view of nature because they believe all of nature is alive. Even inanimate objects, plants, and trees are alive and conscious and have their own spirits or souls. Nature is brimming with life. The earth itself is a living organism, and a life force permeates and infuses all of nature. Starhawk, a witch, says that "the model of the Goddess, who is immanent in nature, fosters respect for the sacredness of all living things. Witchcraft can be seen as a religion of ecology. Its goal is harmony with nature, so that life may not just survive, but thrive."[7]

God. Witches have different views about God. Some are pantheists, believing that all is God and God is all. Others are panentheists, believing that all is in God and God is in all. Most are in some sense polytheists, since they acknowledge many deities. The two primary deities for most witches are the Mother Goddess and the Horned God, but many also believe in a pantheon of other gods and goddesses.

Some believe that the pantheistic "One" (the universal Life Force) is polarized by the female and male deities—the Mother

Goddess and the Horned God. These are dualistic manifestations of the "One." Both these deities are immanent among human beings, and both can be invoked by witches. Popular names for the Mother Goddess include Diana, Aphrodite, and Isis. Popular names for the Horned God include Pan, Adonis, and Apollo.

Magic. Witches make heavy use of magic, including incantations and potions. This magic utilizes the forces of nature to manipulate events in one's favor. In no case is this magic viewed as involving Satan or demons (most witches do not even believe the devil exists).

Rituals. Witches engage in mystical rituals such as "drawing down the moon" and "drawing down the sun." These rituals involve invoking the Mother Goddess (who is associated with the moon) or the Horned God (who is associated with the sun). Witches typically go into a deep trance state during these rituals. The Mother Goddess can possess either a priestess (all female witches are priestesses) or the high priestess of the coven. The Horned God can possess a priest (all male witches are priests) or the high priest of the coven. Sometimes mediumistic messages are communicated during these rituals.[8]

The Occult. Witches are involved in various forms of occultism, including spiritism (contact with departed humans, angels, spirit guides, and the like), crystal gazing, numerology, out-of-body experiences (astral projection), use of tarot cards, and astrology. During coven meetings, witches are often trained in the occultic arts.

Sacredness of Sex. Sex is often used as a sacrament among witches. It is said to be an outward sign of an inward grace. Both heterosexuality and homosexuality are acceptable to witches (tolerance is shown regarding both). Sometimes sex is used in magic rituals.

Jesus Christ. Witches typically redefine the person and work of Jesus Christ. Some say he was a witch with a coven of disciples. His miracles involved the use of magic. Others say he was an occultist who accomplished his feats through the occultic arts. Still others say he embodied divinity just as all of us today can embody divinity. And still others argue that he was a proponent of patriarchal (male-dominated) religion and therefore is to be rejected and opposed. All deny that Jesus was God in human flesh who died for the sins of humankind.

Sin and Salvation. Because human beings are divine, they cannot be evil or sinful. They are not fallen. Therefore, they do not need salvation. If human beings have any need at all, they need to be more in tune with the world of nature and all the life forms that are a part of nature.

Death Is Not the End. Most witches believe in reincarnation. Therefore, death is not the end but a state that leads to new rebirth. Human beings need not be fearful of death. Witches add a new twist to the typical teaching on reincarnation with their view of Summerland (roughly equivalent to the Christian's heaven). Raven Grimassi, author of *The Wiccan Mysteries*, tells us that Summerland is "a metaphysical astral realm of meadows, lakes, and forests where it is always summer. It is a Pagan paradise filled with all the lovely creatures of ancient lore, and the gods themselves dwell there."[9] In Summerland, souls can be refreshed and become ready for rebirth in a new body.

──── APOLOGETIC POWER POINTS ────

God Is Personal. (12)

God Is Transcendent and Immanent. (15)

God Alone Is to Be Worshipped. (25)

Pantheism Is False. (26)

Polytheism Is False. (27)

Jesus Is God. (30)

Jesus Is the Only Way. (36)

Jesus Performed Miracles. (39)

Jesus Atoned for Sin. (40)

Humans Are Fallen in Sin. (67)

Salvation Is by Grace Through Faith. (71)

Death Is Real. (76)

Heaven Is Real. (77)

Hell Is Real. (78)

All People Will Face Judgment (83)

Satan Is a Fallen Angel. (84)

Satan's Titles Reveal His Nature. (85)

Unbelievers Can Be Demon Possessed. (87)

Occultism Is Prohibited. (98)

Spiritism Is Prohibited. (99)

Astrology Is Prohibited. (100)

Witchcraft Is Prohibited. (101)

Chanting Is Prohibited. (102)

Reincarnation Is False. (103)

Relativism Is Illogical. (109)

Claims of Tolerance Are Hollow. (110)

Sexual Immorality Is Prohibited. (113)

Homosexuality Is Prohibited. (115)

41

Zen

ZEN IS A DEEPLY MYSTICAL FORM of Buddhism that emphasizes "non-thinking" and is a means by which one can achieve enlightenment, often by meditating on illogical phrases. J. Isamu Yamamoto tells us that the Sanskrit word for meditation is *Dhyana*, which refers to a highly developed meditative discipline in Hinduism. "Evidently this practice—or a form of this practice—was transmitted to the Chinese, giving rise to the Chinese word *Chan-na*, which is a rendering of the word *Dhyana*. *Ch'an* is the shortened form of *Chan-na*, and also means 'meditation.' The Japanese studied *Ch'an*, and pronounced it 'Zen.'"[1]

Zen Buddhism became firmly established in Japan in the Kamakura period (1185–1333). Two schools of Zen emerged—the Rinzai school and the Soto school. The Rinzai school was founded by Myoan Eisai (1141–1215) and taught that one could obtain sudden flashes of enlightenment or understanding—the same kind of enlightenment achieved by Gautama the Buddha. The Soto school was founded by Dogen (1200–1253) and, in contrast to Rinzai, taught that enlightenment came as a result of an extended process of striving to reach ever-deeper levels of awareness.[2]

Zen Buddhism made its way to America in the late 1800s when Soyen Shaku, a Zen master, accepted an invitation to Chicago to participate in the World's Parliament of Religions. Later, Daisetz Teitaro Suzuki (1870–1966) popularized Zen in the United States, lecturing widely on Zen and writing books on the subject. He advocated the Rinzai version of Zen, emphasizing the attainment of sudden flashes of enlightenment. Suzuki impacted Alan Watts, who himself wrote books on Zen, including *The Way of Zen*. By the 1950s, Zen began to attract a wide audience in the United States. During the 1970s and 1980s, Zen centers spread across the country.

Why has Zen caught on in the United States? One reason is that many Americans are experience oriented, and Zen is all about experience (see below). Further, in a culture where self-reliance is a virtue, the self-effort nature of Zen is appealing to many. Finally, Zen provides an attractive means of eradicating suffering (by ridding oneself of attachments to things).[3]

Beliefs

The Impossibility of Defining Zen. Zen proponents say Zen is impossible to define. It is *beyond* definition. It cannot be described in words. One must simply *experience* it.[4] In a non-thinking state, rational thought is excluded and one can experience the truth. Zen involves "a vigorous attempt to come into direct contact with the truth itself without allowing theories and symbols to stand between the knower and the known."[5]

Everyone Has a Buddha Nature. According to Zen, all people have a Buddha nature that lies dormant within, but they do not realize it. Ignorance is the problem. A recognition of one's true Buddha nature comes through *satori* (ultimate insight or enlightenment). Enlightenment does not come through engaging in external rituals. Rather, *satori* is an experiential realization—a sudden enlightenment—that all things in the universe are "one" (monism), and that duality is an illusion (that is, dualities such as heaven and hell, right and wrong, and life and death). One comes to realize the true nature of things, recognizing that what we see in the external world is simply an illusory manifestation of "the underlying unitary reality that is itself indescribable."[6] One comes to realize one's own nature (as Buddha). Zen Buddhists thus emphasize that they do not place faith in an external being known as Buddha (for the external realm involves illusion); rather, they place faith in the Buddha nature that is within them (which recognizes the "oneness" of all things).

The Koan: A Meditative Aid. A key meditative aid for Zen students is the *koan*. The koan is an irrational question or phrase that the Zen master asks the student in order to bring the student to a nonthinking state—a state in which rational thoughts become excluded. One moves into a state beyond reason. "Koans are designed to 'attack' the mind, to dismantle its reason, logic, history, ordinary consciousness and duality until it finally 'breaks down' and perceives an alternate reality, the monistic perception that Zen considers reality."[7] A famous koan is, "What is the sound of one hand clapping?"

A former Zen disciple commented: "Because they were impossible to answer by thinking about them such questions were supposed to help us stop thinking. By our answers, the master gauged the progress of our 'don't know' minds."[8] There are 1700 koans, though often one is enough to enable a disciple to obliterate rational thought and attain *satori*.

God. Belief in a transcendent God "out there" is a false view of reality. In Buddhism, neither God nor even the Buddha are the object of one's attention. Rather, the Buddha nature within is the sole object of focus. Belief in an external transcendent God is nothing but a hindrance to the recognition of one's true Buddha nature. Zen students reject the God of Christianity, but they prostrate themselves before their Zen masters and worship Buddhist idols.

Jesus Christ. Zen students respect Jesus as a great man and perhaps even a guru, but he was not God in human flesh and was certainly not the Savior of humankind. He accomplished no atonement.

Sin and Salvation. A transcendent God who must be obeyed does not exist, so people cannot possibly offend him. The closest thing to sin is an ignorance of one's true nature as Buddha.

Salvation involves the attainment of *satori*, which is ultimate insight or enlightenment. This experience leads people to awaken to that true nature within. When Zen disciples recognize their Buddha nature, they have joy and peace. Zen teaches that one may reach this state in a single life and does not require multiple lives or reincarnation.

———— APOLOGETIC POWER POINTS ————

God Is Transcendent and Immanent. (15)

Jesus Is God. (30)

Jesus Is the Savior. (35)

Jesus Is the Only Way. (36)

Jesus Atoned for Sin. (40)

Humans Are Fallen in Sin. (67)

Salvation Is by Grace Through Faith. (71)

Heaven Is Real. (77)

Hell Is Real. (78)

Reincarnation Is False. (103)

Mysticism Is Unreliable. (104)

Altered States of Consciousness Are Dangerous. (106)

Idolatry Is Prohibited. (107)

Eastern Meditation Is Prohibited. (108)

42

Apologetic Power Points

The Bible

1. The Bible Is Inspired.

Biblical inspiration is God's superintendence of the human authors so that, using their own individual personalities (and even their writing styles), they composed and recorded without error his revelation to man in the words of the original autographs (2 Timothy 3:16). The Holy Spirit is the agent of inspiration (2 Peter 1:21). By the Holy Spirit "God *moved* and the prophet *mouthed* these truths; God *revealed* and man *recorded* His word."[1]

The Greek word for "inspiration" literally means "God-breathed." Because Scripture is breathed out by God, it is inerrant—exempt from the liability to mistake, incapable of error, and in perfect accord with the truth.

2. The Bible Should Not Be Added To.

God's Word cannot be edited. Deuteronomy 4:2 (NASB) gives this command: "You shall not add to the word which I am commanding you, nor take away from it, that you may keep the commandments of the LORD your God which I command you." Proverbs 30:6 (NASB) instructs, "Do not add to His words or He will reprove you, and you will be proved a liar." Revelation 22:18-19 (NASB) likewise instructs, "I testify to everyone who hears the words of the prophecy of this book: if anyone adds to them, God will add to him the plagues which are written in this book; and if anyone takes away from the words of the book of this prophecy, God will take away his part from the tree of life and from the holy city, which are written in this book."

3. The Bible Is Reliable.

The Bible's reliability is evident in the following factors:

* It is based on eyewitness testimony (1 John 1:1; 2 Peter 1:16).

* So committed were the Bible writers that they gave up their lives defending what they wrote.

* More than 5000 partial and complete manuscript copies of the New Testament exist, many of which date very early (for example, the Bodmer papyrus [P66] dates to AD 200, the Chester Beatty papyrus [P45] dates to the third century AD, and Old Testament manuscripts from the Dead Sea Scrolls date to 150 BC).

* First- and second-century Christian leaders—such as Clement Papias, Justin Martyr, Polycarp, and Irenaeus—all cite from the four gospels as reliable sources.

* First- and second-century secular sources cite events related to the Bible, including Jewish historian Flavius Josephus, Roman historian Cornelius Tacitus, Pliny the Younger, and Suetonius.

* More than 25,000 archeological discoveries have proven the historical accuracy of the Bible.

4. The Gospel Writers Were Reliable.

Some claim the four Gospel writers were biased by theological motives, seeking to convince readers of Jesus' deity. But passionately believing something does not discredit one's historical account of it. In modern times, some of the most reliable reports of the Nazi Holocaust were written by Jews who were passionately committed to seeing such genocide never repeated. The New Testament is not made up of fairy tales but is rather based on eyewitness testimony (2 Peter 1:16; 1 John 1:1). The historical evidence solidly supports the reliability of the Gospel writers.

5. Bible "Contradictions" Are Easily Explained.

The Gospels may have *apparent* contradictions, but they do not have *genuine* contradictions. The differences are not actual contradictions. If all four Gospels were identical, critics would be screaming "collusion."

The Gospel differences represent four different (but inspired) accounts of the same events.

A partial account in a Gospel is not a faulty account. For example, Matthew 27:5 says Judas died by hanging himself. Acts 1:18 says he burst open and his entrails gushed out. These are partial accounts. Taken together we can reconstruct a complete account. Judas hanged himself, the rope later loosened, and he fell on the rocks below, causing his intestines to gush out.

6. The Bible Is Authoritative.

Scripture alone is the supreme and infallible authority for the church and the individual believer (2 Peter 1:21; 2 Timothy 3:16-17; 1 Corinthians 2:13; 1 Thessalonians 2:13). Scripture has final authority because it is a direct revelation from God and carries the very authority of God himself (Galatians 1:12). What the Bible says, God says. Jesus affirmed the Bible's divine inspiration (Matthew 22:43), its indestructibility (Matthew 5:17-18), its infallibility (John 10:35), its final authority (Matthew 4:4,7,10), its historicity (Matthew 12:40; 24:37), and its factual inerrancy (John 17:17; Matthew 22:29). Jesus appealed to Scripture in every matter under dispute—with the Sadducees (Matthew 22:29), the Pharisees (Mark 7:13), and even the devil (Matthew 4:4-10).

7. Esotericism Is Illegitimate.

Esotericism is illegitimate for at least eight reasons:

1. Esotericism violates the Scriptural injunction to rightly handle the Word of God and not distort its meaning (2 Peter 3:16; 2 Corinthians 4:2).

2. Esotericism fails to recognize that each verse of Scripture has only one correct meaning, not multiple meanings.

3. In esotericism, the basic authority in interpretation is not Scripture but the mind of the interpreter.

4. Esotericists rely on their own inner illumination and not the Holy Spirit (1 Corinthians 2:9-11; John 16:12-15).

5. Esotericism superimposes mystical meanings on Bible verses instead of objectively seeking the biblical author's intended meaning.

6. Esotericism ignores the context of Scripture.

7. Esotericism ignores grammar, history, and culture.

8. Esotericism goes against Jesus' example of properly interpreting Scripture, for he always interpreted the Old Testament Scriptures literally (for example, Luke 11:29-32).

8. Sound Hermeneutics Yields Proper Interpretation.

Several hermeneutical instructions help us to understand the Bible rightly:

* Seek the author's intended meaning instead of superimposing a meaning onto the text.

* Interpret each verse in context. Every word is part of a verse, every verse is part of a paragraph, every paragraph is part of a book, and every book is part of the whole of Scripture.

* Consult history to get a better grasp on the historical context in which the biblical book was written.

* Make a correct genre judgment. Biblical genres include history (Acts), the dramatic epic (Job), poetry (Psalms), wise sayings (Proverbs), and apocalyptic writings (Revelation). (This awareness will keep us from interpreting poetry as history, for example.)

* Interpret the Old Testament using the greater light of the New Testament.

* Depend on the Holy Spirit for guidance (John 16:12-15; 1 Corinthians 2:9-11).

9. Joseph Smith's "Inspired Version" Is Untrustworthy.

Joseph Smith did not do any manuscript study whatsoever. He simply rewrote certain Bible passages in the light of supposed new revelations from God. This means that Smith's "translation" cannot be verified by any objective means.

A large group of the world's greatest Bible scholars took years to finish the KJV, but Smith took a mere three years to complete his work—despite the fact that he had no knowledge of the biblical languages.

Moreover, Smith's revision violates scriptural warnings not to add to or subtract from God's Word (for example, Revelation 22:18). His "Inspired Version" is more of a "Contrived Version," written to support Mormon theology.

10. The Book of Mormon Is Unreliable.

The Book of Mormon is unreliable for several reasons:

* The Mormon church has made more than 4000 changes to the original edition of the Book of Mormon. It should not have required *any* changes because Smith allegedly used magic seer stones (guided by God) that infallibly translated one letter at a time for him.

* The book is undermined by its many plagiarisms from the KJV. The Book of Mormon was allegedly penned between 600 BC and AD 421, so how could it contain word-for-word quotations from the AD 1611 KJV?

* Virtually *no* archeological support exists for the cities mentioned in the Book of Mormon.

11. Other "Holy Books" Are Incompatible with the Bible.

The claim that the Bible is one of many holy books and teaches the same truths as other holy books is completely fallacious. If one of these books is correct, then the others are necessarily incorrect because they set forth diametrically opposing ideas on basic doctrines. Regarding the doctrine of God, for example, the Bible teaches the Trinity; the Koran denies the Trinity; the Hindu Vedas teach pantheism and polytheism; Zoroastrian writings present a good God and a bad God; Buddhist writings affirm God is irrelevant. Such radical differences also exist on the doctrines of sin, salvation, Jesus, and the afterlife.

God

12. God Is Personal.

A person is a conscious being—one who thinks, feels, purposes, and carries these purposes into action. A person engages in active relationships with others. You can talk to a person and get a response. You can share feelings and ideas with him. You can argue with him, love him, and even hate him. Surely by this definition God must be understood as a person.

The Bible pictures God as a loving personal Father to whom believers may cry, "Abba" (Romans 8:15). "Abba" is an Aramaic term of great intimacy, loosely meaning "daddy." Jesus often spoke of God as a loving Father. Indeed, God is the personal "Father of compassion" of all believers (2 Corinthians 1:3).

13. God Is a Spirit.

The Scriptures affirm that God is Spirit (John 4:24). A spirit does not have flesh and bones (Luke 24:39). Therefore, God is not a physical being. Because God is a Spirit, he is invisible. He cannot be seen. First Timothy 1:17 refers to God as "the King eternal, immortal, invisible, the only God." Colossians 1:15 speaks of "the invisible God."

If God is a Spirit, how are we to interpret the many references in Scripture to God's face, ears, eyes, hands, strong arm, and the like? This is anthropomorphic language. The biblical writers often described God metaphorically in humanlike language so people could more readily understand God's nature and characteristics. Such language uses figures of speech.

14. God Is Not an Exalted Man.

God is not a man or an exalted man. In Hosea 11:9 God asserts, "For I am God, and not man." Numbers 23:19 tells us that "God is not a man." Romans 1:22-23 (NASB) speaks of idolaters who have changed the glory of God into an image made like corruptible man. Isaiah 45:12 indicates that God is the creator of man. Such verses prove that God is not now nor ever has been a man.

15. God Is Transcendent and Immanent.

The theological phrase "transcendence of God" refers to God's otherness or separateness from the created universe and from humanity. The phrase "immanence of God" refers to God's active presence within the creation and in human history (though all the while remaining distinct from the creation). God is both transcendent *and* immanent, high above his creation but at the same time intimately involved with his creatures.

A plethora of Scripture verses speak of God's transcendence (for example, 1 Kings 8:27; Psalm 113:5-6). Likewise, many verses speak of God's immanence (Exodus 29:45-46; Deuteronomy 4:7). Some verses teach both God's transcendence *and* his immanence (Deuteronomy 4:39; Isaiah 57:15; Jeremiah 23:23-24).

16. God Is All-Powerful.

Scripture portrays God as being omnipotent—he is all-powerful. He has the power to do all that he desires and wills. Some 56 times Scripture declares that God is almighty (for example, Revelation 19:6). God is abundant in strength (Psalm 147:5) and has incomparably great power (2 Chronicles 20:6; Ephesians 1:19-21). No one can hold back God's hand (Daniel 4:35). No one can reverse God (Isaiah 43:13), and no one can thwart Him (Isaiah 14:27). Nothing is impossible with God (Matthew 19:26; Mark 10:27; Luke 1:37), and nothing is too difficult for Him (Genesis 18:14; Jeremiah 32:17,27). The Almighty reigns (Revelation 19:6).

17. God Is Immutable.

God in his essential nature is immutable (unchanging). In Malachi 3:6 God affirms, "I the LORD do not change." Psalm 102:25-27 says of God, "In the beginning you laid the foundations of the earth, and the heavens are the work of your hands. They will perish, but you remain; they will all wear out like a garment. Like clothing you will change them and they will be discarded. But you remain the same, and your years will never end." James 1:17 speaks of "the Father of the heavenly lights, who does not change like shifting shadows." Scripture is also clear that God's eternal plans do not change (Psalm 33:11; Isaiah 46:10; Hebrews 6:17).

18. God's Attributes Reveal His Nature.

God Is Eternal. As an eternal being, God has always existed (Psalm 90:2; 1 Timothy 1:17; Revelation 1:8).

God Is Love. God is the very personification of love (1 John 4:8).

God Is Everywhere-Present. One cannot go anywhere where God is not (Psalm 139:7-8; Jeremiah 23:23-24; Acts 17:27-28).

God Is All-Knowing. God knows all things, both actual and possible

(Matthew 11:21-23). He knows all things past (Isaiah 41:22), present (Hebrews 4:13), and future (Isaiah 46:10).

God Is All-Powerful. His power is limitless (Genesis 18:14; Psalm 147:5; Jeremiah 32:17,27; Revelation 19:6).

God Is Sovereign. God rules the universe, controls all things, and is Lord over all (Psalm 50:1; 66:7; 93:1; Isaiah 40:15).

God Is Holy. God is entirely separate from all evil and is pure in every way (Exodus 15:11; Leviticus 19:2; Psalm 71:22; Isaiah 6:3; Revelation 15:4).

19. God Is the Creator.

God alone is Creator (Isaiah 44:24). Many Old Testament references attribute creation simply to God (Genesis 1:1; Psalm 96:5; Isaiah 37:16; 44:24; 45:12; Jeremiah 10:11-12). Other passages relate the creation specifically to the Father (1 Corinthians 8:6), to the Son (Colossians 1:16; Hebrews 1:2; John 1:3), or to the Holy Spirit (Job 26:13; 33:4; Psalm 104:30; Isaiah 40:12-13). Some people suggest that creation is *from* the Father, *through* the Son, and *by* the Holy Spirit (see 1 Corinthians 8:6).

20. God Is Elohim.

Elohim is a common name for God in the Old Testament. It occurs about 2570 times and literally means "strong one." Its plural ending (*im* in Hebrew) indicates fullness of power. The Old Testament portrays Elohim as the powerful and sovereign governor of the universe, ruling over the affairs of humankind. As related to God's sovereignty, the word Elohim describes him as the "God of all the earth" (Isaiah 54:5), the "God of all flesh" (Jeremiah 32:27 NASB), the "God of heaven" (Nehemiah 2:4), and the "God of gods and Lord of lords" (Deuteronomy 10:17).

21. Jehovah Is Not God's Only Name.

Contrary to the Jehovah's Witnesses, Scripture identifies God in other ways besides the name Jehovah. For example, it refers to God as Yahweh-Nissi, Elohim, El Shaddai, Adonai, and Lord of hosts. This shows that though God is Jehovah (or, more properly, Yahweh), he is also known by other names.

In New Testament times, Jesus never addressed God as Jehovah but rather referred to him as Father. Believers too are privileged to call God "Abba! Father"! (Romans 8:15; Galatians 4:6).

22. God Is a Trinity.

God is one, but the unity of the Godhead includes three coequal and coeternal persons—the Father, the Son, and the Holy Spirit, who are equal in divine nature but distinct in personhood.

Three lines of evidence support the doctrine of the Trinity:

1. Only one true God exists (Isaiah 44:6; 46:9; John 5:44; 17:3; Romans 3:29-30; 16:27; 1 Corinthians 8:4; Galatians 3:20; Ephesians 4:6; 1 Timothy 2:5; and James 2:19).

2. Three persons are God—the Father (1 Peter 1:2), the Son (Hebrews 1:8), and the Holy Spirit (Acts 5:3-4).

3. The Godhead has three-in-one-ness (see Matthew 28:19, which subsumes "the Father," "the Son," and "the Holy Spirit" under a singular "name" of God) (see also 2 Corinthians 13:14).

23. The Trinity Is Not a Pagan Idea.

The doctrine of the Trinity did not derive from paganism. The Babylonians and Assyrians believed in triads of gods who headed up a pantheon of many other gods. These triads constituted three separate gods (polytheism). This is utterly different from the doctrine of the Trinity, which maintains that within the Godhead is only one God (monotheism) with three persons.

24. Modalism Is False.

Modalism views the Father, Son, and Holy Spirit not as persons but as modes of manifestation of the one God. The New Testament refutes this heresy by portraying all three persons in the New Testament together (Matthew 28:19; 2 Corinthians 13:14). Moreover, we read that the Father sent the Son (John 3:17). The Father and Son love each other (John 14:31). The Father speaks to the Son, and the Son speaks to the Father (John 11:41-42). The Holy Spirit comes upon Jesus at the baptism (Matthew 3:16). Jesus and the Father sent the Holy Spirit (John 15:26). Clearly these are distinct persons who interact with each other.

25. God Alone Is to Be Worshipped.

We are to worship God alone (Matthew 4:10; Acts 14:11-18; Revelation 19:10). The Hebrew word for worship, *shaha*, means "to bow down" or "to prostrate oneself" (see Genesis 22:5; 42:6). Likewise, the New Testament word for worship, *proskuneo*, means "to prostrate oneself" (see Matthew 2:2,8,11). In Old English, "worship" was rendered "worthship," pointing to the worthiness of the one and only true God. Such worship is the proper response of a creature to the glorious Creator (Psalm 95:6).

26. Pantheism Is False.

A pantheistic view of God has many problems:

* It destroys all distinctions between creation (finite) and the Creator (infinite). Biblically, God is eternally distinct from what he created (Hebrews 11:3; see also Genesis 1:1; Psalm 33:8-9).

* Pantheism contradicts common sense. If all is truly God, then no difference exists between myself and anything else in the world.

* Pantheism fails to adequately deal with the existence of real evil in the world. If all is God, then both good and evil stem from one and the same essence (God).

* The pantheistic God is an impersonal force, not a personal Being with whom we can establish relationships (see Mark 14:36; Galatians 4:6).

27. Polytheism Is False.

Polytheism is unbiblical. Scripture consistently testifies that only one true God exists. God himself positively affirmed through Isaiah the prophet, "I am the first and I am the last; apart from me there is no God" (Isaiah 44:6; see also 37:20; 43:10; 45:5,14,21-22). God later said, "I am God, and there is no other; I am God, and there is none like me" (46:9; see also Deuteronomy 6:4; 32:39; 2 Samuel 7:22). The New Testament also emphasizes the oneness of God (John 5:44; 17:3; Romans 3:29-30; 16:27; Galatians 3:20; Ephesians 4:6; 1 Thessalonians 1:9; 1 Timothy 1:17; 2:5; 1 John 5:20; Jude 25).

28. Atheism Is False.

A pivotal problem for atheists is that they cannot possibly know from *their own experience* that no God exists. They would have to be omniscient (all-knowing) to be able to say from their own pool of knowledge that God does not exist anywhere in the universe.

Some atheists claim the problem of evil proves God does not exist. Scripture, however, reveals that God has allowed evil for a purpose (1 Peter 1:6-9)—much like I have a purpose in allowing my son and daughter to experience the "evil" of going to the dentist (there is a "good" I am ultimately bringing about). See my book *Why Do Bad Things Happen If God Is Good?* (Harvest House Publishers).

Many atheists give evidence of severe moral problems in their lives. Their atheistic view gives them a false sense of security, ignoring the fact that they must answer to a moral law-giver.

29. God's Name Is Not Jabulon.

The Masonic claim that God's true name is Jabulon—combining "Ja" (for Jehovah), "Bul" (for Baal), and "On" (for Osiris)—is atrocious and highly offensive. Attempting to relate the God of the Bible with Baal is nothing less than blasphemy. Baal worship is the epitome of evil idol worship in the ancient world and included such things as ritual prostitution (Judges 2:17), self-mutilation (1 Kings 18:28), and sacrificing (ritually murdering) little children (Jeremiah 19:4-5). In Judges 3:7 we read, "The Israelites did evil in the eyes of the LORD; they forgot the LORD their God and served the Baals and the Asherahs." From this, we can easily surmise that the Masonic view that God is Jabulon is detestable to the Lord.

Jesus Christ

30. Jesus Is God.

A comparison of the Old and New Testaments provides powerful testimony to Jesus' identity as Yahweh (God Almighty). For example, the Old Testament indicates that *only* God is Savior (Isaiah 43:11), yet the New Testament calls Jesus Savior (Titus 2:13-14). The Old Testament indicates that *only* God is Creator (Isaiah 44:24), yet the New Testament calls Jesus Creator (John 1:3; Colossians 1:16). Likewise, God's glory in the Old Testament (Isaiah 6:1-5) is equated with Jesus' glory in the New Testament (John 12:41).

The New Testament applies divine names like Yahweh and Elohim to Jesus (see Isaiah 40:3; compare with Mark 1:24). Moreover, as Yahweh gives and preserves life in Old Testament times (Psalm 119:25,37,40, 50,88,93,107,149,154,156,159), so Jesus does in New Testament times (John 5:21). As Yahweh's voice is "like the roar of rushing waters" (Ezekiel 43:2), so the same is true of the glorified Jesus (Revelation 1:15).

Further, people worshipped Jesus on many occasions (Matthew 2:11; 8:2; 9:18; 15:25; 28:9; John 9:38; Hebrews 1:6). That Jesus willingly received (and condoned) worship on various occasions says a lot about his true identity, for Scripture says we are to worship God alone (Exodus 34:14).

31. Jesus Is Omniscient.

The apostle John said that Jesus "did not need man's testimony about man, for he knew what was in a man" (John 2:25). Jesus' disciples said, "Now we can see that you know all things" (16:30). After the resurrection, when Jesus asked Peter for the third time if Peter loved him, Peter responded: "Lord, you know all things; you know that I love you" (21:17). Jesus knew just where the fish were in the water (Luke 5:4,6; John 21:6-11), and he knew just which fish contained the coin (Matthew 17:27). He knows the Father as the Father knows him (Matthew 11:27; John 7:29; 8:55; 10:15; 17:25). Jesus is omniscient!

32. Jesus Is Not Lesser than the Father.

Though cults often cite a barrage of biblical verses to "prove" Jesus is lesser than the Father, in each case they misinterpret the passage in question:

* Isaiah 9:6 refers to Jesus as "mighty God," but this does not mean he is a lesser God than God Almighty, for Yahweh is also called "mighty God" in Isaiah 10:21 (NASB).

* John 3:16 makes reference to Jesus as the "Son of God," but this title indicates that Jesus has the same divine nature as the Father (see John 5:18). Among the ancients, "Son of" indicated "Same nature as."

* John 14:28 portrays Jesus saying the Father is greater than him, but he was only speaking positionally (the Father was in heaven, and Jesus was on earth about to be crucified).

* Colossians 1:15 (NASB) calls Jesus the "firstborn," but this phrase throughout the Bible indicates preeminence. In the present case, Jesus is *preeminent* over creation (verse 15) because he *created* the creation (verse 16).

* Mark 13:32 indicates Jesus does not know the hour of his return, but Jesus was speaking only from his human nature. Christ in his divine nature *is* omniscient (see Matthew 11:27; 17:27; Luke 5:4,6; John 7:29; 8:55; 10:15; 16:30; 17:25; 21:17; 21:6-11). To fulfill his messianic mission on earth, Jesus voluntarily chose *not* to use some of his divine attributes on some occasions.

33. Jesus Is the Son of God.

Ancient Near Eastern people used the phrase "Son of" to indicate *likeness or sameness of nature* and *equality of being*. When Jesus claimed to be the Son of God, his Jewish contemporaries fully understood that he was making a claim to be God in an unqualified sense. The Jews insisted, "We have a law, and according to that law he [Christ] must die, because he claimed to be the Son of God" (John 19:7; see also 5:18). Recognizing that Jesus was identifying himself as God, the Jews wanted to kill him for committing blasphemy.

Scripture indicates that Christ's Sonship is an *eternal* Sonship. In keeping with this, Hebrews 1:2 says God created the universe *through* his "Son"—implying that Christ was the Son of God prior to the creation. Moreover, Christ *as* the Son existed "before all things" (Colossians 1:17; see verses 13,14). As well, Jesus, speaking as the Son of God (John 8:54-56), asserts his eternal preexistence before Abraham (verse 58).

34. Jesus Is the Christ.

Jesus *alone* is the Christ. Jesus did not *become* the Christ as an adult but rather was the *one and only* Christ from the very beginning (see Luke 2:11). John's first epistle thus warns us, "Who is the liar? It is the man who denies that Jesus is the Christ. Such a man is the antichrist" (1 John 2:22).

The Old Testament presents hundreds of prophecies regarding the coming of a single Messiah (for example, Isaiah 7:14; 53:3-5; Micah 5:2; Zechariah 12:10). The New Testament counterpart for "Messiah" is "Christ" (see John 1:41). Jesus alone fulfilled these hundreds of prophecies, and therefore, he alone is the Christ.

Notice that when the New Testament acknowledges Jesus as the Christ, Jesus never said, "You too have the Christ within." Instead he warned that others would come falsely claiming to be the Christ (Matthew 24:5).

35. Jesus Is the Savior.

The Old Testament indicates that only God is Savior (Isaiah 43:11). The New Testament refers to Christ as the Savior (Luke 2:11; John 4:42), revealing his divine nature.

In Titus 2:13 Paul encourages Titus to await the blessed hope, the "glorious appearing of our great God and Savior, Jesus Christ." Notice that in Titus 2:10-13; 3:4; and 3:6; the phrases *God our Savior* and *Jesus our Savior* are used interchangeably four times.

Related to this is the fact that Jesus placed himself on an equal par with the Father as the proper object of men's trust. Jesus told the disciples: "Do not let your hearts be troubled. Trust in God; trust also in me" (John 14:1). Had Jesus not been God, this would have been blasphemy.

36. Jesus Is the Only Way.

Speaking of Jesus, Peter proclaimed: "Salvation is found in no one else, for there is no other name under heaven given to men by which we must be saved" (Acts 4:12). The apostle Paul affirmed, "There is one God and one mediator between God and men, the man Christ Jesus" (1 Timothy 2:5). Jesus himself said, "I am the way and the truth and the life. No one comes to the Father except through me" (John 14:6). Jesus also warned his followers about those who would try to set forth a different "Christ" (Matthew 24:4-5). Truly Jesus is the *only* way of salvation.

37. Jesus Is Unique.

Scripture portrays Jesus as completely unique. The Greek word that

John 3:16 uses to describe Jesus ("God's *only begotten* son") is *mono-genes,* meaning "unique" or "one of a kind." Jesus is uniquely God's Son because, like the Father, Jesus is God by nature. John F. Walvoord notes that "the thought is clearly that Christ is the Begotten of God in the sense that no other is."[2] Benjamin Warfield comments, "The adjective 'only begotten' conveys the idea, not of derivation and subordination, but of uniqueness and consubstantiality: Jesus is all that God is, and He alone is this."[3] Further, Jesus proved the veracity of all he said by rising from the dead (Acts 17:31). None of the other leaders of the different world religions ever did that (Romans 1:4).

38. Jesus Was Sinless.

Scripture consistently portrays Jesus as being sinless. When Judas betrayed Jesus, he admitted that he had "betrayed innocent blood" (Matthew 27:4). Jesus has "nothing false" in him (John 7:18), and he always did what pleased the Father (John 8:29). Jesus challenged Jewish leaders, "Can any of you prove me guilty of sin?" (John 8:46). The apostle Paul referred to Jesus as "him who had no sin" (2 Corinthians 5:21). Jesus is one who "loved righteousness and hated wickedness" (Hebrews 1:9). He "was without sin" (Hebrews 4:15) and was "holy, blameless, [and] pure" (Hebrews 7:26). "He committed no sin, and no deceit was found in his mouth" (1 Peter 2:22). Indeed, "in him is no sin" (1 John 3:5).

39. Jesus Performed Miracles.

Scripture often refers to the miracles of Jesus as "signs" (John 4:54; 6:14; 9:16). Jesus performed these signs to *signify* his true identity and glory as the divine Messiah.

John's Gospel tells us that Jesus performed signs in the presence of his disciples, ensuring an adequate witness to the events that transpired (John 20:30). The signs Jesus performed are thoroughly attested.

The Gospels record Jesus performing 35 separate miracles. Of these, Matthew mentioned 20; Mark, 18; Luke, 20; and John, 7. But these are only a selection from among many that he did (Matthew 4:23-24; 11:4-5; 21:14). Scripture records the miracles or signs "that you may believe that Jesus is the Christ, the Son of God" (John 20:31).

40. Jesus Atoned for Sin.

Jesus affirmed that he came into the world for the very purpose of dying (John 12:27). Moreover, he knew his death was a sacrificial offering for the sins of humanity (he said his blood "is poured out for many for the forgiveness of sins," Matthew 26:26-28). Jesus took his sacrificial mission with utmost seriousness, for he knew that without him, humanity would certainly perish (Matthew 16:25; John 3:16) and spend eternity apart from God in a place of great suffering (Matthew 10:28; 11:23; 23:33; 25:41; Luke 16:22-31). Jesus therefore described his mission this way: "The Son of Man did not come to be served, but to serve, and to give his life a ransom for many" (Matthew 20:28).

41. Jesus Was Not a Mere Moral Teacher.

No mere moral teacher would ever claim that the destiny of the world lay in his hands, or that people would spend eternity in heaven or hell depending on whether they believed in him (John 6:26-40). C.S. Lewis said that "a man who was merely a man and said the sort of things Jesus said would not be a great moral teacher. He would either be a lunatic—on the level with the man who says he is a poached egg—or else he would be the Devil of Hell."[4] Certainly for Jesus to convince people that he was God (John 8:58) and the Savior of the world (Luke 19:10) when he was really a mere man would be the ultimate immorality.

42. Jesus Was Not the Archangel Michael.

Colossians 1:16 tells us Christ created all of the angels. Therefore, Jesus cannot be an angel.

Daniel 10:13 calls Michael "one of the chief princes." He is one among a group of chief princes, and is hence not unique. By contrast, Jesus is unique (John 3:16) and is the "KING OF KINGS AND LORD OF LORDS" (Revelation 19:16).

Moreover, Hebrews 1:5 tells us that no angel can ever be called God's son. Jesus is the Son of God, so Jesus cannot possibly be the archangel Michael.

Further, Hebrews 2:5 says the world is not (and will not be) in subjection to an angel. The Bible repeatedly calls Christ the ruler of God's kingdom, so he cannot be the archangel Michael (Luke 1:32-33; Matthew 2:1-2; Revelation 19:16).

Finally, Michael does not have the authority to rebuke Satan (Jude 9), whereas Jesus often does so (for example, Matthew 17:18; Mark 9:25). Therefore, Jesus cannot be Michael.

43. Jesus Was Not the Spirit-Brother of Lucifer.

Colossians 1:16 tells us that Jesus created the entire angelic realm—including Lucifer. Jesus and Lucifer are therefore of two different classes: One is the Creator, and the other is a created being.

The focus of the first three chapters of the book of Hebrews is to demonstrate the superiority of Jesus Christ, including his superiority over the prophets (1:1-3), over the angels (1:4–2:18), and over Moses (3:1-6). How is this superiority demonstrated? Christ is God's ultimate revelation (1:1), he is the Creator and Sustainer of the universe (1:2-3), and he has the very nature of God (1:3). None of these things is true of mere creatures—prophets, angels, or Moses.

44. Jesus Is Not the Father.

Jesus relates to the Father as someone *other* than himself more than 200 times in the New Testament. More than 50 times in the New Testament, the Father and Son are distinct within the same verse (for example, Romans 15:6; 2 Corinthians 1:3; Galatians 1:1,3; Philippians 2:10-11; 1 John 2:1; 2 John 3).[5]

Scripture indicates that the Father sent the Son (John 3:16-17), the Father and Son love each other (John 3:35), and the Father and Son speak to each other (John 11:41-42). Moreover, the Father knows the Son, and the Son knows the Father (Matthew 11:27). Jesus is our advocate with the Father (1 John 2:1). Clearly the Father and Son are two distinct persons.

45. Jesus Is Not the Holy Spirit.

Jesus is not the Holy Spirit. Scripture indicates that the Holy Spirit descended upon Jesus at his baptism (Luke 3:22). The Holy Spirit is another comforter (John 14:16). Jesus sent the Holy Spirit (John 15:26). And the Holy Spirit seeks to glorify Jesus (John 16:14). These facts show that Jesus is not the Holy Spirit, as Oneness Pentecostals say he is. Jesus and the Holy Spirit are two distinct persons.

46. Jesus Did Not Go East.

Jesus did not go to India as a child, but rather grew up in Nazareth (Luke 4:16). During these years, he studied the Old Testament, as did other Jewish boys his age (see Luke 2:52).

Upon reaching adulthood, Jesus was well-known in his community as a long-standing carpenter (Mark 6:3) and as a carpenter's son (Matthew 13:55). This would not be the case had Jesus just returned from India. Luke 4:22 clearly shows the local community's familiarity with Jesus.

Others were offended that Jesus was attracting so much attention, and they treated him with a contempt born of familiarity (Matthew 13:54-57). These people seem to be thinking: "We've known Jesus since he was a child, and now, he's standing before us claiming to be the Messiah. What nerve and audacity he has!" They would not have responded this way if they hadn't had regular contact with him for a prolonged time.

Among those who became angriest at Jesus were the Jewish leaders. They accused him of many offenses, but they never accused him of teaching or practicing anything learned in the East. Had Jesus actually gone to India to study under gurus, the Jews could have easily refuted his claim to be the promised Jewish Messiah. If the Jewish leaders could have accused Jesus of this, they certainly would have.

47. The Incarnate Jesus Had Two Natures.

Before the incarnation, Jesus was one person with one nature (a divine nature). After the incarnation, Jesus was still one person, but now he had two natures—a divine nature and a human nature.

One Person. Though Jesus in the incarnation had both a human and a divine nature, he was only one person—as indicated by his consistent use of "I," "me," and "mine" in reference to himself. Jesus never used the words "us," "we," or "ours" in reference to his human-divine person.

Two Natures. Christ's two natures are distinct. This is one of the most complex aspects of the relationship of Christ's two natures. The Bible never attributes the characteristics of one nature to the other, yet it properly attributes the characteristics of both natures to his one person. Thus Christ at the same moment in time had what seem to be contradictory qualities. He was finite and yet infinite, weak and yet omnipotent, increasing in knowledge and yet omniscient.

The Human-Divine Union Lasts Forever. When Christ became a man in the incarnation, he did not enter into a temporary union of the human and divine natures in one person that ended at his death and resurrection. Rather, the Scriptures make clear that Christ's human nature continues forever (see, for example, Acts 1:11; Matthew 26:64).

48. Jesus Died on a Cross.

The Jehovah's Witnesses' view that Jesus was crucified not on a cross but on a stake is in error. The Greek word in question *(stauros)* can refer to a variety of wooden structures used for execution in ancient days. The term can refer to a structure that looks like the Greek letter *tau* (T), the plus sign (+), two diagonal beams (X), or, infrequently, an upright stake. The Jehovah's Witnesses are guilty of grossly restricting the term to its most infrequent meaning.

The Romans used "nails" (plural) at Christ's crucifixion (John 20:25), one for each hand. (One would have sufficed for a stake.) They placed a sign saying "King of the Jews" above Jesus' head, not above His hands (Matthew 27:37).

Tradition tells us that Peter similarly died by crucifixion, and John 21:18-19 tells us that his arms were outstretched. This would not be possible on a stake.

49. Jesus Completed the Work of Salvation.

Jesus completed the work of redemption at the cross. On the cross he uttered, "It was finished" (John 19:30). This proclamation is fraught with meaning. The Lord was doing more than announcing the termination of his physical life. That fact was self-evident. He was announcing that God through Christ had completed the final sacrifice for sin. The work that prophets and saints had long contemplated, long promised, and long expected was *done* (Isaiah 53:3-5; Zechariah 12:10). He paid in *full* the price of our redemption (2 Corinthians 5:21). By his death "we have been sanctified through the offering of the body of Jesus Christ once for all" (Hebrews 10:10 NASB). And "when He had made purification of sins,

He sat down at the right hand of the Majesty on high" (Hebrews 1:3 NASB), where he remains to this day.

50. Jesus Physically Rose from the Dead.

Jesus physically and bodily rose from the dead, as the following facts show:

* The resurrected Christ said, "See My hands and My feet, that it is I Myself; touch Me and see, for a spirit does not have flesh and bones as you see that I have" (Luke 24:39 NASB). Notice three things here: (1) The resurrected Christ indicates in this verse that he is not a spirit, (2) the resurrected Christ indicates that his resurrection body is made up of flesh and bones, and (3) Christ's physical hands and feet represent physical proof of the materiality of his resurrection from the dead.

* Jesus told the Jews: "'Destroy this temple, and I will raise it again in three days.' The Jews replied, 'It has taken forty-six years to build this temple, and you are going to raise it in three days?' But the temple he had spoken of was his body" (John 2:19-21).

* The resurrected Christ ate physical food on four different occasions. He did this to prove that he had a real, physical body (Luke 24:30; 24:42-43; John 21:12-13; Acts 1:4).

* Different people touched and handled the physical body of the resurrected Christ (Matthew 28:9; Luke 24:39; John 20:17).

* The body that is "sown" in death is the very same body that is raised in life (1 Corinthians 15:35-44).

* The Greek word for "body" (soma), when used of a person, without exception means physical body in the New Testament. We must understand all references to Jesus' resurrection "body" (soma) in the New Testament to mean a resurrected physical body.

51. Jesus Will Return at the Second Coming.

The very same Jesus who ascended into heaven will come again at the second coming. In Acts 1:11 some angels appeared to Christ's disciples (after the ascension) and said to them, "Men of Galilee, why do you stand here looking into the sky? *This same Jesus,* who has been taken from you into heaven, will come back in the same way you have seen him go into heaven" (italics added).

This second coming will be a visible, physical, bodily coming of the glorified Jesus. Every eye will see him (Revelation 1:7). The New Testament uses the Greek word *epiphaneia* for Christ's Second Coming. It carries the basic meaning of "to appear," "to shine forth." In Titus 2:13 (NASB), Paul speaks of "looking for the blessed hope and the *appearing* of the glory of our great God and Savior, Christ Jesus."

52. Jesus' Death Does Not Detract from His Deity.

The Greek word for death *(thanatos)* conveys the idea of separation. When a person physically dies, his immaterial nature (soul and spirit) separates from his physical body. When Jesus died on the cross, the divine person with his divine nature *and* with his human immaterial nature (soul and spirit) departed from his human body. At the resurrection, Christ's real self, including his divine nature and his immaterial human nature, were joined to the same physical body in which he died, now immortal and incorruptible. Jesus' death on the cross therefore does not detract from his deity.

53. Jesus' Temptation Is Not Incompatible with His Deity.

The fact that Jesus was tempted is not a proof against his full deity, as some cultists allege. In the incarnation, Jesus took on an additional nature—a *human* nature. It was *in his humanity* that he experienced temptation, distress, weakness, pain, sorrow, and limitation. Because he was also fully God, however, the temptation stood no chance of success. As the God-man, Christ could not have sinned.

* In his divine nature, he is *immutable* and does not change.
* In his divine nature, he is *omniscient,* knowing all the consequences of sin.
* In his divine nature, he is *omnipotent* in his ability to resist sin.
* Hebrews 4 tells us that he was tempted yet was *without* sin.

     * Christ had no sin nature like all other human beings and was perfectly holy from birth (Luke 1:35).

This does not mean Christ's temptations were unreal. Christ was genuinely tempted, but the temptations stood no chance of luring Christ to sin. They had as much potential as a canoe trying to attack a battleship. The attack is genuine, but it stands no chance of success.

54. Jesus' Praying Is Not Incompatible with His Deity.

The fact that Jesus prayed to the Father does not mean he is not fully God, as some cultists have claimed. In the incarnation, Christ took on a human nature. Christ prayed in his humanity to the Father. Christ came as man, and one of the proper duties of man is to worship, pray to, and adore God, so for Jesus to address the Father in prayer was perfectly proper. As a man, as a Jew, and as our high priest ("made like his brothers in every way," Hebrews 2:17), Jesus could pray to the Father. But this in no way detracts from his intrinsic deity.

55. Jesus Was Not Spineless.

Contrary to Satanists, who argue that Jesus was a spineless wimp, Jesus showed the greatest act of courage known in human history: dying on a common criminal's cross and taking upon himself the sins of all humanity (John 15:13; 1 John 3:16). As well, during his three-year ministry, Jesus took an unbending stance against the most powerful religious men of his day—the Pharisees, the Scribes, and the Sadducees. Not once did Jesus retract or take back anything he said to them. Certainly all human beings will receive abundant evidence of a conquering Christ at his visible, bodily, and glorious second coming (Revelation 19:11-16).

56. Christians Should Pray in Jesus' Name.

We are to pray to God in the name of Jesus Christ. Jesus said, "You may ask me for anything in my name, and I will do it" (John 14:14; see also John 15:16). Jesus also said, "I tell you the truth, my Father will give you whatever you ask in my name. Until now you have not asked for anything in my name. Ask and you will receive, and your joy will be complete" (John 16:23-24). The reason we are to pray in the name of Jesus Christ is that Jesus is the one and only mediator between God and man (1 Timothy 2:5). To leave Jesus out of the equation is to cut oneself off from God.

The Holy Spirit

57. The Holy Spirit Is a Person.

The three primary attributes of personality are mind, emotions, and will.

The Holy Spirit Has a Mind. Romans 8:27 (NASB) tells us that just as the Holy Spirit knows the things of God, so God the Father knows "what the mind of the Spirit is."

The Holy Spirit Has Emotions. Ephesians 4:30 admonishes us, "Do not grieve the Holy Spirit of God." Grief is an emotion.

The Holy Spirit Has a Will. First Corinthians 12:11 (NASB) tells us that the Holy Spirit distributes spiritual gifts "to each one individually just as He wills."

The Holy Spirit's Works Confirm His Personality. The Holy Spirit does things only a person can do—such as teaching believers (John 14:26), testifying (John 15:26), commissioning people to service (Acts 13:4), issuing commands to believers (Acts 8:29), and interceding for believers (Romans 8:26).

The objection that the Holy Spirit's lack of a name indicates that the Spirit is not a person shows faulty reasoning. Scripture does not always name spiritual beings. Scripture rarely names evil spirits but identifies them by their character ("unclean," "wicked," and so forth—see Matthew 12:45). Likewise, by contrast, the Bible identifies the Holy Spirit by his character, which is holiness. Besides, the Holy Spirit is, in fact, related to the name of the other persons of the Trinity in Matthew 28:19.

The objection that since the Holy Spirit fills many people at the same time, the Spirit must not be a person but is rather a force (Acts 2:4) also shows faulty reasoning. Ephesians 3:19 speaks of God filling all the Ephesian believers. Ephesians 4:10 speaks of Christ filling all things, and Ephesians 1:23 (NASB) speaks of Christ as the one who "fills all in all." The Holy Spirit is a person every bit as much as the Father and Son are.

58. The Holy Spirit Is God.

Acts 5:3 indicates that lying to the Holy Spirit and lying to God are virtually equated. Further, 2 Corinthians 3:17-18 calls the Holy Spirit "Lord." The Bible often identifies the Holy Spirit with Yahweh (Acts 7:51; 28:25-27; 1 Corinthians 2:12; Hebrews 3:7-9; 10:15-17; 2 Peter 1:21) and speaks of him as divine (Matthew 12:32; Mark 3:29; 1 Corinthians 3:16; 6:19; Ephesians 2:22). As well, the Bible calls the Holy Spirit the "Spirit of God," thus indicating his full deity (Genesis 1:2; Exodus 31:3; Numbers 24:2; Job 33:4; Ezekiel 11:24; Romans 8:9; 8:14; 1 Corinthians 2:11,14; 1 Peter 4:14; 1 John 4:2). Further, the Holy Spirit has all the attributes of deity, such as omnipresence (Psalm 139:7), omniscience (1 Corinthians 2:10), omnipotence (Romans 15:19), holiness (John 16:7-14), and eternity (Hebrews 9:14).

59. The Spirit of Truth Is the Holy Spirit.

The "Spirit of truth" of John 16 is not Baha'u'llah or some other cultic leader; he is the Holy Spirit. Jesus clearly identifies the Spirit of truth as the Holy Spirit (see John 14:16-17,26). Jesus said almost 2000 years ago that his promise of the Holy Spirit would be fulfilled "in a few days" (Acts 1:5), not in the 1800s, when Baha'u'llah was born. The fulfillment came in Acts 2 on the Day of Pentecost. Moreover, Jesus said one function of the Holy Spirit would be to communicate Jesus' teaching, not replace his teachings with those of another prophet (John 16:14). Finally, Jesus said the Holy Spirit will "be with you forever" (John 14:16). Baha'u'llah lived 75 years and died in 1892. This hardly constitutes "forever."

Humanity

60. Man Is a Creature.

Contrary to the cultic view that man is divine, Scripture says man is a creature, created in the "image of God" (Genesis 1:26-27). Because man is a creature, he is intrinsically weak, helpless, and dependent upon God. In 2 Corinthians 3:5 the apostle Paul affirmed, "Not that we are competent in ourselves to claim anything for ourselves, but our competence *comes from God*" (italics added). In John 15:5 Jesus said, "I am the vine; you are the branches. If a man remains in me and I in him, he will bear much fruit; *apart from me you can do nothing*" (italics added). God wants humans to recognize they are finite creatures who are responsible to him, their Creator (Psalm 100:3). This recognition of creaturehood should lead to humility and a worshipful attitude (Psalm 95:6-7).

61. Man Is Both Material and Immaterial.

God created man with both a material *and* an immaterial nature (Ecclesiastes 12:7). Man has had a spirit and body from the very beginning (Genesis 2:7). The book of James indicates that the body without the spirit is dead (2:26). The Bible affirms that disembodied human spirits go either to heaven or Hades to await the future resurrection of the just and unjust (John 5:29), whereupon God will judge them (Matthew 25:31-32). Human beings are not complete again until the resurrection, when the body is reunited with the spirit (see 1 Corinthians 15).

62. Humans Are Not Divine.

If the essence of human beings is God, and if God is an infinite, changeless being, then how can man (if he is a manifestation of divinity) go through a changing process of enlightenment by which he discovers his divinity? The fact that a man comes to realize he is God proves that he is not God. If he were God, he would never have passed from a state of ignorance to a state of awareness as to his divinity.[6]

If people were divine, one would expect them to display qualities similar to God's. This seems only logical. However, when one compares humankind's attributes with God's (as set forth in Scripture), we find more than ample testimony for the truth of Paul's statement in Romans 3:23 that human beings "fall short of the glory of God." God is all-knowing (Matthew 11:21), but man is limited in knowledge (Job 38:4); God is all-powerful (Revelation 19:6), but man is weak (Hebrews 4:15); God is everywhere-present (Psalm 139:7-12), but man is confined to a single space at a time (John 1:50); God is holy (1 John 1:5), but even man's "righteous" deeds are as filthy garments before God (Isaiah 64:6); God is eternal (Psalm 90:2), but he created man at a point in time (Genesis 1:1,27); God is truth (John 14:6), but man's heart is deceitful above all else (Jeremiah 17:9); God is characterized by justice (Acts 17:31), but man is lawless (1 John 3:4; Romans 3:23); God is love (Ephesians 2:4-5), but man is plagued with numerous vices like jealousy and strife (1 Corinthians 3:3). If man is a god, one could never tell it by his attributes!

63. Humans Do Not Become Angels.

Christ directly created the angels as angels (Colossians 1:16). Psalm 8:5 indicates that human beings were made lower than the angels but shall be made higher than the angels in the afterlife (in heaven). Hebrews 12:22-23 (NASB) indicates that the "myriads of angels" are distinct from the "spirits of righteous men made perfect." First Corinthians 6:3 indicates that a time is coming when believers (in the afterlife) will judge the angels. As well, 1 Corinthians 13:1 draws a distinction between the languages of human beings and those of angels. Clearly, the Bible portrays human beings and angels as different classes of beings.

64. God Created All Races.

God created all races of man. All human beings are completely equal—equal in terms of their creation (Genesis 1:28), their sin problem (Romans 3:23), God's love for them (John 3:16), and God's provision of salvation for them (Matthew 28:19). The apostle Paul affirmed, "From one man he made every nation of men, that they should inhabit the whole earth; and he determined the times set for them and the exact places where they should live" (Acts 17:26). Moreover, Revelation 5:9 (NASB) tells us that God's redeemed will be from "every tribe and tongue and people and nation." Racial discrimination is completely wrong, for all human beings are equal in God's sight.

65. Cain Was Not the Offspring of Satan and Eve.

Genesis 4:1 flatly asserts that "Adam lay with his wife Eve, and she became pregnant and gave birth to Cain. She said, 'With the help of the LORD I have brought forth a man.'" Clearly, Adam and Eve were the biological parents of Cain. The serpent-seed theory (which says Cain was the offspring of Satan and Eve) is thus incorrect.

66. Anglo-Israelism Is Unbiblical.

The ten tribes of Israel (the Northern Kingdom) were never lost during or after the Assyrians brought them into exile in 722 BC. Archeology confirms that some of the Israelites in the ten tribes of the Northern Kingdom fled down to the Southern Kingdom of Judah just before the Assyrian onslaught. Further, by New Testament times all 12 tribes of Israel were clearly still known and in existence. This is why

James addressed his epistle "to the twelve tribes who are dispersed abroad" (James 1:1 NASB). This is also why the apostle Paul could speak of "the promise our twelve tribes are hoping to see fulfilled as they earnestly serve God day and night" (Acts 26:7). Moreover, Anna, the New Testament prophetess who recognized the infant Jesus as the divine Messiah, certainly knew she was of the tribe of Asher (Luke 2:36). The evidence is clear, then, that the tribes did not become lost.

Sin and Salvation

67. Humans Are Fallen in Sin.

Jesus taught that human beings have a grave sin problem that is altogether beyond their means to solve. He taught that human beings are by nature evil (Matthew 12:34; Luke 11:13) and that they are capable of great wickedness (Mark 7:20-23; Luke 11:42-52). He said human beings are utterly lost (Luke 19:10), are sinners (Luke 15:10), and are in need of repentance before a holy God (Mark 1:15; Luke 15:10).

Jesus often spoke of human sin with metaphors that illustrate the havoc sin can wreak in one's life. He described human sin as blindness (Matthew 15:14; 23:16-26), sickness (Matthew 9:12), slavery (John 8:34), and darkness (John 3:19-21; 8:12; 12:35-46). He also taught that this is a universal condition and that all people are guilty before God (see Luke 7:37-48). Moreover, he taught that a person is guilty of sin not only because of external acts but also because of inner thoughts (Matthew 5:28).

68. All Humans Are Infected by Sin (Original Sin).

Adam and Eve's sin did not just affect them in an isolated way. It affected the entire human race. Ever since then, every human being born into the world has been born in a state of sin. The apostle Paul said that "sin entered the world through one man, and death through sin, and in this way death came to all men, because all sinned" (Romans 5:12). Indeed, "through the disobedience of the one man the many were made sinners" (Romans 5:19; see also Psalm 51; 1 Corinthians 15:21-22). This is why Ephesians 2:3 says we are "by nature objects of wrath." Every one of us is born into this world with a sin nature.

69. The Fall Was Not Sexual.

No scriptural foundation exists for the perverted idea that the devil sexually seduced Eve so that they committed fornication in their spiritual bodies, as the Unification Church teaches. Further, Scripture never describes the sexual relationship between Adam and Eve as sinful. They fell by eating the forbidden fruit (Genesis 3:3,6). Moreover, Scripture nowhere indicates that Adam and Eve were supposed to mature to spiritual perfection before engaging in sexual union, as Reverend Moon claims. Following their creation, God instructed Adam and Eve to be fruitful and multiply (Genesis 1:28 NASB). God did not mention a waiting period.

70. The Law Cannot Save.

God did not give us the law as a means of attaining salvation. Romans 3:20 (NASB) emphasizes that "by the works of the Law no flesh will be justified in His sight." So why did God give us the law?

* God gave us the law to show us what sin is. The law also shows us the consequences if we do not measure up to those high standards.

* Another purpose of the law is to provoke sin all the more in human beings. Scripture indicates that the law was given to us so that "trespass [or sin] might increase" (Romans 5:20). God wants us to become so overwhelmed with the sin problem that we cannot deny its reality and our need for a Savior.

* Most important, the law is like a tutor that leads us to Christ (Galatians 3:24-25 NASB). The law does this by showing us our sin and then pointing us to the marvelous grace of Christ.

* Once we have "arrived" to Christ—trusting in him as our Savior—the law has done its job, and it no longer holds sway over us. For believers, "Christ is the end of the law so that there may be righteousness for everyone who believes" (Romans 10:4).

71. Salvation Is by Grace Through Faith.

The word "grace" literally means "unmerited favor." "Unmerited" means this favor cannot be earned. Grace refers to the undeserved, unearned favor of God. Romans 5:1-11 tells us that God gives his incredible grace to those who actually deserve the opposite—that is, condemnation.

Eternal life cannot be earned. It is a free gift of grace that comes as a result of believing in the Savior, Jesus Christ. Jesus said: "Truly, truly, I say to you, he who believes *has* eternal life" (John 6:47 NASB, italics added). "The *free gift of God* is eternal life in Christ Jesus our Lord" (Romans 6:23 NASB, italics added; see also Revelation 21:6). Titus 3:5 (NASB) tells us that God "saved us, not on the basis of deeds which we have done in righteousness, but according to His mercy."

The means of receiving the wonderful grace-package of salvation is by faith in Christ. Recall that in Acts 16:31 the jailer asked Paul and Silas how to be saved. They responded, "Believe in the Lord Jesus, and you will be saved." The jailer believed and immediately became saved. Close to 200 times in the New Testament salvation is said to be by faith alone (see, for example, John 3:15; 5:24; 11:25; 12:46; 20:31).

72. Salvation Involves Justification.

We become "justified" the moment we trust in Christ. Biblical justification is a singular and instantaneous event in which God judicially (legally) declares the believing sinner to be absolutely not guilty and absolutely righteous (Romans 3:25,28,30; 8:33-34; 1 John 1:7–2:2).

This legal declaration is external to man. It does not depend on man's personal level of righteousness. It does not hinge on anything that man does. It depends solely on God's declaration. It is a once-for-all judicial pronouncement that takes place the moment a sinner places faith in Christ. Even while the person is yet a sinner and is experientially not righteous, he is nevertheless righteous in God's sight because of forensic justification (Romans 3:25,28,30).

73. Universalism Is False.

Universalism, the idea that all people will be saved in the end, is a false doctrine. Certain passages—John 12:32; Philippians 2:11; and 1 Timothy 2:4—are typically twisted out of context in support of this viewpoint. Such passages, interpreted properly, do not support universalism.

* John 12:32 says that Christ's work on the cross makes possible the salvation of both Jews and Gentiles. Notice, however, that the Lord—in the same passage—warned of judgment of those who reject Christ (verse 48).

* Philippians 2:10-11 assures us that someday all people will acknowledge that Jesus is Lord, but not necessarily as Savior. (Even those in hell will have to acknowledge Christ's Lordship.)

* First Timothy 2:4 expresses God's desire that all be saved but does not promise that all will be. This divine desire is only realized in those who exercise faith in Christ (Acts 16:31).

In Matthew 13:49 Jesus said, "This is how it will be at the end of the age. The angels will come and separate the wicked from the righteous." He mentions two classes—unbelievers and believers, the wicked and the righteous. Likewise, in Matthew 25:32 Jesus said that following his second coming, "All the nations will be gathered before him, and he will separate the people one from another as a shepherd separates the sheep from the goats." Jesus differentiates between believers and unbelievers by the terms "sheep" and "goats." The sheep will enter into God's kingdom (verse 34) and inherit eternal life (verse 46). The goats go into eternal punishment (verse 46).

74. Tongues Is Not Necessary for Salvation.

Speaking in tongues is not necessary for salvation. The Holy Spirit bestows spiritual gifts on believers (1 Corinthians 12:11), and he does not give every Christian the same gift. We can derive from Scripture a number of scriptural facts about speaking in tongues:

* Speaking in tongues is not an evidence of the baptism of the Holy Spirit. Not all the Corinthians spoke in tongues (1 Corinthians 14:5), but they had all been baptized (12:13).

* The fruit of the Holy Spirit (Galatians 5:22-23) does not include speaking in tongues. Therefore, Christlikeness does not require speaking in tongues.

* Most of the New Testament writers are silent on tongues. Only three books (Acts, 1 Corinthians, and Mark) mention it. (Note that Mark 16:17 is not in the two best Greek manuscripts.)

Significantly, many of the other New Testament books speak a great deal about the Holy Spirit but fail to even mention speaking in tongues.

* Other gifts are more important than tongues, and believers are to seek them (1 Corinthians 12:28,31).

75. Baptism Is Not Necessary for Salvation.

Baptism is not required for salvation. The apostle Paul stated, "For Christ did not send me to baptize, but to preach the gospel—not with words of human wisdom, lest the cross of Christ be emptied of its power" (1 Corinthians 1:17). Paul here draws a clear distinction between baptism and the gospel. Since the gospel saves (1 Corinthians 15:1-2), baptism is clearly not necessary to attain salvation.

That's not to say that baptism is unimportant. Baptism should be the first act of obedience to God following a person's conversion to Christ. But even though we should obey God and get baptized, we must not forget that our faith in Christ is what saves us (Acts 16:31; John 3:16), not baptism. Baptism is a public profession of faith. It says to the whole world, "I am a believer in Christ and have identified my life with him."

Death and the Afterlife

76. Death Is Real.

The New Testament word for "death" carries the idea of separation. At the moment of physical death, man's spirit separates or departs from his body (2 Corinthians 5:8). This is why, when Stephen was being put to death by stoning, he prayed, "Lord Jesus, receive my spirit" (Acts 7:59). At the moment of death "the spirit returns to God who gave it" (Ecclesiastes 12:7). Verses such as these indicate that at death, the believer's spirit departs from the physical body and immediately goes into the presence of the Lord in heaven (Philippians 1:21). For the unbeliever, however, death holds grim prospects. At death, the unbeliever's spirit departs from the body and goes not to heaven but to a place of great suffering (Luke 16:19-31).

77. Heaven Is Real.

Heaven is the splendorous eternal abode of the righteous. The actual splendor of heaven far exceeds anything that we have yet experienced. As the apostle Paul said, "No eye has seen, no ear has heard, no mind has conceived what God has prepared for those who love him" (1 Corinthians 2:9).

Revelation 2:7 makes reference to heaven as the "paradise of God." The word "paradise" literally means "garden of pleasure" or "garden of delight." The apostle Paul in 2 Corinthians 12:4 said he was "caught up to paradise" and "heard inexpressible things, things that man is not permitted to tell." Apparently this paradise of God is so resplendently glorious, so ineffable, so wondrous, that Paul was forbidden to say anything about it to those still in the earthly realm.

This wondrous abode is also called the holy city (Revelation 21:2), the home of righteousness (2 Peter 3:13), and the kingdom of light (Colossians 1:12). It will be a perfect environment.

78. Hell Is Real.

Hell is a real place. But hell was not part of God's original creation, which he called "good" (Genesis 1:31). Hell was created later to accommodate the banishment of Satan and his fallen angels who rebelled against God (Matthew 25:41). Human beings who reject Christ will join Satan and his fallen angels in this infernal place of suffering. The Scriptures use a variety of words to describe the horrors of hell, including the lake of burning sulfur (Revelation 19:20; 20:14,15), eternal fire (Matthew 25:41), fiery furnace (Matthew 13:42), destruction (2 Thessalonians 1:8-9), and eternal punishment (Matthew 25:46). The greatest pain those in hell suffer is that they are forever excluded from the presence of God. If the presence of God brings ecstatic joy (Psalm 16:11), then the eternal absence of his presence will bring utter dismay.

79. Death, Disease, and Sin Are Real.

Simply saying that sin, sickness, and death are unreal—as Christian Science claims—does not make them so. During Mary Baker Eddy's declining years, she was under a doctor's care and received regular morphine injections to ease her pain, wore glasses, had teeth extractions, and eventually died, thus "giving the lie" to all she professed to believe and teach.[7] Her act of denying sin, sickness, and death was itself denied by her own life and death.

80. There Is Conscious Existence After Death.

Scripture indicates that human beings have an immaterial nature that consciously survives death. In Revelation 6:9-10 we read of "the souls of those who had been slain," and they are speaking to God (something that requires consciousness). In Philippians 1:21-23 the apostle Paul speaks of his desire to "depart" and be *with* Christ. In 2 Corinthians 5:6-8 Paul says that to be absent from the body is to be at home with the Lord. The souls of both believers and unbelievers are fully conscious between death and the future day of resurrection. Unbelievers are in conscious woe (see Luke 16:22-23; Mark 9:43-48; Revelation 19:20), while believers are in conscious bliss (Philippians 1:23).

81. Annihilationism Is False.

Matthew 25:46 clearly refutes annihilationism. It tells us that the wicked "will go away to eternal punishment, but the righteous to eternal life." The same word for "eternal" refers to the eternal life of the righteous and the conscious punishment of the wicked. The word comes from the adjective *aionion,* meaning "everlasting," "without end." The wicked will be consciously punished everlastingly and without end, not annihilated out of existence.

Notice that there are no degrees of annihilation. One is either annihilated or one is not. The Scriptures, by contrast, teach that the day of judgment will bring degrees of punishment (Matthew 10:15; 11:21-24; 16:27; Luke 12:47-48; John 16:22; Hebrews 10:29; Revelation 20:11-15; 22:12). The fact that people will suffer varying degrees of punishment in hell shows that the Bible does not teach annihilation or the extinction of consciousness. These are incompatible concepts. Moreover, one cannot deny that for one who is suffering excruciating pain, the extinction of his or her consciousness would actually be a blessing, not a punishment (see Luke 23:30; Revelation 9:6). Any honest seeker after truth must admit that one cannot define "eternal punishment" as an extinction of consciousness.

82. All People Will Be Resurrected.

Both believers and unbelievers will be resurrected from the dead. The resurrection bodies of believers will be specially suited to dwelling in heaven in the direct presence of God—the perishable will be made imperishable and the mortal will be made immortal (1 Corinthians 15:53). Just as the caterpillar has to be changed into a butterfly in order to inherit the air, so we have to be changed in order to inherit heaven. Once we are changed, we will be able to fellowship with God face-to-face.

Unbelievers are resurrected to judgment (John 5:28-29). The resurrection of unbelievers is described in Revelation 20:5-6,11-15. This is an awful spectacle. All the unsaved of all time will be resurrected at the end of Christ's millennial kingdom, judged at the great white throne judgment, and then be cast alive into the lake of fire (Revelation 20:11-15).

83. All People Will Face Judgment.

Both Christians and non-Christians will face a judgment.

Believers. Christians will stand before the judgment seat of Christ (Romans 14:10). God will examine each Christian's deeds done in the body (Psalm 62:12; Ephesians 6:7-8). He will weigh personal motives, intents of the heart, and spoken words (Jeremiah 17:10; 1 Corinthians 4:5). Believers will receive or lose rewards according to their faithfulness (1 Corinthians 3:1-10).

Unbelievers. The horrific judgment unbelievers face is the great white throne judgment, which leads to their banishment to the lake of fire (Revelation 20:11-15). Christ will be the divine judge of the unsaved dead of all time. The judgment takes place at the end of the millennial kingdom. Christ will judge unbelievers on the basis of their works (Revelation 20:12-13).

Angels and Demons

84. Satan Is a Fallen Angel.

God created Lucifer in a state of perfection (Ezekiel 28:12,15), and Lucifer remained perfect in his ways until iniquity was found in him. What was this iniquity? We read in verse 17, "Your heart became proud on account of your beauty, and you corrupted your wisdom because of your splendor." Lucifer was so impressed with his own beauty, intelligence, power, and position that he began to desire for himself the honor and glory that belonged to God alone. The sin that corrupted Lucifer was self-generated pride (see Isaiah 14:12-17). God rightfully judged this mighty angelic being: "I threw you to the earth" (Ezekiel 28:17).

85. Satan's Titles Reveal His Nature.

We learn much about Satan and his work by the various names and titles used of him.

* Satan is our *adversary* (1 Peter 5:8 NASB). Satan opposes us and stands against us in every way he can.

* Satan is *Beelzebub* (Matthew 12:24). This word literally means "lord of the flies," carrying the idea "lord of filth." He corrupts everything he touches.

* Satan is the *devil* (Matthew 4:1). This word carries the idea of "adversary" as well as "slanderer."

* Satan is the *evil one* (1 John 5:19). He opposes all that is good.

* Satan is the *father of lies* (John 8:44). Satan was the first and greatest liar.

* Satan is a *murderer* (John 8:44). This word literally means "man killer" (see 1 John 3:12,15).

* Satan is the *god of this age* (2 Corinthians 4:4). Satan is the head of the current evil age.

* Satan is a *roaring lion* (1 Peter 5:8). He is strong and destructive.

* Satan is the *tempter* (Matthew 4:3). His constant purpose is to incite man to sin.

86. Fallen Angels Hurt Believers.

* Satan tempts believers to sin (Ephesians 2:1-3; 1 Thessalonians 3:5).

* Satan tempts believers to lie (Acts 5:3).

* Satan tempts believers to commit sexually immoral acts (1 Corinthians 7:5).

* Satan hinders the work of believers (1 Thessalonians 2:18).

* Satan and demons wage war against believers (Ephesians 6:11-12).
* Satan sows tares among believers (Matthew 13:38-39).
* Satan incites persecutions against believers (Revelation 2:10).
* Demons hinder answers to the prayers of believers (Daniel 10:12-20).
* Satan plants doubt in the minds of believers (Genesis 3:1-5).
* Demons seek to instigate faction among believers (James 3:13-16).

87. Unbelievers Can Be Demon Possessed.

Demon possession involves a demon residing in a person to control and influence him or her. A demon-possessed person may manifest unusual, superhuman strength (Mark 5:2-4). He may act in bizarre ways such as going nude and living among tombs rather than in a house (Luke 8:27). He may engage in self-destructive behavior (Matthew 17:15; Mark 5:5).

Because the Holy Spirit perpetually indwells Christians (1 Corinthians 6:19), Christians cannot be demon possessed. They can be afflicted by demons externally but not internally. Christians have been delivered from Satan's domain (Colossians 1:13). "The one who is in you is greater than the one who is in the world" (1 John 4:4).

88. There Are Six Judgments Against Satan.

1. Satan was cast from his original position of privilege in heaven following his initial rebellion against God (Ezekiel 28:16).
2. He was judged in the Garden of Eden following his role in leading Adam and Eve into sin (Genesis 3:14-15).
3. He was judged at the cross (John 12:31).
4. He will be cast out of heaven in the middle of the future seven-year tribulation period (Revelation 12:13).
5. He will be confined in the abyss during the future 1000-year millennial kingdom over which Christ will rule (Revelation 20:2).

6. He will be cast into the lake of fire at the end of the millennial kingdom, where he will dwell for the rest of eternity (Revelation 20:10; Matthew 25:41).

89. Christians Should Test the Spirits.

Every book in the New Testament except Philemon has something to say about false teachers, false prophets, false gospels, and heresies. Jesus Himself sternly warned about false prophets (Matthew 7:15-23) and false Christs (Matthew 24:5). The apostle Paul warned of a different Jesus, a different spirit (2 Corinthians 11:4), false apostles (2 Corinthians 11:13-15), and those who preach "another gospel" (Galatians 1:8). First John 4:1 understandably urges believers to "test the spirits." Believers are to use Scripture to test all teachings from spirits (see Acts 17:11).

Church-Related Issues

90. The Mormon Church Is Not the Restored Church.

Church history is well preserved, and so we have an accurate picture not only of the teachings of the early church but also of the deviations from orthodoxy that took place, including Gnosticism, Arianism, and Sabellianism. If Mormonism were the restored church, then we would expect to find early evidence for such unique doctrines as the plurality of Gods, human beings becoming Gods, and God the Father having once been a man. But we do not find even a hint of any of these in ancient church history.

91. Christians Should Tithe as They Are Able.

Christians today are not under the Old Testament 10-percent tithe system. The New Testament supports giving by grace. We are to freely give as we have freely received. And we are to give as we are able (2 Corinthians 8:12). For some, this will mean less than 10 percent. For others whom God has materially blessed, this will mean much more than 10 percent.

The starting point for a right attitude toward giving is giving ourselves to the Lord. The early church is our example: "They gave themselves first to the Lord and then to us in keeping with God's will"

(2 Corinthians 8:5). Only when we have given ourselves to the Lord will we have a proper perspective on money (see Romans 12:1).

92. There Are Not Two Peoples of God.

The Bible does not present two peoples of God, one group of 144,000 with a heavenly destiny and another "large crowd" with an earthly destiny, as Jehovah's Witnesses teach. Jesus taught that *all* people should seek the kingdom and that whoever sought it would find it (Matthew 10:37-39). A heavenly destiny awaits *all* who believe in Christ, not just a select group of 144,000 (Ephesians 2:19; Philippians 3:20; Colossians 3:1; Hebrews 3:1; 12:22; 2 Peter 1:10-11). *All* who believe in Christ are "heirs" of the eternal kingdom (Galatians 3:29; 4:28-31; Titus 3:7; James 2:5). All believers will be together in one flock under one shepherd (John 10:16).

93. Baptism Is Trinitarian.

The idea of baptism "in the name of Jesus only" is based on a misinterpretation of Acts 2:38: "Repent and be baptized, every one of you, in the name of Jesus Christ for the forgiveness of your sins." The phrase "in the name of" in biblical times carried the meaning "by the authority of." Acts 2:38 indicates a baptism according to the authority of Jesus. Such a baptism makes sense in the context of Acts 2 because the Jews ("men of Judea," verse 14 NASB), to whom Peter was preaching, had rejected Christ as the Messiah. It is logical that Peter would call them to repent of their rejection of Jesus and publicly identify with him through baptism. However, a strict formulaic baptism "in the name of Jesus" for believers of all time is uncalled for. Jesus instructed that people be baptized in the name of the Father, the Son, and the Holy Spirit (Matthew 28:19).

94. The Mormon Priesthoods Are Unbiblical.

The New Testament does not include a single example of a believer ever being ordained to the Melchizedek priesthood. Hebrews 7:24 calls Jesus' Melchizedek priesthood "permanent" or "unchangeable." The *Theological Dictionary of the New Testament* tells us, "In the New Testament Hebrews 7:24 says that Christ has an eternal and imperishable priesthood, not just in the sense that it cannot be transferred to anyone else, but in the sense of 'unchangeable.' "[8] This, combined with the fact that Scripture asserts that the Aaronic priesthood has permanently passed away (Hebrews 7:11-12), renders the Mormon claim of a "restored priesthood" false.

Prophecy

95. All Messianic Prophecies Point to Jesus.

From Genesis to Malachi, the Old Testament abounds with anticipations of the coming Messiah. Numerous predictions—fulfilled to the "crossing of the *t*" and the "dotting of the *i*" in the New Testament—relate to his birth, life, ministry, death, resurrection, and glory. Jesus himself often indicated to listeners that he was the specific fulfillment of messianic prophecy:

* "This has all taken place that the writings of the prophets might be fulfilled" (Matthew 26:56).

* "Beginning with Moses and all the Prophets, he explained to them what was said in all the Scriptures concerning himself" (Luke 24:27).

* "Everything must be fulfilled that is written about me in the Law of Moses, the Prophets and the Psalms" (Luke 24:44).

* "If you believed Moses, you would believe me, for he wrote about me" (John 5:46).

* "Today this scripture is fulfilled in your hearing" (Luke 4:21).

Included in the hundreds of prophecies fulfilled in Jesus are his virgin birth (Isaiah 7:14), his birthplace of Bethlehem (Micah 5:2), his ministry of miracles (Isaiah 35:5-6), his being betrayed for 30 shekels (Zechariah 11:12), his crucifixion (Psalm 22:16; Isaiah 53:12), and his resurrection (Psalm 16:10; 22:1,4,18).

96. False Prophets Are Recognizable.

Deuteronomy 18:21-22 indicates that false prophets give false prophecies that do not come true. False prophets sometimes cause people to follow false gods or idols (Exodus 20:3-4; Deuteronomy 13:1-3), they often deny the deity of Jesus (Colossians 2:8-9), they sometimes deny the humanity of Jesus (1 John 4:1-2), they sometimes advocate abstaining from certain foods for spiritual reasons (1 Timothy 4:3-4), they sometimes deprecate marriage (1 Timothy 4:3), they often promote immorality (Jude 4-7), and they often encourage legalistic self-denial (Colossians 2:16-23). If a so-called prophet says anything that clearly contradicts any part of God's Word, his teachings are to be rejected (Acts 17:11; 1 Thessalonians 5:21).

97. Setting Prophetic Dates Is Foolish.

There are at least ten good reasons why Christians should avoid setting dates for eschatological events.

1. During the past 2000 years, those who have predicted and/or expected "the end" have been 100 percent wrong.

2. Those who succumb to the date-setting mentality may end up making harmful decisions for their lives (like joining a survivalist sect).

3. Christians who succumb to the date-setting mentality may end up damaging their faith when their expectations fail.

4. If one loses confidence in the prophetic portions of Scripture, biblical prophecy ceases to be a motivation to holiness (Titus 2:12-14).

5. Christians who succumb to the date-setting mentality may damage the faith of new and immature believers when predicted events fail to materialize.

6. Setting dates may lead to "prophetic agnosticism." People may believe that we can't be sure of what the future holds.

7. Date setters tend to be sensationalistic, and sensationalism is unbefitting to a follower of the Lord Jesus (Mark 13:32-37).

8. Christians who get caught up in the date-setting mentality can potentially do damage to the cause of Christ (humanists, skeptics, and atheists mock Christians in their date-setting).

9. Christians who succumb to the date-setting mentality may get sidetracked from their first priority—living righteously and in holiness in daily fellowship with the Lord Jesus Christ.

10. The timing of end-time events is completely in God's hands (Acts 1:7), and he hasn't given us the precise details.

Cultic Ideas and Occultism

98. Occultism Is Prohibited.

Deuteronomy 18:9-12 reveals that all forms of occultism are detestable to God. Exodus 22:18 instructs that sorceresses are to be put to death, a penalty that demonstrates how serious the sin of divination is. Leviticus 19:26 commands, "Do not practice divination or sorcery." In Acts 19:19 we read that many who converted to Christ in Ephesus rightly destroyed all their paraphernalia formerly used for occultism and divination.

99. Spiritism Is Prohibited.

Deuteronomy 18:10-11 is clear: "Let no one be found among you...who is a medium or spiritist or who consults the dead." Leviticus 19:31 instructs, "Do not turn to mediums or seek out spiritists, for you will be defiled by them." We read in Leviticus 20:27, "A man or woman who is a medium or spiritist among you must be put to death." In 1 Samuel 28:3 we read that Saul rightly "expelled the mediums and spiritists from the land." Later, we read that "Saul died because he was unfaithful to the Lord; he did not keep the word of the Lord, and even consulted a medium for guidance" (1 Chronicles 10:13).

100. Astrology Is Prohibited.

Astrology is strictly off-limits for the Christian. In Isaiah 47 we find a strong denunciation of astrologers and their craft. Verse 15 explicitly states that "each of them goes on in his error," and "there is not one that can save you." The book of Daniel confirms that astrologers lack true discernment and that the only source of accurate revelation is God Almighty (Daniel 2:2,10). Further, anything bordering on worship of heavenly bodies is strictly forbidden (Deuteronomy 4:19). As well, astrology is a form of occultism, and Scripture condemns occultism in all forms (Deuteronomy 18:9-12; 2 Kings 17:16-18; Jeremiah 10:2; Acts 7:42).

Aside from these biblical warnings against astrology, we should note several other problems:

* Different astrologers often give different interpretations even though they are looking at the same horoscope chart.

* Astrologers do not agree on the number of signs of the zodiac. Many say twelve, others say eight, or ten, or fourteen, or twenty-four. The number of signs influences how one interprets the data.

* What is the basis of authority in matters relating to astrology? Who definitively determines how many signs of the zodiac exist? How do we definitively know the meanings of the various planets? All this seems arbitrary.

* How do we explain the different experiences of twins? Consider Jacob and Esau as an example. If astrology were really true, why would we see so much difference in their lives?

* How do we explain disasters where many people of different zodiac signs experience the same fate (like a plane crash)?

* Scientific studies show a prediction failure rate of 90 percent or worse for astrologers.[9]

101. Witchcraft Is Prohibited.

No clearer denunciation of witchcraft exists than the warning contained in Deuteronomy 18:9-13, part of which says: "Let no one be found among you who...engages in witchcraft, or casts spells....Anyone who does these things is detestable to the LORD, and because of these detestable practices the LORD your God will drive out those nations before you." Witchcraft is prohibited!

102. Chanting Is Prohibited.

Chanting, or endless babbling, goes against the clear teachings of Scripture. In Jesus' instructions about prayer, he taught his followers: "And when you pray, do not keep on babbling like pagans, for they think they will be heard because of their many words" (Matthew 6:7). We find an example of such endless babbling in 1 Kings 18:26: "They called on the name of Baal from morning till noon. 'O Baal, answer us!' they shouted." The belief was that endless repetition of specific requests endeared the petitioner to God, and God would be obligated to answer.

Likewise, endless chanting, as proponents of Nichiren Shoshu Buddhism and other cults engage in, violates the spirit of these passages.

103. Reincarnation Is False.

* *Reincarnation is not fair.* Why is one punished by means of karma for something one cannot remember having done in a previous life?

* *Reincarnation does not work.* If karma progressively rids humanity of its selfish desires, why hasn't human nature improved noticeably after all the millennia of reincarnations?

* *Reincarnation makes one socially passive.* It teaches that one should not interfere with someone else's bad karma (bad circumstances).

* *Reincarnation is fatalistic.* The law of karma guarantees that whatever we sow in the present life, we will invariably reap in the next life. It works infallibly and inexorably. No grace!

* *Reincarnation is inconsistent with the Hindu/New Age worldview.* If all in the universe is "one" and all is God, how can individual souls reincarnate?

* *Reincarnation offers little to look forward to.* Absorption into Brahman (the Universal Soul) has little appeal when compared to the possibility of living eternally with the living and personal God (Revelation 22:1-5).

* *Reincarnation is unbiblical.* Each human being lives once as a mortal on earth, dies once, and then faces judgment (see Hebrews 9:27).

104. Mysticism Is Unreliable.

Mystical revelations are uncertain and are not a strong foundation for our knowledge of God. The Bible stresses the importance of objective, historical revelation. In John 1:18 we read, "No one has ever seen God, but God the One and Only [Jesus], who is at the Father's side, has made him known" (John 1:18). In the empirical world of ordinary sense perceptions, human beings saw and heard Jesus as God's ultimate revelation to humankind. No wonder Jesus said, "If you really knew me, you would know my Father as well" (John 14:7).

Those who place faith in mysticism seem blind to the possibility of spiritual deception. What if that which mystics assume to be genuine "god-consciousness" is in fact less than God or at worst Satan, the great impersonator of God and father of lies (John 8:44)?

105. Visualization Can Be Dangerous.

Man's imagination has been thoroughly marred by sin (Genesis 6:5; Romans 8:7; Ephesians 4:18). Visualizers are using faulty equipment. Moreover, visualization sessions can induce an altered state of consciousness that can have extremely dangerous consequences, including opening oneself up to demonic affliction and deeper involvement in occultism. John Ankerberg and John Weldon note that "books on visualization carry numerous anecdotes of how even the well-intentioned and seemingly non-occult use of visualization catapulted people into the New Age movement, psychic development, and/or spirit contact."[10]

106. Altered States of Consciousness Are Dangerous.

Altered states of consciousness are dangerous and can lead to harmful consequences. For example, some people have found Transcendental Meditation to be harmful.[11] Altered states of consciousness led to contact with spirits.[12] Moreover, some deep meditators have developed increased anxiety, confusion, and depression.[13] Too much deep meditation can hinder logical thought processes.[14] One researcher found that "as a person enters or is in an ASC [altered state of consciousness], he often experiences fear of losing his grip on reality, and losing his self-control."[15]

107. Idolatry Is Prohibited.

Idolatry is the worship of false gods and idols. Pagan nations typically believed in a plethora of gods, often represented as statues of human beings or animals. People bowed down to worship these images. Such idolatry was common to nations like the Babylonians, the Assyrians, the Philistines, and the Egyptians. Often these pagan nations believed the different gods were behind various aspects of the world of nature. To be successful in life, one must please these gods, or they would treat him cruelly.

Unlike the God of the Bible, who is just, holy, and righteous in all his dealings, the pagan deities of the Babylonians, Assyrians, Philistines, and Egyptians—often represented as human beings—typically act like human beings. They could love or they could hate, be merciful or be cruel, engage in a peaceful relationship or cause a fight. They could be just as fickle as humans. God consistently condemns idolatry in all its forms (Exodus 20:4; Leviticus 26:1; 2 Kings 9:22).

108. Eastern Meditation Is Prohibited.

Eastern forms of meditation are prohibited for at least three reasons. First, Eastern meditation's goal of transforming one's state of mind into a monistic ("all is one") if not an outright pantheistic ("all is God") outlook is in direct contradiction to the biblical view of the eternal distinction between God the Creator and his creatures (Isaiah 44:6-8; Hebrews 2:6-8). Second, Eastern meditation's goal is to provide the practitioner a way (if not *the* way) to ultimate truth and freedom through sheer human effort, thus advocating a form of self-salvation by works instead of what the Bible explicitly teaches (Ephesians 2:8-9). Third, such altered states of consciousness can open one up to spiritual affliction and deception by the powers of darkness.

Christians should practice biblical meditation. This involves objective contemplation and deep reflection on God's Word (Joshua 1:8) as well as his Person and faithfulness (Psalm 119; see also 19:14; 48:9; 77:12; 104:34; 143:5).

Truth

109. Relativism Is Illogical.

A relativistic view of truth is not logically satisfying. Is the statement "all truth is relative" *absolutely* true? Such a statement is self-defeating. Or is the statement *relatively* true? Such a statement is ultimately meaningless. In contrast to such a view, absolute truth and morals are grounded in the absolutely true and moral God of the Bible (1 Kings 17:24; Psalm 25:5; 43:3; 100:5; 119:30; John 1:17; 8:44; 14:17; 17:17;

2 Corinthians 6:7; Ephesians 4:15; 6:14; 2 Timothy 2:15; 1 John 3:19; 3 John 4,8).

110. Claims of Tolerance Are Hollow.

Consider the Unitarian Universalists as an example. Though they claim tolerance of all religions, they are actually intolerant of Christians who worship Jesus as the one way of salvation. They speak of accepting other religions, but their words for evangelical Christianity include "myth," "rubbish," "a sham," "primitive," and "nonsense."[16] They often view Christian doctrines as mere superstitions. They consider those who believe the Bible is the infallible Word of God as imbeciles.

More often than not, those making accusations of intolerance in others are the most intolerant. They claim to be tolerant of the beliefs of all people, but they are unbendingly intolerant of Christians who love Jesus. As one thinker recently put it, "The fundamentalism of tolerance is just as dogmatic as any other fundamentalism, only it is deceptive in its profession of tolerance....It may actually prove to be less tolerant, since it does not seem to recognize the right of others to reject its relativistic view."[17]

111. Science Does Not Disprove the Bible.

Science depends upon observation and replication. Miracles, such as the incarnation and the resurrection, are by their very nature unprecedented events. No one can replicate these events in a laboratory. Science therefore cannot be the judge and jury of the veracity of these events.

The scientific method is useful for studying nature but not supernatural events. Just as football stars are speaking outside their field of expertise when they appear on television to tell you what razor you should buy, so scientists are speaking outside their field when they address theological issues like miracles or the resurrection.

God has communicated to humankind both by general revelation (nature, or the observable universe) and special revelation (the Bible). Both of these revelations come from God—and God does not contradict himself—so we must conclude these two revelations are in agreement with each other. One's *interpretation* of the observable universe and one's *interpretation* of the Bible may conflict, but the contradictions are not real.

We might say that science is a fallible human interpretation of the observable universe, and theology is a fallible human interpretation of the Scriptures. Nature and Scripture do not contradict; rather, science (man's fallible interpretation of nature) and theology (man's fallible interpretation of Scripture) sometimes fall into conflict.

112. The World Religions Do Not Teach the Same Doctrines.

One cannot rationally claim that the various world religions are teaching the same basic truths. Consider the doctrine of God as an example. According to the Christian Bible, Jesus affirmed one personal God who is triune in nature (Mark 12:29; John 4:24; 5:18-19). Muhammad in the Muslim Koran affirmed only one God and that God cannot have a son. Confucius was polytheistic. The words of Krishna represent a combination of polytheism and pantheism. Zoroaster set forth religious dualism—that is, both a good god and a bad god. Buddha taught that the concept of God was essentially irrelevant. Clearly, the leaders of the world's major religions, as indicated in their "holy books," held completely contradictory views regarding the nature of God.

Other differences are significant. The Koran and Vedas offer a works-oriented view of salvation whereas the Bible says salvation is a free gift for those who trust in Christ alone (Ephesians 2:8-9). Hinduism and Buddhism teach reincarnation, but Christianity denies this doctrine and teaches that we live once, die once, and then face the judgment (Hebrews 9:27). Christianity teaches that Jesus is God, but the Baha'i Faith calls him a mere manifestation of God, and Islam calls him just a prophet of God (lesser than Muhammad).

The bottom line is that with such radical and irreconcilable points of difference between the Bible, the Vedas, the Koran, and other "holy books," if one is right, the others must be wrong. If the Bible is God's Word, then the others cannot be God's Word.

Sexual Deviations

113. Sexual Immorality is Prohibited.

God created sex, and "everything created by God is good" (1 Timothy

4:4 NASB). But it is good only within the confines of the (male-female) marriage relationship, which he himself ordained (Hebrews 13:4; see also Genesis 2:24; Matthew 19:5; Ephesians 5:31).

Christians are commanded to abstain from fornication (Acts 15:20). The apostle Paul strongly affirmed that the body is not for fornication and that a man should flee it (1 Corinthians 6:13,18). We must not forget that the body is the temple of the Holy Spirit (1 Corinthians 6:19). The Ephesians were instructed that fornication should not be even once named or spoken of among them (Ephesians 5:3).

Adultery is also strongly condemned in Scripture: "You shall not commit adultery" (Exodus 20:14). Old Testament adulterers were to be put to death (Leviticus 20:10). Jesus pronounced adultery wrong even in its basic motives (Matthew 5:27-28). Paul called it an evil work of the flesh (Galatians 5:19), and John envisioned in the lake of fire some of those who practiced it (Revelation 21:8).

114. Polygamy Is Prohibited.

The Scriptures repeatedly warn against having multiple wives (Deuteronomy 17:17) and violating the principle of monogamy—one man for one wife (1 Corinthians 7:2). Monogamy is God's standard for the human race. This is clear from the following facts:

* From the very beginning God set the pattern by creating a monogamous marriage relationship with one man and one woman, Adam and Eve (Genesis 1:27; 2:21-25).

* Following from this God-established example of one woman for one man, this was the general practice of the human race (Genesis 4:1) until interrupted by sin (Genesis 4:23).

* The Law of Moses clearly commands, "You shall not multiply wives" (Deuteronomy 17:17).

* Our Lord affirmed God's original intention by creating one "male and [one] female" and joined them in marriage (Matthew 19:4).

* The New Testament stresses that "each man should have his own wife, and each woman her own husband" (1 Corinthians 7:2).

* Likewise, Paul insisted that a church leader should be "the husband of one wife" (1 Timothy 3:2,12).

* Monogamous marriage is a prefiguration of the relation between Christ and his bride, the church (Ephesians 5:31-32). God never sanctioned polygamy for any people under any circumstances.

115. Homosexuality Is Prohibited.

The Bible states that "neither fornicators...nor homosexuals...will inherit the kingdom of God" (1 Corinthians 6:9 NASB). The Scriptures repeatedly and consistently condemn homosexual practices (see Leviticus 18:22 and Romans 1:26). The Bible condemns all types of fornication—which would therefore include homosexuality (Matthew 15:19; Mark 7:21; John 8:41; Galatians 5:19-21; 1 Thessalonians 4:3; Hebrews 13:4). God intends sex only for the (male-female) marriage relationship (Hebrews 13:4).

Other

116. The Space Brothers Are Demons in Disguise.

When modern New Agers and spiritists claim they are receiving revelations from space brothers, they are likely to be in contact with demonic spirits. Consider the evidence:

* Experts who have long investigated UFOs have noted the strong similarity between the UFO experience and typical manifestations of demonism. Alleged abduction experiences are quite similar to the experiences of shamans during shamanistic ceremonies.

* Most people who claim to have an abduction experience have had some kind of past involvement in occultism.

* The messages space brothers communicate consistently go against biblical Christianity, yet they are perfectly in tune with New Age religion and various forms of occultism (for example, the Bible is not God's Word, Jesus is not the unique Son of God, salvation is unnecessary, and death is not to be feared).

* The apostle Paul warned, "Satan himself masquerades as an

angel of light. It is not surprising, then, if his servants masquerade as servants of righteousness" (2 Corinthians 11:14). Demons may be masquerading as space brothers.

117. The Ascended Masters Are Demons in Disguise.

When modern New Agers and spiritists claim they are receiving revelations from Ascended Masters, evidence indicates that they are actually in contact with demonic spirits. The messages communicated by these Ascended Masters consistently go against biblical Christianity, yet they are perfectly in tune with New Age religion and various forms of occultism (for example, the Bible is not God's Word, Jesus is not the unique Son of God, salvation is unnecessary, and death is not to be feared). Let us not forget the apostle Paul's warning: "Satan himself masquerades as an angel of light. It is not surprising, then, if his servants masquerade as servants of righteousness" (2 Corinthians 11:14). Demonic spirits are probably masquerading as Ascended Masters in order to deceive human beings away from the truth of Scripture.

118. Healing Is Subject to God's Will.

God's will is not always to heal. Sometimes God may have a purpose for allowing a believer to go through a time of sickness. God allowed Epaphroditus (Philippians 2:25-27), Trophimus (2 Timothy 4:20), Timothy (1 Timothy 5:23), Job (Job 1–2), and Paul (2 Corinthians 12:9) to suffer through periods of sickness. He does the same with us.

The healing of our bodies in our mortal state is not guaranteed in the atonement, but ultimate healing (in terms of our resurrection bodies) is guaranteed in the atonement. Our resurrection bodies will never get sick, grow old, or die (see 1 Corinthians 15:50-51).

Today when Christians get sick, they should certainly pray for healing (James 5:15). As well, they should not be hesitant about going to the doctor. God can heal directly, or he can heal through a doctor (Matthew 9:12). If we remain sick, however, we must continue to trust in God and rely on his grace, as did the apostle Paul (2 Corinthians 12:9).

Notes

1—Defining Cults
1. Alan Gomes, *Unmasking the Cults* (Grand Rapids: Zondervan, 1995), p. 7.

2—The Aetherius Society
1. Aetherius Society home page: www.aetherius.org.
2. "What Is the Aetherius Society?" Aetherius Society Web page: www.aetherius.org.
3. The Watchman Expositor, "Index of Cults and Religions," Watchman Fellowship, vol. 14 no. 3, p. 4, posted at www.watchman.org.
4. "Frequently Asked Questions," Aetherius Society website: www.aetherius.org.
5. Ibid.
6. Ibid.
7. "What Is the Aetherius Society?"
8. "Frequently Asked Questions."
9. Sidney Jansma, *UFO's and Evolution* (n.p., 1981), pp. 77-78.
10. "Frequently Asked Questions."

3—Anthroposophy
1. Timothy P. Weber, "Anthroposophy," *Evangelical Dictionary of Theology,* ed. Walter Elwell (Grand Rapids: Baker, 1984), p. 54.
2. Rudolf Steiner, *The Reappearance of the Christ in the Etheric* (Spring Valley: Anthroposophic Press, 1983), pp. 127-28.
3. Rudolf Steiner, *Jesus and Christ* (Spring Valley: Anthroposophic Press, 1976), pp. 16-17.
4. Rudolf Steiner, *The Four Sacrifices of Christ* (Spring Valley: Anthroposophic Press, 1944), pp. 19-20.
5. Rudolf Steiner, *Knowledge of the Higher Worlds and Its Attainment* (Spring Valley: Anthroposophic Press, 1984), pp. 1-34.
6. Steiner, *Knowledge of the Higher Worlds and Its Attainment,* p. 31.

4—The Arcane School
1. Alice Bailey, *The Unfinished Autobiography* (New York: Lucis Publishing, 1951), p. 197.
2. Bailey, *The Unfinished Autobiography,* p. 36.
3. Alice Bailey, *The Externalization of the Hierarchy* (New York: Lucis Publishing, 1957), p. 10.
4. Alice Bailey, *The Reappearance of the Christ* (New York: Lucis Publishing, 1979), pp. 105-6.
5. George Trevelyan, *A Vision of the Aquarian Age* (Walpole: Stillpoint, 1984), p. 171.
6. Trevelyan, p. 171.
7. Bailey, *The Externalization of the Hierarchy,* p. 592.

5—The Association for Research and Enlightenment

1. Mary Carter and William McGarey, *Edgar Cayce on Healing* (New York: Paperback Library, 1972), pp. 8-9.
2. Philip Swihart, *Reincarnation, Edgar Cayce, and the Bible* (Downers Grove: InterVarsity, 1978), p. 18.
3. Anne Read, *Edgar Cayce: On Jesus and His Church* (New York: Warner, 1970), p. 70.
4. Ibid., p. 142.
5. See the official Edgar Cayce web site: www.edgarcayce.org.

6—Astrology

1. John Ankerberg and John Weldon, *Cult Watch* (Eugene, OR: Harvest House Publishers, 1991), p. 210.
2. Lloyd Shearer, "The Woman Behind the Woman Behind Ronald Reagan," Parade, April 1, 1990, p. 16.
3. Shearer, p. 16.
4. Ibid.
5. Ibid.
6. George Mather and Larry Nichols, *Dictionary of Cults, Sects, Religions and the Occult* (Grand Rapids: Zondervan, 1993), p. 30.
7. Charles Strohmer, "Astrology in Perspective," in *Contend for the Faith,* ed. Eric Pement (Chicago: EMNR, 1992), p. 200.
8. Ankerberg and Weldon, p. 222.

7—The Baha'i Faith

1. William Hatcher and Douglas Martin, *The Baha'i Faith* (San Francisco: Harper & Row, 1984), pp. 62-63. See John Ankerberg and John Weldon, *Encyclopedia of Cults and New Religions* (Eugene: Harvest House Publishers, 1999), p. 8.
2. J. Esslemont, *Baha'u'llah and the New Era* (Wilmette: Baha'i Publishing Trust, 1980), p. 71.
3. *Gleanings from the Writings of Baha'u'llah* (Wilmette: Baha'i Publishing Trust, 1969), pp. 78, 95, 217, 287.
4. Baha'i World Faith website: www.bahai.org.
5. *Selections from the Writings of the Bab,* trans. Habib Taherzadeh (Haifa: Baha'i World Center, 1978), pp. 11-17, 47, 54-55.
6. Esslemont, pp. 23-24.
7. *The Baha'is: A Profile of the Baha'i Faith and Its Worldwide Community* (United Kingdom: Baha'i Publishing Trust, 1994), p. 37.
8. *The Baha'is: A Profile,* p. 35.
9. Ankerberg and Weldon, p. 19.
10. Huschmand Sabet, *The Heavens Are Cleft Asunder* (Oxford: Ronald, 1975), p. 112.
11. Hatcher and Martin, p. 113.
12. Peter Simple, *Baha'i Teachings, Light for All Regions* (Wilmette: Baha'i, 1970), p. 21.
13. *The Baha'is: A Profile,* p. 35.

8—Christadelphians

1. "Christadelphian," *Encyclopedia Britannica,* online edition.
2. Harry Tennant, *Christadelphians: What They Believe and Preach* (Birmingham: The Christadelphian, 1986), pp. 84-87.
3. "Doctrines to be Rejected," Christadelphian website: www.christadelphian.org.

4. "Response to Mainstream Christianity: The Nature of Christ," Christadelphian website: www.christadelphian.org.

5. "Our Faith and Beliefs," Christadelphian website: www.christadelphian.org.

6. "Doctrines to be Rejected."

7. Tennant, p. 75.

8. *The Christadelphian Messenger,* No. 46, "The Word Made Flesh," p. 3.

9. *Christadelphian Answers,* ed. Frank Jannaway (Houston: Herald Press, 1920), p. 25.

10. Tennant, p. 74.

11. *Christadelphian Answers,* p. 24.

12. "Our Faith and Beliefs."

13. Both quotes are from Tennant, p. 115.

14. "Doctrines to be Rejected."

15. "Response to Mainstream Christianity: The Nature of Man," Christadelphian website: www.christadelphian.org.

16. Ibid.

17. "Doctrines to be Rejected."

18. George Mather and Larry Nichols, *Dictionary of Cults, Sects Religions and the Occult* (Grand Rapids: Zondervan, 1993), p. 58.

19. "Doctrines to be Rejected."

9—Christian Identity

1. Richard Abanes, *Cults, New Religious Movements, and Your Family* (Wheaton: Crossway Books, 1998), p. 95.

2. "Doctrinal Statement," Kingdom Identity Ministries website, www.kingidentity .com.

3. Ibid.

4. Ibid.

5. Arnold Murray, "Grace: Baptism" (cassette #404) (Gravette: Shepherd's Chapel, n.d.).

6. Michael Barkun, *Religion and the Racist Right: The Origins of the Christian Identity Movement* (Chapel Hill: University of North Carolina Press, 1996).

7. "Christian Identity," *Watchman Expositor,* Watchman Fellowship website: www.watch man.org.

10—Christian Science

1. Willa Cather and Georgine Milmine, *The Life of Mary Baker G. Eddy and the History of Christian Science* (Lincoln: University of Nebraska Press, 1993), p. 12.

2. Todd Ehrenborg, *Mind Sciences* (Grand Rapids: Zondervan, 1996), p. 8.

3. Walter Martin, *The Kingdom of the Cults* (Minneapolis: Bethany, 1985), pp. 128-33.

4. Ehrenborg, p. 11.

5. Mary Baker Eddy, *The First Church of Christ Scientist and Miscellany* (Boston: Trustees under the Will of Mary Baker G. Eddy, 1913), p. 238.

6. Mary Baker Eddy, *Science and Health with Key to the Scriptures* (Boston: Trustees under the Will of Mary Baker G. Eddy, 1934), p. 44.

7. Eddy, *Science and Health,* p. 46.

11—The Church of Jesus Christ of Latter-day Saints
1. Joseph Fielding Smith, *History of the Church of Jesus Christ of Latter-day Saints* (hereafter *History*) (Salt Lake City: Deseret, 1973), 1:3-8.
2. Ibid., 1:28.
3. Ibid., 1:34,35.
4. David Whitmer, *An Address to All Believers in Christ* (Concord: Pacific Publishing, 1887), p. 12.
5. Smith, *History*, 1:40-42.
6. Ibid., 4:461.
7. James Talmage, *A Study of the Articles of Faith* (Salt Lake City: Church of Jesus Christ of Latter-day Saints, 1982), p. 236.
8. Orson Pratt; cited in Bill McKeever and Eric Johnson, *Questions to Ask Your Mormon Friend* (Minneapolis: Bethany, 1994), p. 47.
9. Bruce McConkie, *Mormon Doctrine* (Salt Lake City: Bookcraft, 1977), p. 383.
10. Joseph Smith, Genesis 40:33, Inspired Version.
11. Milton Hunter, *The Gospel Through the Ages* (Salt Lake City: Deseret, 1958), p. 104.
12. McConkie, p. 278.
13. Orson Pratt, *The Seer* (Washington, DC, 1853), pp. 37-38.
14. Brigham Young, *Journal of Discourses* (London: Latter-day Saints, 1854-56), 3:93.
15. *Gospel Principles* (Salt Lake City: Church of Jesus Christ of Latter-day Saints, 1986), p. 290.
16. Smith, *History*, p. 327.
17. McConkie, pp. 546-47.
18. LeGrand Richards, *A Marvelous Work and a Wonder* (Salt Lake City: Deseret, 1958), p. 98.
19. *Articles of Faith* (Salt Lake City: The Church of Jesus Christ of Latter-day Saints, 1982), #2.
20. *Gospel Principles*, p. 19.
21. *Church News*, 18 March 1989, p. 16.
22. Joseph Fielding Smith, *Answers to Gospel Questions* (Salt Lake City: Deseret, 1958), 2:208.

12—The Church Universal and Triumphant
1. Walter Martin, *The New Cults* (Ventura: Regal, 1978), p. 214.
2. Mark and Elizabeth Clare Prophet, *The Lost Teachings of Jesus 3* (Livingston: Summit, 1988), pp. 273-74.
3. Mark and Elizabeth Clare Prophet, *Climb the Highest Mountain* (Los Angeles: Summit, 1974), p. 228.
4. Ibid., p. 160.
5. Mark and Elizabeth Clare Prophet, *The Lost Teachings of Jesus 2* (Livingston: Summit, 1988), p. 254.
6. Ibid., p. 62.
7. Prophet, *Climb the Highest Mountain*, pp. 279-80.
8. Ibid., p. 443.
9. Elizabeth Clare Prophet, *The Lost Years of Jesus* (Livingston: Summit, 1987), pp. 218-46.
10. Nicolas Notovitch, *The Life of Saint Issa*, cited by Joseph Gaer, *The Lore of the New Testament* (Boston: Little Brown and Co., 1952), p. 118.

11. Nicolas Notovitch, cited by Per Beskow, *Strange Tales about Jesus* (Philadelphia: Fortress, n.d.), p. 59.
12. Notovitch, in Prophet, *The Lost Years of Jesus,* p. 219.
13. Ibid., 222-23.

13—Eckankar

1. "About Eckankar: An Overview," Eckankar website: www.eckankar.com.
2. "A Glossary of ECK Terms," Eckankar website: www.eckankar.com.
3. Sri Harold Klemp, "Spiritual Exercises of ECK," Eckankar website: www.eckankar.com.
4. "Soul Travel," Eckankar website: www.eckankar.com.
5. "A Glossary of ECK Terms."
6. "What Is Eckankar?" Eckankar website: www.eckankar.com.
7. "A Glossary of ECK Terms."
8. "Eckankar," Christian Apologetics and Research Ministry website: www.carm.org.
9. "About Eckankar: An Overview."

14—The Family (The Children of God)

1. Ron Enroth, *The Lure of the Cults* (Downers Grove: InterVarsity, 1987), p. 85.
2. Richard Abanes, *Cults, New Religious Movements, and Your Family* (Wheaton: Crossway, 1998), p. 166.
3. Moses David, "The Flirty Little Fishy!" in *The Basic Mo Letters* (London: Children of God, 1974), 2340-43.
4. Moses David, "The Flirty Little Fishy," p. 528.
5. Deborah Davis, *The Children of God: The Inside Story* (Grand Rapids: Zondervan, 1984), pp. 122-23.
6. David Moses, cited in *Time,* August 22, 1977, p. 48.
7. David Berg; quoted in Walter Martin, *The New Cults* (Ventura: Regal, 1978), p. 175.
8. Moses David, *Love vs. Law!* (Rome: Children of God, 1977), p. 4.
9. In 1984, Deborah Davis published *The Children of God: The Inside Story.*
10. Joe Maxwell, "Children of God Revamp Image, Face Renewed Opposition," *Christian Research Journal,* Fall 1993, p. 5.
11. Paul Carden, "Raids Rock COG," *Christian Research Newsletter,* September/October 1993, p. 11.
12. Ibid., p. 11.
13. The Family website: www.thefamily.org.

15—Hare Krishna (ISKCON)

1. Garuda Dasa, "Sankirtana: The Perfection of Glorifying God," *Back to Godhead* 16, no. 11 (1981), p. 6.
2. J. Isamu Yamamoto, "Hare Krishna," in *A Guide to Cults and New Religions,* ed. Ron Enroth (Downers Grove: InterVarsity, 1983), p. 92.
3. Irvine Robertson, *What the Cults Believe* (Chicago: Moody, 1983), p. 118.
4. *Back to Godhead,* no. 47, p. 1.
5. J. Isamu Yamamoto, *Hinduism, TM & Hare Krishna* (Grand Rapids: Zondervan, 1998), p. 18.
6. Vishal Mangalwadi, *When the New Age Gets Old* (Downers Grove: InterVarsity, 1993), p. 65.
7. Francine Daner, *The American Children of Krsna* (New York: Holt, Rinehart and Winston, 1976), p. 67.

8. Yamamoto, "Hare Krishna," in *A Guide to Cults and New Religions*, p. 95.

16—The I AM Movement

1. Guy and Donald Ballard, *Purpose of the Ascended Masters "I AM" Activity* (Chicago: Saint Germain, 1942), pp. 24, 35, 110.
2. Louis Berkhof, *A History of Christian Doctrines* (Grand Rapids: Baker, 1981), p. 47.
3. Ballard, p. 110.
4. Ibid., p. 35.
5. Godfre King, *The "I AM" Discourses* (Schaumburg: St. Germain, 1999), pp. 273-74.
6. "I AM Movement," *Encyclopedia Britannica*, online edition.

17—Jehovah's Witnesses

1. *The Watchtower*, 15 January 1983, p. 22.
2. *The Watchtower*, 15 August 1987, p. 29.
3. *You Can Live Forever in Paradise on Earth* (Brooklyn: Watchtower, 1982), p. 143.
4. *Aid to Bible Understanding* (Brooklyn: Watchtower, 1971), p. 1395.
5. *Should You Believe in the Trinity?* (Brooklyn: Watchtower Bible and Tract Society, 1989), p. 20.
6. *Reasoning from the Scriptures* (Brooklyn: Watchtower Bible and Tract Society, 1989), p. 380.
7. *The Watchtower*, 1 April 1947, 204.
8. *The Watchtower*, 15 August 1972, 491.
9. *You Can Live Forever in Paradise on Earth*, p. 88.

18—Kabbalism

1. Elliot Miller, "Cabala," Fact Sheet, Christian Research Institute, P.O. Box 7000, Rancho Santa Margarita, CA, 92688.
2. Miller.
3. *The Sorcerer's Handbook;* cited in E.M. Storms, *Should a Christian Be a Mason?* (Kirkwood: Impact, 1999), p. 20.
4. Storms, p. 20.
5. Ibid., pp. 20-21.
6. Kenneth Boa, Cults, *World Religions, and You* (Wheaton: Victor, 1986), p. 138.
7. "What Is Kabbalah?" Kabbalah Centre website: www.kabbalah.com.
8. John Ankerberg and John Weldon, *The Secret Teachings of the Masonic Lodge* (Chicago: Moody, 1990), p. 219.
9. Albert Pike, *Morals and Dogma* (Montana: Kessinger, n.d.), p. 741.
10. Ibid., p. 625.
11. Albert Mackey, *Mackey's Revised Encyclopedia of Freemasonry* (Richmond: Macoy, 1966), p. 375, insert added.
12. Vindex, *Light Invisible* (Boston: Masonic Publishers, 1996), p. 11.
13. David Rowan, "Kabbalah Centre: Secrets of a Celebrity Sect," *Evening Standard* (England), October 3, 2002, online edition.

19—The Masonic Lodge

1. Michael Baigent and Richard Leigh, *The Temple and the Lodge* (New York: Arcarde, 1989), p. 126.
2. Henry Coil, *A Comprehensive View of Freemasonry* (Richmond: Macoy, 1973), p. 378.

3. Alphonse Cerza, *Let There Be Light* (Silver Spring: Masonic Service Association, 1983), p. 1.
4. Joseph Newton, *The Religion of Masonry* (Richmond: Macoy, 1969), pp. 58-59.
5. Richard Thorn, *The Boy Who Cried Wolf* (New York: Evans, 1994), p. 83.
6. John Robinson, *Born in Blood* (New York: Evans, 1989), p. 255.
7. Thorn, p. 22.
8. Robinson, pp. 206-07.
9. Ibid., pp. 207-08.
10. Vindex, *Light Invisible* (Boston: Masonic Publishers, 1996), p. 40.
11. Coil, p. 192.
12. J. Acker, *Strange Altars* (St. Louis: Concordia, 1959), p. 37.
13. Martin Wagner, *Freemasonry: An Interpretation* (Columbiana: Missionary Service and Supply, n.d.), pp. 338-39.
14. Jack Harris, *Freemasonry: The Invisible Cult in Our Midst* (Chattanooga: Global, 1983), p. 112.
15. Albert Mackey, *Revised Encyclopedia of Freemasonry* (Richmond: Macoy, 1966), 1:269.
16. H.L. Haywood, *Great Teachings of Masonry* (Kingsport: Southern Publishers, 1923), p. 94.
17. Pike, pp. 22, 23.
18. Vindex, p. 9.

20—The Nation of Islam
1. Henry Young, *Major Black Religious Leaders Since 1940* (Nashville: Abingdon, 1979), pp. 66-67.
2. Elijah Muhammad, *Message to the Blackman in America* (Chicago: Final Call, 1965), p. 164.
3. Eric Lincoln, *The Black Muslims in America* (Boston: Beacon, 1961), pp. 16-17.
4. Malcolm X, *The Autobiography of Malcolm X* (New York: Grove Press, 1964), p. 294.
5. Eric Pement, "Louis Farrakhan and the Nation of Islam," Statement DI-175, Christian Research Institute, Rancho Santa Margarita, CA, 92688.
6. "11,000 Flock to Hear Farrakhan in D.C.," *The Final Call*, September 1985, pp. 10, 14.
7. Muhammad, *Message to the Blackman in America*, p. 89.
8. Elijah Muhammad, *Our Savior Has Arrived* (Newport News: United Brothers, n.d.), p. 152.
9. Ibid., *Our Savior Has Arrived*, p. 97.
10. Jerry Buckner, "Witnessing to the Nation of Islam," Statement DI-209, Christian Research Institute, Rancho Santa Margarita, CA, 92688.
11. Muhammad, *Message to the Blackman in America*, pp. 117, 119.
12. Muhammad, *Our Savior Has Arrived*, p. 35.
13. Ibid., *Our Savior Has Arrived*, p. 26.
14. Muhammad, *Message to the Blackman in America*, p. 9.
15. Muhammad, *Our Savior Has Arrived*, p. 96.
16. Muhammad, *Message to the Blackman in America*, p. 219.

21—The New Age Movement
1. Elliot Miller, *A Crash Course on the New Age Movement* (Grand Rapids: Baker Books, 1989), p. 15.

2. Stephan Schuhmacher and Gert Woerner, eds. *The Encyclopedia of Eastern Philosophy and Religion* (Boston: Shambhala, 1989), p. 224.
3. David Gershon and Gail Straub, *Empowerment* (New York: Dell, 1989), p. 21.
4. Jennifer Donavan, "Seth Followers Spoon Up Fun," *Dallas Morning News,* July 1, 1986.
5. David Spangler, *The Laws of Manifestation* (Forres, Scotland: Findhorn, 1983), pp. 23-24.
6. Benjamin Creme, *The Reappearance of the Christ and the Masters of Wisdom* (Los Angeles: Tara Center, 1980), p. 115.
7. Spangler, *Reflections on the Christ* (Forres, Scotland: Findhorn, 1981), p. 8; David Spangler, *Towards a Planetary Vision* (Forres, Scotland: Findhorn, 1977), p. 30.
8. Levi Dowling, *The Aquarian Gospel of Jesus the Christ* (London: Fowler, 1947), p. 87.
9. Elizabeth Clare Prophet, *The Lost Years of Jesus* (Livingston: Summit University, 1987), pp. 218-46.
10. Dowling, p. 54.
11. Spangler, *Reflections on the Christ,* p. 28.
12. Shirley MacLaine, *Dancing in the Light* (New York: Bantam, 1985), p. 354.
13. Ibid., p. 15.
14. Ibid., p. 263.
15. Shirley MacLaine, *Out on a Limb* (New York: Bantam, 1984), p. 347.
16. David Spangler, *Cooperation with Spirit* (Middleton: Lorian, 1982), p. 4.
17. Spangler, *Towards a Planetary Vision,* p. 108.

22—The New Thought Movement
1. Horatio Dresser, *A History of the New Thought Movement* (London: Harrap, n.d.), pp. 160-61; Dean Halverson, "Mind Power," *SCP Newsletter* (Spring 1985), Vol. 11, No. 1.
2. Halverson, p. 9.
3. Stephen Gottschalk, *The Emergence of Christian Science in American Religious Life* (Berkeley: University of California, 1973), p. 128.
4. Ralph Trine, *In Tune with the Infinite* (New York: Crowell, 1897), p. 11.
5. Ibid., p. 13.
6. William Warch, *The New Thought Christian* (Anaheim: Christian Living, 1977), p. 91.
7. Trine, p. 29.
8. Halverson, p. 8.
9. Phineas Quimby, *The Quimby Manuscripts,* ed. Horatio Dresser (New Hyde Park: University Books, 1961), p. 283.
10. Horatio Dresser, *Spiritual Health and Healing* (New York: Crowell, 1922), p. 19.
11. Dresser.
12. *New Thought,* Spring 1979, p. 18.

23—Nichiren Shoshu Buddhism
1. "Nichiren Buddhism," *Encyclopedia Britannica,* online edition.
2. John Ankerberg and John Weldon, *Encyclopedia of Cults and New Religions* (Eugene, OR: Harvest House Publishers, 1999), p. 66.
3. J. Isamu Yamamoto, *Buddhism, Taoism, & Other Far Eastern Religions* (Grand Rapids: Zondervan, 1998), p. 17.

4. "The Road to True Happiness," Nichiren Shoshu Buddhism website: www.nst.org.
5. Ibid.
6. "The Practice of Faith in Nichiren Shoshu," Nichiren Shoshu Buddhism website: www.nst.org.
7. Yamamoto, p. 17.
8. Ibid., p. 17.
9. Ankerberg and Weldon, p. 68.
10. Walter Martin, *The New Cults* (Ventura: Regal, 1978), p. 335.
11. Daisaku Ikeda, "Soka Gakkai," in *Lectures on Buddhism* (Tokyo: Seikyo, 1969), 4:15; cited in Yamamoto, p. 52.

24—Occultism
1. Ron Enroth, "The Occult," *Evangelical Dictionary of Theology*, ed. Walter Elwell (Grand Rapids: Baker, 1984), p. 787.
2. Enroth, p. 787.
3. Elliot Miller, *A Crash Course on the New Age Movement* (Grand Rapids: Baker, 1990), p. 141.
4. George Mather and Larry Nichols, *Dictionary of Cults, Sects, Religions and the Occult* (Grand Rapids: Zondervan, 1993), p. 86.
5. John Ankerberg and John Weldon, *The Facts on Life After Death* (Eugene, OR: Harvest House Publishers, 1992), p. 10.
6. Ibid., p. 11.
7. Kenneth Ring; cited in Ankerberg and Weldon, p. 21.
8. Brooks Alexander, "Machines Made of Shadows," *SCP Journal*, 17:1-2, 1992, p. 11.
9. John Weldon with Zola Levitt, *UFOs: What On Earth Is Happening?* (Eugene, OR: Harvest House Publishers, 1975), p. 101.
10. David Wimbish, *Something's Going On Out There* (Old Tappan: Revell, 1990), p. 158.
11. Wimbish, p. 164.
12. Dave Hunt, *The Cult Explosion* (Eugene, OR: Harvest House Publishers, 1978), p. 19.
13. Rick Fields, *Chop Wood, Carry Water* (Los Angeles: Tarcher, 1984), p. 186.
14. Elliot Miller, "The Christian, Energetic Medicine, and 'New Age Paranoia,'" *Christian Research Journal*, Winter 1992, p. 26.
15. Ibid., p. 26.

25—Oneness Pentecostalism
1. Note that Oneness Pentecostalism is different from mainstream Pentecostalism. The former is heretical. The latter is not.
2. George Mather and Larry Nichols, *Dictionary of Cults, Sects, Religions and the Occult* (Grand Rapids: Zondervan, 1993), p. 213.
3. Calvin Beisner, *"Jesus Only" Churches* (Grand Rapids: Zondervan, 1998), p. 70.
4. Gregory Boyd, *Oneness Pentecostals and the Trinity* (Grand Rapids: Baker, 1992), p. 10.
5. John Ankerberg and John Weldon, *Encyclopedia of Cults and New Religions* (Eugene, OR: Harvest House Publishers, 1999), p. 369.
6. David Bernard, *The Oneness of God* (Hazelwood: Word Aflame, 1983), p. 66.
7. Kenneth Reeves, *The Godhead* (St. Louis: Trio, 1999), pp. 79, 85.

8. Gordon Magee, *Is Jesus in the Godhead or Is the Godhead in Jesus?* (Hazelwood: Word Aflame, 1988), p. 15.

9. Bernard, p. 208.

10. Magee, p. 42.

11. Bernard, p. 177.

26—The Raelian Movement

1. "The History of the Raelian Movement," Raelian website: www.raelian.org.

2. Claude Vorilhon, *Let's Welcome Our Fathers from Space* (Tokyo: AOM, 1986).

3. "Quick Summary," Raelian website: www.raelian.org.

4. "The History of the Raelian Movement."

5. "Where Do We Come From?" PR Newswire, 21 May 1997.

6. William Alnor, "UFO Cults Are Flourishing in New Age Circles," *Christian Research Journal,* Summer 1990, p. 35.

7. "Quick Summary."

8. Ibid.

9. "Why Do They Need An Embassy?" Raelian website: www.raelian.org.

10. Ibid.

11. Elif Kaban, "Swiss Cultists Gather for Sensual Meditation," Reuters, 6 August 1997, downloaded from AR-Talk, Internet.

12. *The Gods Have Landed,* ed. James Lewis (New York: State University of New York Press, 1995), p. 107.

27—Religious Science

1. Ernest Holmes, *Science of Mind* (magazine), February 1979, p. 40.

2. Fenwicke Holmes, *Ernest Holmes: His Life and Times* (New York: Dodd, Mead and Co., 1970), back cover.

3. Ernest Holmes, *What Religious Science Teaches* (Los Angeles: Science of Mind, 1975), p. 10.

4. Ibid., pp. 9-10.

5. Ernest Holmes, *The Science of Mind* (New York: Dodd, Mead and Co., 1938), p. 362.

6. Holmes, *What Religious Science Teaches,* p. 61.

7. Ibid., p. 64.

8. Ibid., p. 65.

9. Fenwicke L. Holmes, p. 294.

10. Holmes, *The Science of Mind,* p. 388.

11. Ernest Holmes, "What I Believe," (pamphlet) (n.p., n.d.), p. 3.

12. Holmes, *What Religious Science Teaches,* pp. 24-25.

13. Ibid., p. 65.

14. Ibid., p. 50.

15. Ibid., p. 21.

16. Ibid., p. 19.

17. Holmes, *The Science of Mind,* p. 361.

18. Holmes, *What Religious Science Teaches,* p. 12.

19. Ibid., p. 55.

20. Ibid., p. 20.

21. Holmes, *The Science of Mind,* p. 359.

22. Holmes, *What Religious Science Teaches,* p. 20.

28—The Rosicrucian Fellowship
1. "The Journey into Self and the Mystical Path," AMORC website: www.rosicrucian.org.
2. "The Rosicrucian Order is Unique," AMORC website: www.rosicrucian.org.
3. "Developing Your Highest Potential," AMORC website: www.rosicrucian.org.
4. "The History of Rosicrucianism," AMORC website: www.rosicrucian.org.
5. "Rosicrucianism—The Ancient and Mystical Order Rosae Crucis," Watchman Fellowship website: www.watchman.org.
6. Walter Martin, *The Kingdom of the Cults* (Minneapolis: Bethany, 2003), p. 645.
7. "About the Rosicrucian Order," AMORC website: www.rosicrucian.org.
8. "Rosicrucianism," Watchman Fellowship website: www.watchman.org.
9. "The History of Rosicrucianism."
10. "Rosicrucian," in the *Encyclopedia Britannica,* online edition.
11. Martin, p. 646.
12. Max Heindel, *The Rosicrucian Cosmo-Conception* (San Jose: AMORC, n.d.), p. 376.
13. Max Heindel, *The Rosicrucian Philosophy in Questions and Answers* (Oceanside: Rosicrucian Fellowship, 1922), p. 54.

29—Satanism
1. Craig Hawkins, "The Many Faces of Satanism," *Forward,* Fall 1986, p. 1.
2. Bob and Gretchen Passantino, *Satanism* (Grand Rapids: Zondervan, 1995), p. 7.
3. Larry Kahaner, *Cults That Kill* (New York: Warner, 1988), p. 70.
4. Arthur Lyons, *Satan Wants You* (New York: Mysterious Press, 1988), p. 9.
5. Richard Abanes, *Cults, New Religious Movements, and Your Family* (Wheaton: Crossway, 1998), p. 53.
6. Jon Trott, "About the Devil's Business," *Cornerstone,* vol. 19 Issue 93, p. 10.
7. Passantino, pp. 40-41.
8. Blanche Barton, *The Secret Life of a Satanist* (Los Angeles: Ferel, 1990), pp. 74f.
9. Neville Drury and Gregory Tillett, *The Occult Sourcebook* (London: Routledge and Kegan Paul, 1978), p. 77.
10. Anton LaVey, *The Satanic Bible* (New York: Avon, 1969), p. 25.
11. Burton Wolfe, *The Devil's Avenger* (New York: Pyramid, 1974), p. 35.
12. Passantino, p. 76.

30—Self-Realization Fellowship
1. "Aims and Ideals of Self-Realization Fellowship," Self-Realization Fellowship (SRF) website: www.yogananda-srf.org.
2. "The Life of Paramahansa Yogananda," SRF website: www.yogananda-srf.org.
3. Cited in "The Life of Paramahansa Yogananda."
4. "About Self-Realization Fellowship," SRF website: www.yogananda-srf.org.
5. *Undreamed of Possibilities: An Introduction to Self-Realization* (Los Angeles: Self-Realization Fellowship, 1982), pp. 9.
6. Swami Sri Yukteswar, *The Holy Science* (Los Angeles: Self-Realization Fellowship, 1984), p. 21.
7. Paramahansa Yogananda, *The Science of Religion* (Los Angeles: Self-Realization Fellowship, 1982), p. 21.
8. Elliot Miller, "Swami Yogananda and the Self-Realization Fellowship," Statement DS-213, Christian Research Institute, Rancho Santa Margarita, CA, 92688.

9. Paramahansa Yogananda, cited in "About Self-Realization Fellowship."

31—Spiritism

1. Elliot Miller, *A Crash Course on the New Age Movement* (Grand Rapids: Baker, 1989), p. 141.
2. Russell Chandler, *Understanding the New Age* (Dallas: Word, 1991), pp. 8-11.
3. Jon Klimo, *Channeling* (Los Angeles: Tarcher, 1987), chapter 2.
4. Miller, p. 142.
5. Kevin Ryerson and Stephanie Harolde, *Spirit Communication* (New York: Bantam, 1989), pp. 46-48.
6. Ryerson and Harolde, p. 46.
7. Ibid., p. 48.
8. Levi Dowling, *The Aquarian Gospel of Jesus the Christ* (London: Fowler, 1947), p. 54.
9. Ibid., p. 97.
10. Ibid., p. 56.
11. Ibid., p. 126.
12. Ibid., p. 63.
13. Ibid., p. 56.
14. Ibid., p. 63.

32—Swedenborgianism

1. "About Swedenborg," Swedenborg website: www.swedenborg.org.
2. N. Crompton, *Swedenborg: The Man Who Wanted to Know* (New York: Swedenborg, 1993), pp. 8-9.
3. Emanuel Swedenborg, cited in Cyriel Sigstedt, *The Swedenborg Epic* (New York: Bookman, 1952), p. 198.
4. "Swedenborg, Emanuel," *Encyclopedia Britannica,* online edition.
5. "History," Swedenborg website: www.swedenborg.org.
6. "The Church Today," Swedenborg website: www.swedenborg.org.
7. "Tenets," Swedenborg website: www.swedenborg.org.
8. Emanuel Swedenborg, *The Arcana Caelestia,* vol. 12 (New York: Swedenborg, 1978), paragraph 10325.
9. "Tenets."
10. Samuel Warren, *Compendium of Swedenborg's Theological Writings* (London: Swedenborg, 1954), p. 86.
11. "Beliefs," Swedenborg website: www.swedenborg.org.
12. "Tenets."
13. Ibid.
14. "Beliefs."
15. "Tenets."
16. Emanuel Swedenborg, *Life After Death* (New York: New-Church, n.d.), p. 10.

33—Theosophy

1. C. Leadbeater, *A Textbook of Theosophy* (India: Theosophical Publishing House, 1954), pp. 20-21.
2. Helena Blavatsky, *The Key to Theosophy* (Pasadena: Theosophical University Press, 1972), p. 61.
3. Ibid.

4. Helena Blavatsky, *The Secret Doctrine* (Wheaton: Theosophical Publishing House, 1966), pp. 168-89.

5. Annie Besant, *Esoteric Christianity* (Wheaton: Theosophical Publishing House, 1953), pp. 90-91.

6. Cited by Jan Karel Van Baalen, *Chaos of the Cults* (Grand Rapids: Eerdmans, 1956), p. 52.

34—Transcendental Meditation

1. Cited in Ronald Enroth, *The Lure of the Cults* (Downers Grove: InterVarsity, 1987), p. 42.

2. Patricia Hemingway, *The Transcendental Meditation Primer* (New York: McKay, 1975), p. xvii. Kenneth Boa, *Cults, World Religions, and You* (Wheaton: Victor, 1979), p. 156.

3. Walter Martin, *The New Cults* (Ventura: Regal, 1980), p. 96.

4. John Noss, *Man's Religions* (New York: Macmillan, 1974), p. 101.

5. Lewis Hopfe, *Religions of the World* (New York: Macmillan, 1991), p. 100.

6. John Hick, *Death and Eternal Life* (New York: Harper & Row, 1976), p. 315.

7. Vishal Mangalwadi, *When the New Age Gets Old* (Downers Grove: InterVarsity, 1993), p. 77.

8. Cited in Josh McDowell, *A Ready Defense* (Nashville: Nelson, 1992), p. 354.

35—The Unarius Academy of Science

1. Duane Noriyuki, "Age of Unarius," *Los Angeles Times,* April 7, 1997, p. A-3.

2. *The Gods Have Landed,* ed. James Lewis (New York: State University of New York Press, 1995), pp. 86, 88.

3. Ibid., p. 88.

4. Ibid., p. 90.

5. Ibid., pp. 90, 92.

6. Noriyuki, "Age of Unarius," p. 3.

7. Ibid.

8. *The Gods Have Landed,* pp. 90, 92.

9. "Frequently Asked Questions," Unarius website: www.unarius.org.

10. Paul Hoversten, "With 2000 Near, UFO Believers Taking Off," *USA TODAY,* March 31, 1997, p. 02A.

11. Hoversten, p. 02A.

36—The Unification Church

1. Nansook Hong, *In the Shadow of the Moons* (Boston: Little, Brown and Company, 1998), p. 18.

2. James Beverley, "The Unification Church," in *Evangelizing the Cults,* ed. Ronald Enroth (Ann Arbor: Servant, 1990), p. 75.

3. Carroll Stoner and Jo Anne Parke, *All God's Children* (Radnor: Chilton, 1977), pp. 154-55.

4. J. Isamu Yamamoto, "Unification Church," in *A Guide to Cults and New Religions* (Downers Grove: InterVarsity, 1983), p. 157.

37—Unitarian Universalism

1. John Ankerberg and John Weldon, *Encyclopedia of Cults and New Religions* (Eugene, OR: Harvest House Publishers, 1999), p. 503.

2. John Sias, *100 Questions that Non-Members Ask About Unitarian Universalism* (Nashua: Transition, 1999), p. 19.
3. *The Unitarian Universalist Pocket Guide,* ed. John Buehrens (Boston: Skinner, 1999), p. ix.
4. David Robinson, *The Unitarians and the Universalists* (Westport: Greenwood, 1985), pp. 3-4, 61-65.
5. Buehrens, p. xxii.
6. Philip Hewett, *The Unitarian Way* (Toronto: Canadian Unitarian Council, 1985), p. 89.
7. Karl Chworowsky and Gist Raible, "What is a Unitarian Universalist?" in *Religions in America,* ed. Leo Rosten (New York: Simon and Schuster, 1975), p. 272. Marta Flanagan, "We are Unitarian Universalists," UUA online pamphlet, p. 1; Unitarian Universalist website: www.uua.org.
8. Kathleen Elgin, *The Unitarians* (New York: McKay, 1971), p. 82.

38—The Unity School of Christianity
1. Walter Martin, *The Kingdom of the Cults* (Minneapolis: Bethany, 1985), p. 280.
2. James Freeman, *The Story of Unity* (Unity Village: Unity, 1978), p. 60.
3. Charles and Myrtle Fillmore, *Modern Thought* (magazine), 1889, p. 42.
4. James Dillet Freeman, *What Is Unity?* (Lees Summit: Unity, n.d.), p. 5.
5. Elizabeth Turner, *What Unity Teaches* (Lees Summit: Unity, 1952), p. 4.
6. Emilie Cady, *Lessons in Truth* (Lees Summit: Unity, 1962), pp. 8-9.
7. Charles Fillmore, *The Metaphysical Dictionary* (Lees Summit: Unity, 1962), p. 629.
8. Cady, p. 6.
9. "Unity Statement of Faith" (Lees Summit: Unity, n.d.), Art. 22.
10. Marcus Bach, *The Story of Unity* (Englewood Cliffs: Prentice-Hall, 1962), pp. 15960.
11. Charles Fillmore, *What Practical Christianity Stands For* (Lees Summit: Unity, 1947), p. 5.
12. Turner, p.3.
13. *Unity* (magazine) Vol. 57, no. 5, p. 464; and Vol. 72, no. 2, p. 8.
14. "Unity Statement of Faith," Art. 24.

39—The Way International
1. George Mather and Larry Nichols, *Dictionary of Cults, Sects, Religions and the Occult* (Grand Rapids: Zondervan, 1993), p. 309.
2. Ruth Tucker, *Another Gospel* (Grand Rapids: Zondervan, 1989), p. 218.
3. Elena Whiteside, *The Way: Living in Hope* (New Knoxville: American Christian, 1972), p. 178.
4. *This is the Way* (New Knoxville: The Way, n.d.), pamphlet.
5. Ibid.
6. Victor Paul Wierwille, cited in Kenneth Boa, *Cults, World Religions, and You* (Wheaton: Victor, 1986), p. 197.
7. John Juedes, "The Way Tree Is Splintering," Statement DW-100, Christian Research Institute website: www.equip.org.
8. Victor Paul Wierwille, *Jesus Christ Is Not God* (New Knoxville: American Christian, 1975), book jacket.
9. Ibid., p. 5.

10. Victor Paul Wierwille, *The Word's Way* (New Knoxville: American Christian, 1971), p. 26.
11. Ibid., p. 37.
12. Wierwille, *Jesus Christ Is Not God*, p. 79.
13. Victor Paul Wierwille, *Receiving the Holy Spirit Today* (New Knoxville: American Christian, 1972), pp. 258-90.
14. Wierwille, *Jesus Christ Is Not God*, p. 128.
15. Walter Martin, *The New Cults* (Ventura: Regal, 1980), p. 72.
16. Victor Paul Wierwille, *Power for Abundant Living* (New Knoxville: American Christian, 1972), p. 258.
17. Wierwille, *Jesus Christ Is Not God*, p. 131.
18. Victor Paul Wierwille, *The New Dynamic Church* (New Knoxville: American Christian, 1971), p. 123.
19. Victor Paul Wierwille, *The Bible Tells Me So* (New Knoxville: American Christian, 1971), p. 84.
20. Wierwille, *The New Dynamic Church*, p. 31.

40—Wicca / Witchcraft
1. Craig Hawkins, *Goddess Worship, Witchcraft and Neo-Paganism* (Grand Rapids: Zondervan, 1998).
2. Craig Hawkins, *Witchcraft: Exploring the World of Wicca* (Grand Rapids: Baker, 1996), pp. 18-21.
3. Raymond Buckland, *Buckland's Complete Book of Witchcraft* (St. Paul: Llewellyn, 1986), p. 99.
4. Rosemary Giuley, *Encyclopedia of Witches and Witchcraft* (New York: Checkmark, 1999), p. 376.
5. Scott Cunningham, *The Truth About Witchcraft Today* (St. Paul: Llewellyn, 1999), p. 66.
6. Craig Hawkins, "The Modern World of Witchcraft," *Christian Research Journal,* Winter/Spring 1990.
7. Starhawk, *The Spiral Dance* (New York: Harper & Row, 1989), p. 23.
8. Hawkins, *Witchcraft: Exploring the World of Wicca,* pp. 41-46.
9. Raven Grimassi, *The Wiccan Mysteries* (St. Paul: Llewellyn, 2000), p. 32.

41—Zen
1. J. Isamu Yamamoto, "North Americans Embrace a Contemplative School of Buddhism," Christian Research Institute website: www.equip.org.
2. "Zen," *Encyclopedia Britannica,* online edition; J. Isamu Yamamoto, *Buddhism, Taoism, & Other Far Eastern Religions* (Grand Rapids: Zondervan, 1998), p. 16.
3. Yamamoto, "North Americans Embrace a Contemplative School of Buddhism."
4. Stephen Short, "Zen and the Art of Not Knowing God," Christian Research Institute website: www.equip.org.
5. Alan Watts, *The Spirit of Zen* (New York: Grove Press, 1958), p. 18.
6. John Ankerberg and John Weldon, *Encyclopedia of Cults and New Religions* (Eugene, OR: Harvest House, 1999), p. 630.
7. Ibid., p. 634.
8. Short, "Zen and the Art of Not Knowing God."

42—Apologetic Power Points
 1. Norman Geisler and William Nix, *A General Introduction to the Bible* (Chicago: Moody, 1968), p. 28.
 2. John Walvoord, *Jesus Christ Our Lord* (Chicago: Moody, 1980), p. 44.
 3. Benjamin Warfield, *The Person and Work of Christ* (Philadelphia: Presbyterian and Reformed, 1950), p. 56.
 4. C.S. Lewis, *Mere Christianity* (New York: Macmillan, 1960), pp. 40-41.
 5. Gregory Boyd, "Sharing Your Faith with a Oneness Pentecostal," *Christian Research Journal* (Spring 1991), p. 7.
 6. Norman Geisler and Ronald Brooks, *Christianity Under Attack* (Dallas: Quest, 1985), p. 43.
 7. Orville Swenson, *The Perilous Path of Cultism* (Briercrest, Canada: Briercrest, 1987), p. 51.
 8. *Theological Dictionary of the New Testament*, eds. Gerhard Kittel and Gerhard Friedrich (Grand Rapids: Eerdmans, 1985), p. 772.
 9. André Kole and Terry Holley, *Astrology & Psychic Phenomena* (Grand Rapids: Zondervan, 1998), pp. 74-75.
10. John Weldon and John Ankerberg, "Visualization: God-Given Power or New Age Danger?" Part 2, *Christian Research Journal,* Fall 1996, p. 21.
11. Kenneth Boa, *Cults, World Religions, and You* (Wheaton: Victor, 1986), p. 163.
12. Tal Brooke, *Riders of the Cosmic Circuit* (Batavia: Lion Publishers, 1986), pp. 39-50.
13. James Hassett, "Caution: Meditation Can Hurt," *Psychology Today,* November 1978, pp. 125-26.
14. Vishal Mangalwadi, *When the New Age Gets Old* (Downers Grove: InterVarsity, 1993), p. 81.
15. Arnold M. Ludwig, *Altered States of Consciousness*, p. 16; cited in Josh McDowell and Don Stewart, *Answers to Tough Questions* (Nashville: Nelson, 1993), p. 83.
16. Ankerberg and Weldon, p. 508.
17. Elliot Miller, "The 1993 Parliament of the Worlds Religions: The Fundamentalism of Tolerance," *Christian Research Journal,* Winter 1994, CRI website, www.equip.org.

Bibliography

Abanes, Richard. *Cults, New Religious Movements and Your Family.* Wheaton, IL: Crossway, 1998.

Ankerberg, John and John Weldon. *Cult Watch.* Eugene, OR: Harvest House Publishers, 1992.

_____. *Encyclopedia of Cults and New Religions.* Eugene, OR: Harvest House Publishers, 1999.

Bach, Marcus. *The Story of Unity.* Englewood Cliffs, NJ: Prentice-Hall, 1962.

Baha'i World Faith. Wilmette, IL: Baha'i Publishing Trust, 1956.

Baigent, Michael and Richard Leigh. *The Temple and the Lodge.* New York: Arcarde Publishing, 1989.

Bailey, Alice. *The Externalization of the Hierarchy.* New York: Lucis Publishing Co., 1957.

Ballard, Guy and Donald Ballard. *Purpose of the Ascended Masters "I AM" Activity.* Chicago: Saint Germain Press, 1942.

Barker, Eileen. *The Making of a Moonie.* Cambridge, MA: Basil Blackwell, 1984.

Barkun, Michael. *Religion and the Racist Right: The Origins of the Christian Identity Movement.* Chapel Hill, NC: University of North Carolina Press, 1996.

Barton, Blanche. *The Secret Life of a Satanist.* Los Angeles: Ferel House, 1990.

Beisner, Calvin. *"Jesus Only" Churches.* Grand Rapids, MI: Zondervan Publishing House, 1998.

Bernard, David. *The Oneness of God.* Hazelwood, MO: Word Aflame Press, 1983.

Besant, Annie. *Esoteric Christianity.* Wheaton, IL: Theosophical Publishing House, 1953.

Bjornstad, James. *Counterfeits at Your Door.* Ventura, CA: Regal Books, 1979.

Blavatsky, Helena. *The Key to Theosophy.* Pasadena: Theosophical University Press, 1972.

Boa, Kenneth. Cults, *World Religions, and the Occult.* Wheaton, IL: Victor Books, 1990.

Bowman, Robert. *Why You Should Believe in the Trinity.* Grand Rapids, MI: Baker, 1989.

Boyd, Gregory. *Oneness Pentecostals and the Trinity.* Grand Rapids, MI: Baker, 1992.

Buckland, Raymond. *Buckland's Complete Book of Witchcraft.* St. Paul: Llewellyn Publications, 1986.

Carter, Mary, and William McGarey. *Edgar Cayce on Healing.* New York: Paperback Library, 1972.

Cather, Willa and Georgine Milmine. *The Life of Mary Baker G. Eddy and the History of Christian Science.* Lincoln, NE: University of Nebraska Press, 1993.

Coil, Henry. *A Comprehensive View of Freemasonry.* Richmond, VA: Macoy Publishing and Masonic Supply Company, 1973.

Creme, Benjamin. *The Reappearance of the Christ and the Masters of Wisdom.* Los Angeles: Tara Center, 1980.

Crompton, N. *Swedenborg.* New York: Swedenborg Foundation, 1993.

Cunningham, Scott. *The Truth About Witchcraft Today.* St. Paul: Llewellyn Publications, 1999.

Daner, Francine. *The American Children of Krsna.* New York: Holt, Rinehart and Winston, 1976.

David, Moses. *FFer's Handbook!,* ed. Justus Ashtree. Rome: Children of God, 1977.

Davis, Deborah. *The Children of God: The Inside Story.* Grand Rapids, MI: Zondervan Publishing House, 1984.

Dowling, Levi. *The Aquarian Gospel of Jesus the Christ.* London: L.N. Fowler, 1947.

Dresser, Horatio. *A History of the New Thought Movement.* London: George G. Harrap, n.d.

Drury, Neville and Gregory Tillett. *The Occult Sourcebook.* London: Routledge and Kegan Paul, 1978.

Eddy, Mary Baker. *Science and Health with Key to the Scriptures.* Boston: Trustees under the Will of Mary Baker G. Eddy, 1934.

Ehrenborg, Todd. *Mind Sciences.* Grand Rapids, MI: Zondervan Publishing House, 1996.

Elgin, Kathleen. *The Unitarians.* New York: David McKay Company, 1971.

Enroth, Ronald. *The Lure of the Cults & New Religions.* Downers Grove, IL: InterVarsity Press, 1987.

Esslemont, J. *Baha'u'llah and the New Era.* Wilmette, IL: Baha'i Publishing Trust, 1980.

Fillmore, Charles. *The Metaphysical Dictionary.* Lees Summit, MO: Unity School of Christianity, 1962.

Freeman, James Dillet. *The Story of Unity.* Unity Village, MO: Unity Books, 1978.

Gershon, David and Gail Staub. *Empowerment.* New York: Dell, 1989.

Giuley, Rosemary Ellen. *The Encyclopedia of Witches and Witchcraft.* New York: Checkmark Books, 1999.

Gleanings from the Writings of Baha'u'llah, trans. Shoghi Effendi. Wilmette, IL: Baha'i Publishing Trust, 1969.

Gomes, Alan W. *Unmasking the Cults.* Grand Rapids, MI: Zondervan, 1995.

Gottschalk, Stephen. *The Emergence of Christian Science in American Religious Life.* Berkeley: University of California Press, 1973.

Grimassi, Raven. *The Wiccan Mysteries.* St. Paul: Llewellyn Publications, 2000.

Groothuis, Doug. *Unmasking the New Age.* Downers Grove, IL: InterVarsity Press, 1986.

Gruss, Edmond. *Cults and the Occult.* 3rd ed. Phillipsburg, NJ: Presbyterian & Reformed, 1994.

Hammond, William E. *What Masonry Means.* Richmond, VA: Macoy Publishing, 1952.

Harris, Jack. *Freemasonry.* Chattanooga: Global, 1983.

Hatcher, William S. and J. Douglas Martin. *The Baha'i Faith.* San Francisco: Harper & Row Publishers, 1984.

Hawkins, Craig. *Goddess Worship, Witchcraft and Neo-Paganism.* Grand Rapids, MI: Zondervan, 1998.

Heindel, Max. *The Rosicrucian Cosmo-Conception.* San Jose, CA: AMORC, n.d.

Hemingway, Patricia. *The Transcendental Meditation Primer.* New York: David McKay Company, 1975.

Hewett, Philip. *The Unitarian Way.* Toronto: Canadian Unitarian Council, 1985.

Holmes, Ernest. *The Science of Mind.* New York: Dodd, Mead and Co., 1938.

_____. *What Religious Science Teaches.* Los Angeles: Science of Mind Publications, 1975.

Holmes, Fenwicke. *Ernest Holmes: His Life and Times.* New York: Dodd, Mead and Co., 1970.

Hong, Nansook. *In the Shadow of the Moons: My Life in the Reverend Sun Myung Moon's Family.* Boston: Little, Brown and Company, 1998.

King, Godfre Ray. *The "I AM" Discourses.* Schaumburg, IL: St. Germain Press, 1999.

Kirby, Richard. *The Mission of Mysticism.* London: SPCK, 1979.

Koch, Kurt. *Between Christ and Satan.* Grand Rapids, MI: Kregel, 1972.

Kole, André, and Terry Holley. *Astrology & Psychic Phenomena.* Grand Rapids, MI: Zondervan, 1998.

LaVey, Anton. *The Satanic Bible.* New York: Avon Books, 1969.

Leadbeater, C. *A Textbook of Theosophy.* Adyar, Madras, India: The Theosophical Publishing House, 1954.

Lincoln, Eric. *The Black Muslims in America.* Boston: Beacon Press, 1961.

Lyons, Arthur. *Satan Wants You.* New York: Mysterious Press, 1988.

Mackey, Albert. *Mackey's Revised Encyclopedia of Freemasonry.* Richmond, VA: Macoy, 1966.

MacLaine, Shirley. *Dancing in the Light.* New York: Bantam, 1985.

_____. *Out on a Limb.* New York: Bantam, 1984.

Magee, Gordon. *Is Jesus in the Godhead or Is the Godhead in Jesus?* Hazelwood, MO: Word Aflame Press, 1988.

Malcolm X. *The Autobiography of Malcolm X.* New York: Grove Press, 1964.

Mangalwadi, Vishal. *When the New Age Gets Old.* Downers Grove, IL: InterVarsity Press, 1992.

Martin, Walter. *The New Cults.* Ventura, CA: Regal Books, 1985.

_____. *The Kingdom of the Cults.* Minneapolis: Bethany, 1997.

Mather, George and Larry Nichols. *Dictionary of Cults, Sects, Religions, and the Occult.* Grand Rapids, MI: Zondervan, 1993.

McConkie, Bruce. *Mormon Doctrine.* Salt Lake City: Bookcraft, 1977.

McKeever, Bill and Eric Johnson. *Questions to Ask Your Mormon Friend.* Minneapolis: Bethany, 1994.

Melton, Gordon. *Magic, Witchcraft and Paganism in America.* New York: Garland, 1982.

Miller, Elliot. *A Crash Course on the New Age.* Grand Rapids, MI: Baker Book House, 1989.

Muhammad, Elijah. *Message to the Blackman in America.* Chicago: The Final Call, 1965.

_____. *Our Savior Has Arrived.* Newport News, VA: United Brothers Communications Systems, n.d.

Newton, Joseph Fort. *The Religion of Masonry.* Richmond, VA: Macoy, 1969.

Passantino, Bob and Gretchen Passantino. *Answers to the Cultist at Your Door.* Eugene, OR: Harvest House Publishers, 1981.

_____. *Satanism.* Grand Rapids, MI: Zondervan, 1995.

Pike, Albert. *Morals and Dogma.* Montana: Kessinger Publishing Co., n.d..

Pratt, Orson. *The Seer.* Washington, D.C.: n.p., 1853-1854.

Prophet, Elizabeth Clare. *The Lost Years of Jesus.* Livingston, MT: Summit University Press, 1987.

Prophet, Mark and Elizabeth Clare. *The Lost Teachings of Jesus 2.* Livingston, MT: Summit University Press, 1988.

Read, Anne. *Edgar Cayce: On Jesus and His Church.* New York: Warner Books, 1970.

Reasoning from the Scriptures. Brooklyn: Watchtower Bible and Tract Society, 1989.

Reed, David. *Jehovah's Witnesses Answered Verse by Verse.* Grand Rapids, MI: Baker, 1986.

Reeves, Kenneth. *The Godhead.* St. Louis: Trio Printing Company, 1999.

Robinson, David. *The Unitarians and the Universalists.* Westport, CA: Greenwood, 1985.

Robinson, John. *Born in Blood: The Lost Secrets of Freemasonry.* New York: Evans, 1989.

Robinson, Stephen and Craig Blomberg. *How Wide the Divide?* Downers Grove, IL: InterVarsity Press, 1995.

Ryerson, Kevin and Stephanie Harolde. *Spirit Communication.* New York: Bantam, 1989.

Saliba, John A. *Understanding New Religious Movements.* Grand Rapids, MI: Eerdmans, 1995.

Should You Believe in the Trinity? Brooklyn, NY: Watchtower Bible and Tract Society, 1989.

Sias, John. *100 Questions that Non-Members Ask About Unitarian Universalism.* Nashua: Transition Publishing, 1999.

Siegel, Bernie. *Peace, Love & Healing.* New York: Harper & Row Publishers, 1989.

Sigstedt, Cyriel. *The Swedenborg Epic.* New York: Bookman, 1952.

Simple, Peter. *Baha'i Teachings, Light for All Regions.* Wilmette, IL: Baha'i, 1970.

Smith, Joseph Fielding. *History of the Church of Jesus Christ of Latter-day Saints.* Salt Lake City: Deseret, 1973.

Spangler, David. *The Laws of Manifestation.* Forres, Scotland: Findhorn Publications, 1983.

Steiner, Rudolf. *Knowledge of the Higher Worlds and its Attainment.* Spring Valley, NY: Anthroposophic Press, 1984.

Storms, E. *Should a Christian Be a Mason?* Kirkwood: Impact Christian Books, 1999.

Strohmer, Charles. *What Your Horoscope Doesn't Tell You.* Wheaton, IL: Tyndale, 1988.

Swedenborg, Emanuel. *Life After Death.* New York: The New Church Press, n.d.

Swihart, Philip. *Reincarnation, Edgar Cayce, and the Bible.* Downers Grove, IL: InterVarsity Press, 1978.

Talmage, James. *A Study of the Articles of Faith.* Salt Lake City: The Church of Jesus Christ of Latter-day Saints, 1982.

Tanner, Jerald and Sandra. *The Changing World of Mormonism.* Chicago: Moody Press, 1980.

Tennant, Harry. *Christadelphians.* Birmingham, England: The Christadelphian, 1986.

The Baha'is: A Profile of the Baha'i Faith and its Worldwide Community. United Kingdom: Baha'i Publishing Trust of the United Kingdom, 1994.

The Gods Have Landed: New Religions from Other Worlds, ed. James R. Lewis. New York: State University of New York Press, 1995.

The Unitarian Universalist Pocket Guide, ed. John A. Buehrens. Boston: Skinner House Books, 1999.

Trevelyan, George. *A Vision of the Aquarian Age.* Walpole, NH: Stillpoint Publishing, 1984.

Tucker, Ruth. *Another Gospel.* Grand Rapids, MI: Zondervan Publishing House, 1989.

Turner, Elizabeth Sand. *What Unity Teaches.* Lees Summit, MO: Unity School of Christianity, 1952.

Undreamed of Possibilities: An Introduction to Self-Realization Fellowship. Los Angeles: Self-Realization Fellowship, 1982.

Vallee, Jacques. *UFO Chronicles of the Soviet Union.* New York: Ballantine Books, 1992.

Van Gordon, Kurt. *Mormonism.* Grand Rapids, MI: Zondervan, 1995.

Vindex. *Light Invisible: The Freemason's Answer to "Darkness Visible."* Boston: Masonic Publishers, 1996.

Vorilhon, Claude. *Let's Welcome Our Fathers from Space: They Created Humanity in Their Laboratories.* Tokyo: AOM Corporation, 1986.

Wagner, Martin. *Freemasonry.* Columbiana, AL: Missionary Service and Supply, n.d.

Warch, William A. *The New Thought Christian.* Anaheim, CA: Christian Living, 1977.

Warren, Samuel. *Compendium of Swedenborg's Theological Writings.* London: Swedenborg Society, 1954.

Watts, Alan. *The Spirit of Zen.* New York: Grove Press, 1958.

Wierwille, Victor Paul. *Jesus Christ Is Not God.* New Knoxville, OH: American Christian Press, 1975.

_____. *Power for Abundant Living.* New Knoxville, OH: American Christian Press, 1972.

Wilson, Clifford and John Weldon. *Occult Shock and Psychic Forces.* San Diego: Master Books, 1987.

Yamamoto, Isamu. *Buddhism, Taoism, & Other Far Eastern Religions.* Grand Rapids, MI: Zondervan, 1998.

_____. *Hinduism, TM & Hare Krishna.* Grand Rapids, MI: Zondervan, 1998.

Yogananda, Paramahansa. *The Science of Religion.* Los Angeles: Self-Realization Fellowship, 1982.

Young, Brigham. *Journal of Discourses.* London: Latter-day Saint's, 1854-1856.

Other Books by Ron Rhodes

Find It Fast in the Bible
A quick reference that lives up to its name! With more than 400 topics and 8000-plus references, this comprehensive, topical guide provides one-line summaries of each verse. Perfect for research, discussions, and Bible studies.

The 10 Things You Should Know About the Creation vs. Evolution Debate
This helpful guide demonstrates why the two sides of the debate are mutually exclusive. Readers will deepen their appreciation for the wonder of creation and see how it points to the reality of the Creator.

The 10 Most Important Things You Can Say to a Catholic
If you want to witness to Catholic friends or be more informed about their beliefs, this fact-filled book discusses use of the Apocrypha, the role of tradition, purgatory, Mary worship, and much more.

The 10 Most Important Things You Can Say to a Jehovah's Witness
Essential information for effectively witnessing to Jehovah's Witnesses. Includes a look at errors in the New World Translation Bible, false prophecies of the sect's leaders, and their unbiblical views. Great for Bible studies, youth groups.

The 10 Most Important Things You Can Say to a Mormon
If you want to witness to Mormons, this is a must-have, covering the Mormon view of the Bible and the Book of Mormon's origins. Stresses the importance of the Trinity, salvation by grace not works, and more.

Reasoning from the Scriptures with Muslims

Who was Muhammad? What kind of inspiration and authority does the Quran have? How can Muslims be reached with the good news? Each chapter examines a Muslim belief and compares it with biblical Christianity.

Reasoning from the Scriptures with Catholics

This thorough, easy-to-use reference examines Catholic beliefs and practices and outlines verses typically cited to support those views. A must-have tool for sharing the good news of salvation by faith alone with Catholics.

Reasoning from the Scriptures with the Mormons

Powerful tools for sharing the truth of God's Word in a loving and gracious way are presented in a simple, step-by-step format.

Reasoning from the Scriptures with the Jehovah's Witnesses

Many outstanding features make this the *complete* hands-on guide to sharing the truth of God's Word in a loving, gracious way. Includes favorite tactics used by the Witnesses and effective biblical responses.

The Complete Guide to Christian Denominations

Ron Rhodes has compiled his extensive research into a handy, easy-to-use manual that provides accurate, straightforward information about various churches. Includes each denomination's brief history, its most important doctrinal beliefs, and distinctive teachings.

The Complete Book of Bible Promises

Bible promise books abound—but not like this one! Two hundred alphabetized categories of verses include explanatory headings, insights from the original languages, and deeply moving quotes from famous Christian authors and hymns.

Quick Reference Guides

In 16 pages of concise, reader-friendly information, these booklets present the major points and arguments of the religion or subject discussed. Side-by-side comparisons with biblical teachings are provided for a scriptural perspective. Ideal for at-a-glance reference or for giving away.

> Believing in Jesus: What You Need to Know
> Islam: What You Need to Know
> Jehovah's Witnesses: What You Need to Know

Why Do Bad Things Happen If God Is Good?

Bible scholar Ron Rhodes addresses the problem of pain with the heart of a pastor and the mind of an apologist. Ron explores the unshakable biblical truths that provide a strong foundation in stormy times.

Angels Among Us

What are angels like? What do they do? Are they active today? Taking you on a fascinating and highly inspirational tour of God's Word, Ron provides solid, biblically based answers to these questions and more.